HOW TO STUDY T

Pembrokes.
Learning P

How to Study Literature
Series editors: John Peck and Martin Coyle

IN THE SAME SERIES

How to Begin Studying English Literature (second edition)
    Nicholas Marsh
How to Study a Jane Austen Novel *Vivien Jones*
How to Study Chaucer *Robert Pope*
How to Study a Joseph Conrad Novel *Brian Spittles*
How to Study a Charles Dickens Novel *Keith Selby*
How to Study an E. M. Forster Novel *Nigel Messenger*
How to Study a Thomas Hardy Novel *John Peck*
How to Study a D. H. Lawrence Novel *Nigel Messenger*
How to Study a James Joyce Novel *John Blades*
How to Study Milton *David Kearns*
How to Study Modern Drama *Kenneth Pickering*
How to Study Modern Poetry *Tony Curtis*
How to Study a Novel (second edition) *John Peck*
How to Study a Poet (second edition) *John Peck*
How to Study a Renaissance Play *Chris Coles*
How to Study Romantic Poetry *Paul O'Flinn*
How to Study a Shakespeare Play (second edition) *John Peck and Martin Coyle*
How to Study Television *Keith Selby and Ron Cowdery*
Literary Terms and Criticism (second edition) *John Peck and Martin Coyle*
Practical Criticism *John Peck and Martin Coyle*

How to Study Television

Keith Selby and Ron Cowdery

MACMILLAN

First published 1995 by
MACMILLAN PRESS LTD
Houndmills, Basingstoke, Hampshire RG21 6XS
and London
Companies and representatives
throughout the world

ISBN 0–333–56965–2

A catalogue record for this book is available
from the British Library.

10   9   8   7   6   5   4   3   2
03   02   01   00   99   98   97   96

Printed in Malaysia

Contents

For Susan and Debbie

List of figures

List of tables

Editors' preface

IF you are a student taking Media or Communication Studies, the chances are that you are looking for a book on television that will not only help you to come to grips with the technical aspects of media production, but also help you to formulate your critical response in a clear, analytical way. The aim of *How To Study Television* is to offer you guidance on both these important tasks by providing not only the sort of technical information you need, but also a critical method that will allow you to explore your insights and ideas about a range of different types of television programme.

The opening chapter introduces you to the five main areas of analysis when dealing with television: Construction, Audience, Narration, Category and Agency. These terms are then explored in Chapter 2 in relation to a single still – an advertisement for airmail letters. Chapter 3 develops the analysis of the advertisement further by discussing the effect of camera angles and visual and cultural codes. These two chapters are intended to offer you points of reference for your own work and also for the chapters that follow. These deal, in turn, with how to analyse an episode from a police series (*The Bill*), from a TV sitcom (*Fawlty Towers*), from a news broadcast (*News at Ten*), and an episode from a TV soap – *Neighbours*. In each case, practical advice is given on what to look for and how to interrelate all the areas that make television the complex social, political and aesthetic medium it is.

Following these chapters on the different kinds of television programme is a chapter on essay-writing and how to organise a written response. The chapter takes for its example television gameshows, but the advice given will help you with writing about all types of television output. Finally, at the end of the book, is an extensive glossary of terms used in the discussion and production of television programmes. Understanding such terms is best done by seeing them put into practice, which is exactly what *How To Study Televison* does. At once a guide to current ideas about the media and a practical textbook that will help you develop your own critical responses, *How To Study Television* is also a rich source of suggestions that should further your enjoyment of studying television.

John Peck
Martin Coyle

Acknowledgements

WE should like to thank those who have helped us in the writing of this book. In particular we are grateful to Cathryn Tanner for her interest and constructive comments during her time as Commissioning Editor for Macmillan Press; to John Peck and Martin Coyle for their unstinting editorial guidance and support; and to Margaret Bartley (Senior Editor, Macmillan), who directed the book so genially through its final production. We also wish to thank John Foster for the interview he gave us in connection with *The Bill*, and for reading and commenting upon early drafts of Chapter 4 of this book. Any errors which remain are, of course, our own.

The authors and publishers are grateful to the Post Office for permission to reproduce the advertisement 'Melt her to the Coeur', and to Independent Television News Ltd for the use of photographs from its *News at Ten* studios.

1

Studying television

To many people, television is just flickering wallpaper, moving pictures in the corner of the room. As a medium, television is notoriously easy to watch without, apparently, requiring a great deal of effort from the viewer. While it is easy to watch television, however, it is hard to write analytically about it. If you are studying communications, media studies, social studies, humanities or English, you will probably need either to write about a television programme, or to prepare and present a project about television at some point in the course of your studies. Most students find this very difficult. Precisely because television is so easy to watch it seems to resist our efforts to analyse it critically.

This problem can sometimes be made much worse by the mass of theory which surrounds the study of television. Some critics concentrate on the effects of the media on audiences, in an attempt to identify links between, for example, violence and television. Others concentrate on the importance of the director as the author or creator of the finished product. Others still focus on the way in which social groups or classes are represented by the media, and on how this reinforces stereotyping of people – such as the young and the elderly, homosexuals, women, the working classes, or people of other races and nationalities.

Another problem about which you are probably thinking by now is the complexity of a television programme. It is quite likely that you will feel daunted by the sheer diversity of the elements which go to make up a TV programme – economic, political, legal, technological, artistic, institutional, cultural – and that in attempting to piece all this information together you will feel like a detective at the scene of a crime with far too many clues.

A further difficulty is that the people who made the programme have long since left, so it is unlikely that you will be able to find out what decisions were made, who made them, or why. And yet you know that there is not only the writer's script lurking somewhere at the back of the programme, but there are also camera technicians, directors, producers, designers, make-up artists, actors, sound engineers, the artistic and technical decisions taken at production stage, and so on.

Even if you have managed to find your way through the complexities of the theory surrounding television studies, you can still feel baffled by the intricacies of the production process itself. Added to this, you probably feel that while you have plenty to say about what you liked or did not like about a particular TV programme, you cannot see how to fit it into an analysis of the programme as a media text. Part of the problem, then, is that television can overwhelm the student simply by its bulk and complexity once we start to analyse it. Commonly, the student just does not know where to begin. But this is where you can start to establish a method. Indeed, without a clear method from which to work, you probably will not have anything very coherent to say about a television programme at all.

This is the aim of this book: to show you how, working from just a few basic principles, you can build your own response to any television programme. A central point, which will be stressed all the time, is that the best way to build an analytical response is to start with a few clear ideas about the various areas you need to consider and to use these to direct and shape all your subsequent thinking. Of course, we cannot cover every aspect of every television programme ever made, and so have restricted ourselves to just the general, workaday output of TV as an industry – the type of output about which most students find it so difficult to write. In fact, the following two chapters, in which we map out the details of the method we are recommending to you, are both concerned with the analysis of an advertising still, and not a piece of television at all. But the method we will be recommending can be applied to any media text, no matter what type it is. The reason we are starting with a single still from an advertising campaign is because you first of all need to learn how to 'read' a visual image, in much the same way as, when you first started school, you learned to read words on a page. When you have mastered this area of visual literacy you will be much better equipped to follow the type of analysis we are illustrating in this book as a whole.

What we are going to establish first, then, are the areas of the media text to which you should be directing your attention when you start to build your analysis. These have been the subject of considerable discussion in the academic and practical criticism of media texts and are based on the most recent thinking on the subject. If you can get hold of these principles at the outset, you will soon have a clear idea of the kinds of areas you need to consider in your own analysis.

THE MEDIA TEXT: PRINCIPLES OF ANALYSIS

WHEN you first see a picture of any type, whether a still or moving picture, you are likely to be so absorbed by details that you might miss any sense of a larger pattern at work. It is often very easy, when you think back about a still or TV programme, for example, to recall some detail of colour, a particular sequence of shots, an actor's voice or a theme tune, and yet be quite at a loss when it comes to trying to fit this into the way you feel about the picture or TV programme as a whole. This is really because you do not know how to start ordering, structuring or shaping a response to the media text. In consequence, certain details will spring to mind as memorable, even though you cannot say how or why they are so effective. However, once you have a sense of a central tension at work in the text, then you will be able to begin thinking about television critically. In this book we will be using an approach which will help you to develop this sense of a central tension by drawing together many different but related approaches so that you can see the larger pattern of the text.

In more traditional forms of writing about the media – such as television criticism or appreciation – responses tend to be largely impressionistic. That is, the writer describes his or her personal response to the work. However, to write a *critical* response to a work you need to understand and to use particular theoretical concepts. This critical vocabulary will help you to make clear statements about the ways in which any media text works. In this book we have built an approach which uses all the major theoretical concepts currently found in communications and media studies and have broken these down into a series of steps which will allow you to analyse a television programme in a complete and coherent manner.

The first thing to grasp about a visual image is that it is a **Construction**. When we talk about a media text as a 'Construction', however, we are not talking about the celluloid or magnetic tape upon which the programme is stored. What we mean by the use of the term Construction is the idea that all media texts are constructed using a media language. For example, if you were to commission a professional photographer to take your portrait then s/he would make certain choices about whether to use soft or sharp focus, whether to light you from above or below, whether to include the tops of your shoulders or to focus in tightly on just your face, whether to photograph you from an angle or face-on, etc. Such choices are described as codes, and it is these codes which make up media languages. In deciding how to compose your portrait, a photographer will be considering codes of focus, lighting, framing, and many others, and it is the use of these codes which will affect the way we feel about the finished portrait. This is an important point to grasp. A media text is not only constructed using a media language, but the codes which are chosen also convey certain information.

We can demonstrate this by thinking again of the codes that make up the media language of photography. For example, a soft focus may be used to convey things like 'romance' or 'a dream', or, depending on its context, a flashback to the past. But it would be very difficult to make a soft focus photograph mean 'threatening menace'. To create this effect quite different codes would have to be used, such as a low camera angle and harsh, contrastive lighting. So specific codes carry certain meanings with them. This is because we all take a certain cultural knowledge to a visual image and our reading of it will be affected by the type of cultural knowledge we possess.

It is a short step from this to saying that the reality created in a television programme is itself the product of various cultural pressures and constraints, which can take one of two forms. First, media output is to a considerable extent dictated by outside pressures which will significantly affect the selection and representation of society by the media. These constraints may be both financial (the media are part of an industry and are in competition with other businesses to make a profit) and moral, having to do with censorship or public taste. Second, another, less-obvious pressure upon the media in constructing and representing reality directs attention to the question of whether the media's product is actually like reality. That is, the quality of a programme may be judged by how representative it is of reality. But you have to be careful here. There is no point in complaining that, say, M.A.S.H. tells us little about the realities of the Korean War. This may or may not be true. Certainly, however, the programme does tell us about the kinds of forces that bond relationships in a particular situation, and about the ways in which individuals attempt to cope with the ever-present threat of death. The presence of the Korean War merely heightens that threat, and the characters' awareness of it. To a considerable extent, therefore, the Korean War functions only as a backdrop to the programme's real concerns and interests. This means that characters in a TV programme may sometimes be represented as stereotypes or caricatures which perhaps bear little resemblance to real characters in those real situations: while Hawkeye and BeeJay are represented as fully-fleshed-out characters, Hot Lips Houghlan tends to remain exactly what her name suggests, a pair of hot lips waiting for fulfilment and gratification from the fully realised male characters that surround her. This draws our attention to the fact that in a media representation of reality certain characters may often be represented as some form of stereotypical foil against which other characters can be played, and perceived as such by the audience.

This takes us on to the next idea that you need when thinking about media texts in a critical and analytical way. Media texts are not only constructed out of certain media languages, but are also read by **Audiences**. This reveals something significant about the theoretical framework we will be suggesting in this book: that none of the concepts can be considered in isolation, for as soon as you begin to analyse the way that a TV programme is constructed, you will also need to consider its relation to its Audience.

But the way in which we read a media text can depend upon many things, such as our education and social class, our political and religious views and beliefs, and our race and gender. Of course, we cannot remove all the prejudices that go along with each of these groups, but we can look at the way that each of these various groups will extract different meanings from a media text. This is an important idea: that a media text cannot be reduced to a single, fixed and coherent 'meaning', but will instead be open to various interpretations by its various audiences. Indeed, the media text will be 'used' quite differently by its different audiences, and this is likely to affect quite radically the audience's response to the way in which it presents information as Narrative.

Narrative is something so fundamental to television that it is easy to overlook its significance. When we watch a television programme of any type we are presented with a series of events that *seems* quite logical and natural, but which is actually the result of narrative construction. Because we have no control over the way in which narrative events unfold before us, television tends to give rise to a strong impression that things could not have been other than the way that they are represented. In fact, of course, the way in which the narrative unfolds is far from natural, but is rather the result of manipulating the overall effect of a programme through editing information together. The point here is that narrative involves concealing such things, for example, as the manipulation of time through selective editing by making it seem a natural part of the telling of the tale.

This leads us on to the next area we want to identify: media **Categories**. When we watch a TV programme we bring to it a considerable amount of knowledge and understanding about media texts in general. For example, if you walked into a room where there was a television programme on, you could very quickly categorise it as being, say, a documentary, or a sitcom, or as belonging to the genre of science fiction, and this causes us to respond to the text in particular ways. Think, for example, of the American TV series, *Star Trek*.

If you went into a room and found that *Star Trek* was being shown on the television, you could quite rapidly make several observations about the type of media Category to which it belongs. First, you'd notice that it is a programme which is recognisably within the conventions of science fiction. There are many ways in which we can see this, but one of the most obvious is the fact that the central conflict or tension in the programme is that between the rationality, reason and cold logic of Mr Spock and the warmth, understanding and humanity of Captain James Kirk. This is the central conflict in all science fiction, in which one of the central questions posed focuses upon the problem of what happens to humanity in the face of the rapid development of science and technology. It is the repetition of such conflicts which allows us to identify the genre of science fiction.

Second, you know it is on television, which would lead you to expect a different form of media text from what you would find if you had walked into a darkened cinema to see *2001: A Space Odyssey*, and your response would be tempered by those expectations. Television programmes are made for domestic consumption; because people do not pay the same kind of attention to the TV screen as to the cinema screen the programmes tend to be segmented, broken down into a number of incidents which are almost free-standing. This is an aspect of television production which was pioneered by programmes such as

Z Cars in the 1960s and has characterised much television since. Also, the differences in the means of production of film and television create differences in the final products themselves. Much British television drama of the 1950s, for example, was filmed entirely in studio, and this created a sense of smallness or claustrophobia in comparison with the cinema-film tradition of the same period. A television, studio-based production of a film such as *A Taste of Honey* (1961) would be incapable of generating the sense of documentary realism which characterises the filmic original.

The third and final aspect of categorization has to do with the aesthetic patterning of the text. By this we mean the internal, formal characteristics of the medium. *Star Trek*, for example, opens each episode with a reading from the Captain's log, which seems to suggest elements of documentary truth to locate the programme in time and space. However, since in this matter-of-fact reading from the Captain's log there are references to a 'Stardate 2044', the 'Starship Enterprise' and the planet 'Arkon Four', we know we have to locate this reading from the Captain's log within the context of science fiction. This can help us to draw several conclusions about the aesthetic form of science fiction as a genre. One of the things we can notice, as in the above example, is that the text provides us with enough information to ground the story firmly within the realms of reality, and yet allows us to enjoy the pleasure of seeing a fictional form take shape before us. If a text excites us in this way it is very easy for us to become caught up in the story it has to tell.

However, to write critically about media products we also need to take account of the institutions or **Agencies** in which they were produced. Take, for instance, a single photographic image. This might be seen in a newspaper, a book, on an advertising hoarding or in an art gallery. Images are hardly ever found in isolation. We nearly always come across them within an institutional setting, whether that is television, the press or advertising. Yet more important is the way in which the meaning of the image is influenced by its institutional setting and also by our perceptions of that image in that context. If we see a photograph in an art gallery we may find ourselves interested by its formal qualities of lighting and composition, things we would be unlikely to notice in front of an advertising hoarding, or when scanning an advertisement in the daily paper. Consequently, the concept of Agency is wider than the question of who owns and controls the media. A wide range of financial, technological, cultural and political issues come into play as well as the professional and industrial practices that are particular to each media Agency.

It is easy, in media and communication studies, to be blind to these forces, all of which have shaped and moulded the programmes we watch. But these pressures are very real ones, and take us from textual study to contextual study, that is, to a consideration of the organisational context of TV scheduling, broadcasting policy, the influence of financial considerations, the question of the State and of public funding, of political bias, etc. So, in media and communications studies we are looking at the connections and the conflicts that exist both within and between Agencies.

For the moment, all the above might seem very abstract and not very applicable to the task you have in mind, so rather than confuse things by tackling a whole television programme now, what we are going to do in the next chapter is to look at a single still to show you how, if you concentrate on just the five areas outlined above, you will be able to build a clear, reasoned and critical response of your own. Then, in Chapter 3, we will develop our analysis of the same still to show you how, using the information from your basic analysis, you can develop your analysis to concentrate on just one aspect of any media text, just as you are expected to do in any project or essay in communications or media studies.

You may be wondering why we are not taking a still from a TV programme – we actually use an advert for airmail letters. First, it would make little sense to analyse a single still, taken out of context from a TV programme, without discussing the rest of the programme, and we want to leave these broader discussions until later in the book, when they will make more sense. Second, television is, above all, a visual medium, and it is vitally important that we introduce you to the techniques of visual analysis at the outset. Building on this technique of close visual analysis we can then show how, using a simple, step-by-step method, you can build an analysis of a complex television programme using each of the five media aspects discussed above. These are the key areas for all our discussions and provide you with a firm foundation of knowledge on which to build both an informed and yet also personal view of a media text.

This, then, is the shape of the book. The next two chapters concentrate on analysing a single still. After these introductory chapters come a sequence of chapters showing how to analyse various types of television programme using a step-by-step method. These will show you how to construct a basic analysis of a programme and then how to look at a specific aspect of a media text in more detail. After these chapters comes a chapter on how to write an essay on television programmes, with particular reference to game shows. In addition, there is a glossary at the end which gives you definitions of terms used in the book, though these are explained whenever we use them.

What will be new to most students are the five key areas used to discuss media texts. Before we move on to the next chapter it is worthwhile simply summarising those areas so that you begin to get to know them more fully:

1. *Construction*: **the idea that all media texts are constructed using a media language and that the codes which are chosen convey certain cultural information also;**
2. *Audience*: **that a media text cannot be reduced to a single, fixed and coherent 'meaning', but will instead be open to various interpretations by its various audiences;**
3. *Narrative*: **the way in which the narrative unfolds is far from natural, but is instead the result of manipulating and editing information together;**
4. *Categorisation*: **that when we watch a TV programme we bring to it a considerable amount of knowledge and understanding about media texts in general and that part of the enjoyment of the text involves the pleasure of seeing a fictional form take shape before us;**
5. *Agency*: **involving a consideration of the organizational context of TV scheduling, broadcasting policy, the influence of financial considerations, the question of the State and of public funding, of political bias etc. In Media and Communications Studies we are looking at the connections and the conflicts that exist both within and between institutions.**

2

Analysing a media text

I   CONSTRUCTING AN OVERALL ANALYSIS

THE aim of this book is to introduce you to a method of analysing any television programme, and you may think it a little strange that we're starting with an advertising still to do this. As we said in the previous Chapter, our reason for this is simple: we want to make sure that the basic principles upon which this whole book is based are clear from the outset, and it seems sensible to take things one stage at a time, rather than just dropping you straight into a detailed analysis of a complicated full-length TV programme.

This is not, of course, to imply that advertisements are simple, as you will soon find out by looking at various approaches taken to the analysis of advertising. Some writers will tell you that because they celebrate success and consumerism, advertisements are just reflections of an overtly materialistic capitalist society, whilst others will praise the creativity and imagination to be found in advertisements, claiming that they are an art form in their own right. And some people (usually those who have never spent any time analysing a media text) will claim that because advertisements are so much a part of the ephemera of everyday life, they are not worthy of the same close scrutiny that a novel, play or poem might demand. It is only when we start to look at advertisements in a more analytical way that we realise that there really is more to most of them than meets the eye.

Obviously we cannot discuss all the advertisements that have occurred in the British media over even the last thirty days let alone the past thirty years. The steps in an analysis, however, remain essentially the same no matter which media text you are studying. This is the point we want to stress: if you follow the steps in analysis that we use in this book, then you will be able to produce your own, informed and valid reading of any media text. This is very important, because, if you are new to media or communications studies, you will probably feel that what others have written about film and television has much more validity than your own views. And if the only thing you can remember about a particular Carling Black Label or Heineken advertisement is that it made you laugh, then you are bound to feel fairly daunted when you turn to a book that uses a lot of jargon and does not seem to make any mention of your own feelings about the ad. Such books may have many important things to say about the role of the media in contemporary society but they usually presuppose a prior knowledge of the key issues and concepts involved. The aim of this book, however, is slightly different in that we are trying to help you to carry out your own analysis of any television programme. We shall stress that the best way to do this is to start with a few clear and simple ideas about the work as a whole and then to use those key ideas to direct and shape your subsequent thinking.

As you will remember from chapter 1, we have suggested that there are five major areas you need to consider when preparing an analysis of any media text. Even if you still find one or two of these terms confusing, do not be put off, as this chapter aims to clarify each concept in turn as we come to discuss it. Here again are the five major concepts you need to consider when preparing an overall analysis:

- Construction;
- Audience;
- Narrative;
- Categorisation;
- Agency.

Before we start on any of these, however, what we want you to do is to step back a little and think about the image we are going to analyse in this chapter. Turn to Figure 2.1 and take a good long look at the Royal Mail advertisement then consider the following question: What things strike you as in some way significant about this image? You might notice that there is a pun of some sort going on in the title above the advertisement. Even if you do not happen to know that the French word 'coeur' means 'heart, feelings, emotions', the pun on 'coeur' (core), and the look on the girl's face seems to suggest that she is opening what we can assume to be a love letter. This is backed up by the setting. In the background we can see the Eiffel

Figure 2.1 'Melt her to the Coeur'

Tower and a bridge over the river Seine, both of which have distinctly romantic connotations. Also, the photograph is shot using black and white, which seems to give the image a more documentary or realistic feel, probably because most of the photographs that we now see in black and white are in newspapers. It also seems to distance the image in the recent past, when most photographs were shot in black and white, and, implicitly, to return us to an easier, bygone and more carefree age.

This is supported by the props associated with the girl. The girl's hair style is reminiscent of the 1960s, and of the freedom we associate with that period. Also, next to the girl we see a roadster bicycle, which matches the carefree atmosphere of the setting and the way in which the girl is dressed. And finally, we are told that Royal Mail delivers all this by Airmail, and International Airmail at that. We have a French, carefree atmosphere, suggesting that we can talk to the ones we love simply by writing to them, no matter where they are, and that we can rely upon Royal Mail to make this possible.

These, at least, are some of the ideas that seem to us to be generated by the image. You might like to add to these impressions, but, for the moment, we have made some attempt to locate the advertisement as a media text and to account for the kind of story it is telling. Just doing this – looking at the image and trying to account for what we see – is a valuable first step in trying to build a detailed and personal response, because it helps you to start thinking about the details of the text. And yet it is a step all too often not taken by students, simply because they feel swamped by the mass of details confronting them in any media text.

However, although this first step is a useful one to take, if you want to go beyond an introductory and impressionistic response, you will need to turn your attention more specifically to the five areas we have already mentioned: Construction, Audience, Narrative, Categories and Agency. This is less daunting than it seems once you realise, for example, that virtually everything you are likely to be able to say about the image in terms of a first response will have to do with things like setting and props, which all come under Construction.

2.1 Construction

(The idea that all media texts are constructed using a media language and that the codes which are chosen also convey certain cultural information.)

The two aspects of Construction which we need to consider are (i) *mise-en-scène* (see Glossary) and (ii) the technical codes of construction. *Mise-en-scène* analysis looks at only those aspects which overlap with the theatre – setting, props, behaviour of the actors or figures, costumes and make-up. Technical codes of composition include camera angle, lighting and so on. In controlling these elements the director of the film or advertisement is staging the event for the camera, and you need to be quite clear about how these various techniques are used to create specific effects.

2.1.1   mise-en-scène: formal codes of construction
(a)   Setting
(b)   Props
(c)   Codes of non-verbal communication
(d)   Codes of dress

We will be looking at each of these areas in more detail in the next chapter. For the moment, all we really want to do is to introduce you to the way we can use the above headings to start to build an analysis. Further complexities and subtleties can come later.

2.1.1a   Setting   In looking at this advertisement, we can say that the setting is clearly Paris (the Eiffel Tower is there just in case we confuse the bridge over the Seine with one of the bridges over the Thames). Paris has been chosen because we associate particular meanings with it: romance and affairs of the heart, sophistication, culture, *joie de vivre*, the city of young lovers, youthfulness, etc. If the young woman were standing next to the Houses of Parliament then none of these connotations would arise.

2.1.1b   Props   Moving to props, we can say that the bicycle shown, a woman's 'roadster', has particular associations for most people. Because it is an older style of bicycle it conjures up images of tradition and stability. Such cycles are solidly constructed and their design has hardly changed over the years. Bicycles of this sort sold today differ little from those of thirty years ago; we tend to think of them as above the changes and whims of fashion. Choppers and mountain bikes may come and go but the roadster is here to stay. Such machines are also favoured by students, and so the bicycle also conjures up the freedoms of student life.

An interesting point to note here is that all the things we have said about props could have been said about the setting of the advertisement also – its timeless quality, its connection with certain traditional values and feelings. The traditional feeling in this advertisement is, quite obviously, love. That the young woman is reading a love letter is supported by the setting and props, and this fits in well with the overall scheme of things and helps to support the general message of the advertisement.

2.1.1c Codes of non-verbal communication (NVC)   When we turn to codes of non verbal communication (you can abbreviate this to NVC – Non-Verbal Communication), the advertisement is particularly interesting. It is always important to remember that the actors or models whom we see in advertisements *are* acting or modelling and are posed for the camera: the girl in our Royal Mail advertisement did not just happen to be leaning on the bridge in this particular way with this expression on her face. This may seem an obvious point but it is often overlooked. For example, consider the girl's posture.

The ways in which models or actors use their bodies tells us much about what they are supposed to be feeling or thinking. The young woman in the advertisement adopts a 'natural' pose. But of course this is still a pose; she leans on the base of the bridge lamp with an air of relaxed informality. Such a posture would look out of place in the hustle and bustle of New York or Tokyo City, but in Paris it seems just right.

Moving on from NVC as it relates to posture, we need also to think about NVC in relation to facial expression. A good tip to follow when you need to write about gesture or posture in an advertisement is to cover up the heads of the people whom you are trying to comment upon. If you cover the girl's head in the ad, you will note that we see details of the letter almost apparently by chance: a photograph of a male (presumably the distant lover) looking out from between the letter's pages, the letter is hand-written (it is clearly not an electricity bill). These details, in drawing our attention to them, suggest that the girl's attention will be drawn to them also. And, when we uncover the girl's head, we see that she directs her gaze to the letter. It would be obviously inappropriate for her to look out at us. This 'directed' gaze in which the model seems wrapped up in the 'product' – in this case an airmail letter, the service being advertised – portrays her as being slightly dreamy or drifting, and suggests that her mind is elsewhere – presumably with the person who has written her the love letter, and this again fits in well with all our impressions so far.

2.1.1d Codes of dress Codes of NVC lead us on rather usefully to codes of dress. The woman in the Royal Mail ad, with her patterned chunky-knit cardigan, jeans, her T-shirt and waistcoat, evokes a relaxed and slightly Bohemian quality that we might associate with student life or the arts.

Let us summarise here what we can say about the Royal Mail advertisement in terms of *mise-en-scène*: formal codes of Construction.

(a) **Setting.** Overall, the setting has been staged in such a way as to give a realistic or documentary feel. Paris has been chosen because we associate particular meanings with it: romance and affairs of the heart, sophistication, culture, *joie de vivre*, the city of young lovers, youthfulness, etc. Because it is set in Paris, then, this conjures up images of romance and freedom.

(b) **Props** (such as the woman's 'roadster' bicycle) enhance the advertisement's message by placing images of tradition and stability alongside images of freedom, romance and youth.

(c) **Non-verbal communication (NVC)** further reinforce this air of secure romance: the woman leans on the base of the bridge lamp with an air of relaxed informality – just the right pose for a relaxed and informal city – and she looks at ease and secure in her surroundings. This impression is enhanced by the woman's 'directed' gaze in which she seems enthralled by the product – in this case an airmail letter – and suggests that the service being advertised is stable, secure and reliable, as well as allowing for the freedom associated with other images in the advertisement.

(d) **Dress codes** – the patterned chunky-knit cardigan, jeans, T-shirt and waistcoat, evoke a relaxed and slightly Bohemian quality which reinforce the sense of freedom, youth and romance.

What is starting to come through from the advertisement is that the aim here is to suggest that this 'realistic' setting (beautiful young girl, in love, free, in Paris) could be our own everyday reality, too. All we have to do is to use the Royal Mail International Airmail Service to achieve it.

2.1.2 Technical codes

Even if the only form of 'media production' in which you have been involved has been taking holiday snapshots you will still realise that a number of decisions face anyone about to use a piece of media equipment. You have to compose your snapshot in what you feel to be an acceptable way, not cropping off the tops of heads or having lamp-posts or palm trees growing out from behind them. You will probably also think about the lighting and camera angle and about how close you wish to be to your subject. All these choices come under the heading of technical codes and can be analysed as:

(a) Shot size
(b) Camera angle
(c) Lens type
(d) Composition
(e) Focus
(f) Lighting codes
(g) Colour and film stock codes

2.1.2a   Shot size   So, what can we say about the advertisement in terms of shot size? We will be going into the technical details of shot-size later, but for the moment we can make the point that the young woman in the Royal Mail advertisement is in what is termed **medium-shot** (neither close to us, as in **close-up**, nor distant from us, as in **long shot** or **extreme long shot**). This choice of shot size enables us to see a fair amount of detail in her face (the smile, which is also important under codes of NVC), but we do not lose sight of the setting either, which is of equal importance in establishing the overall meaning of the advertisement. Another important aspect of the medium-shot is that it creates an impression of closeness without intimacy; we are aware of watching a scene before us, almost as if we have somehow stumbled upon it. And this in turn means that we tend not to be aware of the artistry of the advertisement, even though, of course, it has been carefully planned and created to produce a specific effect.

2.1.2b   Camera angle   The decision over which camera angle to use is very important because it affects our response to the subject. In the 'Melt her to the Coeur' advertisement the camera angle opens up clear sky in the background, and this seems to intimate the sense of a romance blossoming in a clear, untroubled future, which again supports the kinds of things we have found from our analysis of the mise-en-scène .

2.1.2c   Lenses.   This has to do with a basic choice being made between the three main types of lens: wide angle, standard and telephoto. Do not worry just now about the technical details of this, since we will be looking at these later, but for the moment we can say that using different lenses affects how we respond to what we see. The Royal Mail advertisement has been shot using a standard, perhaps slightly wide angle lens, and this creates the impression that the viewer is a witness to the scene, reinforcing the effects gained under shot size.

2.1.2d   Codes of composition.   There are still some choices left for our photographer. S/he may have decided on the distance (shot size), the camera angle, and the lens, but there are other choices to be made regarding the composition of the shot. Although there are many ways of composing pictures it is, nevertheless, possible to isolate two main sets of choices: **symmetrical** or **asymmetrical composition** on the one hand; and **static** or **dynamic composition** on the other.

Broadly speaking, a symmetrical composition is one in which the subject is in the centre of the picture and the two sides of the picture are similar, if not the same. In an asymmetrical composition the subject is usually to one side or the other of the frame. The Royal Mail advertisement is obviously asymmetrically composed as the young woman is well to the right of the frame. This has the effect of creating a sensation of calm repose, since the image does not appear overtly patterned or structured. Once again, the image relies upon hiding the fact that it has been very carefully staged or posed so as to reinforce the illusion of order, stability and calm which is so central to its overall effect.

As well as making a distinction between symmetrical and asymmetrical composition, you need to distinguish between static and dynamic composition. In the Royal Mail advertisement most of the lines of vision are horizontals and verticals (the bridge, the Eiffel Tower, the buildings on the bank, the girl's reasonably upright pose etc.), rather than lots of angles and perspectives. This makes it what is termed a static composition. However, you do need to note that 'static' is not being used to imply criticism here, we are not saying that the photograph is boring. Instead, the term is used to say something about the nature of the image: that the lines and shapes give a restful sense to the picture. Had the photographer taken the photograph from ground level, holding the camera at an unusual angle, then the picture would have had a dynamic composition, placing the woman at an unusual or distorted angle to the viewer, and this would have changed the overall sense of the advertisement considerably. The type of composition we have in the Royal Mail advertisement, then, is asymmetrical and static, and both these aspects of the advertisement's composition work to create the effect of calm, tranquillity, order and repose.

2.1.2e   Codes of focus   A photographer can also choose which elements of a scene to put in focus. In the Royal Mail advertisement both the foreground and the background are kept in focus in the shot; thus the photograph is in what is called '**deep**' **focus**. The foreground (the young woman), the middle ground (the bridge behind her), and the background (the buildings in the distance) are all sharp and in focus. Because the Royal Mail advertisement is shot in deep focus this means that we see all aspects of the image in equal clarity, so that each part of the advertisement (particularly setting and props) is of equal importance in creating and reinforcing the general effect of the image.

2.1.2f   Codes of lighting   The way in which these various codes are put together, through codes of lighting, reinforces the various messages we are receiving. When considering the lighting in any advertisement there are two variables of which you need to be aware: lighting key and lighting contrast. We will be going into the technical details of key and contrast later, but for the moment the following should clarify what is meant by each term:

(i)   **Lighting key**: refers to the brilliance of the picture as a whole. A picture which is fairly bright, such as our Royal Mail advertisement, is described as **high key**, one which is dark is said to be **low key**.

(ii)   **Contrast**: some pictures are described as 'contrasty' by photographers. By this photographers mean that the dark areas of the image are nearly black and the brightest areas brilliant white. Such images are described as being '**high contrast**'; a **low-contrast** picture is one which has a much narrower range of tones, with many greys but no areas of deep black or bright white.

Always try to avoid the temptation to discuss lighting solely in technical terms when analysing any media text. You must remember that the director has chosen to use a particular form of lighting because it conveys the required mood. So, in terms of codes of lighting, we can say that the Royal Mail advertisement is a high key and fairly low contrast image. Generally speaking, a high-key image conveys an air of relaxation, and low contrast is often used to suggest an element of documentary realism. In the Royal Mail advertisement, these two lighting codes work together to convey a feeling of both happiness (high key) and 'everydayness' (low contrast).

2.1.2g Colour and film stock   Colour is a powerful element in any advertisement. Because of this advertisers often use just one predominant colour to create a particular effect; a coffee advertisement, for example, will be shot in mellow browns and beiges, while an advertisement for a soft drink is more likely to contain bright reds and oranges. We will be discussing the use of colour and the type of film used to create an image later on, but for now, the most significant thing which we can notice about the Royal Mail advertisement is that it is obviously shot using black and white and not colour.

This is significant in itself for fairly obvious reasons. Black and white images tend to suggest realism, quality and restraint, and some of this would be lost if the advertisement were in colour. We can notice, too, that the image in the Royal Mail advertisement is sharp and what is called 'close-grained'. Film comes in varying degrees of graininess. You have probably seen shots in newspapers and magazines which use a very grainy film stock. This gives a feeling of gritty realism to the event. This 'gritty realism' would obviously be inappropriate in the Royal Mail advertisement and because of this the photographer has chosen to use what is termed a 'fine' or 'close' grain film which gives a very smooth look to the picture. Even simple choices, such as the graininess of the film, have a big effect on the overall meaning. What, then, is significant about the Royal Mail advertisement in terms of colour codes is the fact that it is shot in black and white and uses a close grained film: black and white serves to give the advertisement a 'realistic' feel, while the close-grained black and white image means that the advertisement is not a picture-postcard type of picture, and this in turn conjures up a sense of restraint, order and balance.

One way of summarising all this information is to write out in continuous prose your response to each of the above. However, you will find it useful if you get into the habit of summarising this information in the form of a chart, if for no other reason than it helps you to produce the beginnings of an analytical response fairly quickly so that you can begin to build a complete response to any media text, no matter how long or complex it appears. You will need to complete charts for both *mise-en-scène* and another for technical codes of construction. Apart from being useful in clarifying your ideas so far, a chart of this type will help you considerably when you come to develop your thinking about any media text, as we will be showing you in the next chapter. Tables 2.1 and 2.2 illustrate how we have summarised our analysis of the Royal Mail advertisement in terms of construction.

Table 2.1 Construction: *mise-en-scène*

Code	Selection	Meanings/Effects
(a) Setting	Paris	Romance, *joie de vivre*
(b) Props	Bicycle	Student life, freedom, tradition.
(c) Non-verbal codes	Relaxed posture	Coy, demure eyes averted.
(d) Dress codes	Jeans, T-shirt, waistcoat, jumper	Youth, casualness

Table 2.2 Construction: technical codes

Code	Selection	Meanings/Effects
(a) Shot size	Mid-shot	Closeness without intimacy
(b) Camera angle	Low	Emphasises the clear sky
(c) Lens type	Standard (perhaps slightly wide angle)	We feel as if we are a witness to this scene
(d) Composition	Static and asymmetrical	Feeling of calm and repose
(e) Focus	Deep	Everything is of importance in the shot
(f) Lighting codes	Natural	'Everyday' quality
(g) Colour codes	Black-and-white image	Realistic, documentary/ news quality

As we have said, what we have done so far is merely to introduce you to some of the major concepts involved in an analysis of our first area, construction. The next chapter will be concerned with construction in much more detail, and will allow us to develop the points we have been making in these first sections. However, any media text is not only 'made', but it is also made to be 'used', or 'consumed' by an audience.

2.2 Audience

(The idea that a media text cannot be reduced to a single, fixed and coherent 'meaning', but will instead be open to various interpretations by its various audiences.)

On first analysis it would seem to be very difficult to say anything of much significance about the audience of the 'Melt her to the coeur' advertisement. Its audience has no doubt been massive: hundreds of thousands of people will have walked, jogged, cycled or driven past this poster on its various hoarding sites up and down the country. How can we even begin to make any sort of informed comment about this audience?

In writing about audience, there are several areas you need to consider, but the single most important question to ask concerns the nature of the targeted audience itself.

2.2.1 What was the nature of the target Audience?

It is a very important first step to grasp that all advertisements are targeted at a particular audience. Consequently, the style of the advertisement, or, indeed, of any media text, has to be appropriate for its targeted audience: media texts are not just aimed at anyone who cares to look at them, they are produced with a particular audience in mind. A useful way to help you specify the nature of this intended Audience is to consider the following variables:

(a)   What is the Audience's likely educational background?
(b)   What is the Audience's likely age?
(c)   What is the Audience's likely gender?
(d)   What is the Audience's likely economic status?
(e)   What is the Audience's likely social class?

These variables are described in communications and media studies, and, indeed, within the advertising industry itself, as demographic variables, and you can be sure that any advertisement you have chosen to analyse will have been planned and produced bearing such variables in mind. Of course, some of these will be given greater consideration than others in the planning of any advertisement, because of the nature of the product being advertised, and its likely target audience. Thus, in our 'Melt her to the Coeur' advertisement , we might say that (a), above, was important because not everyone would know the meaning of the French word 'coeur'. Also, in terms of (b), above, it would seem that the advertisement is aimed particularly at a younger age group (in fact, the advertisement itself was part of a hoarding campaign composed of posters aimed at different age groups). Given that the advertisement contains a young woman one might be tempted to argue, in terms of (c), above, that it is aimed exclusively at young men; however, we feel that it is more accurate to say that it was aimed at 'young romantics' of both sexes. Both d) and (e) concern the particular social groups targeted in this advertise-ment. In order to consider this issue in more detail we need to look at the categories that are used within the advertising and media industries to classify audiences. These are:

A: Higher managerial, administrative or professional
B: Intermediate managerial, administrative or professional
C1: Supervisory or clerical, and junior managerial, administrative or professional
C2: Skilled manual worker
D: Semi-skilled and unskilled manual workers
E: State pensioners or widows (no other earner in household), casual or lower grade workers, and unemployed.

Okay, you might be saying, perhaps someone from the top of the scale might be more likely to send an airmail letter than someone at the bottom, but is there really a strong class dimension to this particular advertisement? Certainly it is true that class is a very broad and rather ambiguous term, which we all tend to define in our own particular way. Some people think that a person's wealth is the most important indicator of their class; others that professional standing is of greater significance (making a doctor of a higher class than, say, a builder – even if the latter is more wealthy). And there are still some people who will argue that 'breeding' is the most important factor;

thus if someone has an aristocratic or upper class background but has fallen on hard times this does not affect their superior class standing.

Class, then, is a rather general term and we must be clear about the way in which we are using it. It is also, though, a very important term, for most of us employ it when thinking about our lives and the world around us. What we might conclude from this is that any remarks we may wish to make about our advertisement in terms of its class dimension would have to be tentative, for our own assumptions and prejudices are likely to influence our reading. We might, for instance, argue that the advertisement was aimed at broadly middle-class social groups because of its use of location (Paris, a cosmopolitan European city), its slightly Bohemian quality, and even the nature of the postal service itself. However, this is not to deny that there are working-class people who value European culture, Bohemianism and who are regular letter writers to friends, relations or loved ones abroad. Equally, there may be a substantial percentage of middle-class people who have no interest in such areas and activities. Nevertheless, it would seem reasonable to claim that the culture suggested by our advertisement is closer to the conventions, customs and values of the middle class and middle-class young people (as opposed to those of the working class and working-class youth).

It is because of the problems inherent in trying to identify just what is meant by the concept of class that advertisers have more recently begun to use a new way of identifying audiences. Instead of attempting to divide audiences in terms of their class, advertisers tend now to identify them in terms of their needs, aspirations, attitudes, motivations and lifestyle. These variables are termed **psychographic variables** (as opposed to **demographic variables**), and it is an approach which suggests that people tend to choose a particular brand not simply because it is value for money but because, more importantly, it expresses their sense of self-identity.

The task of the creative advertising team, therefore, is to give a product or service a meaning (this is sometimes referred to as the 'brand identity') to which the consumer can relate his/her own lifestyle, aspirations, etc. This is why we associate After Eight Mints with elegance and sophistication, Coca Cola with a fun, outgoing lifestyle and so on. Even our simple Royal Mail Airmail service is given a particular meaning, insofar as it is associated with the emotional importance of staying in touch with loved ones. Using such psychographic variables makes it very much easier to identify the precise nature of a target audience.

For example, research in the advertising industry has broken down the aspirations of the younger audience into a number of psychographic variables. These are:

(a) Trendies   Those who crave the admiration of their peers.
(b) Egoists   Those who seek pleasure.
(c) Puritans   Those who wish to feel virtuous.
(d) Innovators   Those who wish to make their mark.
(e) Rebels   Those who wish to remake the world in their image.
(f) Groupies   Those who just want to be accepted.
(g) Drifters   Those who are not sure what they want.
(h) Drop-outs   Those who shun commitments of any kind.
(i) Traditionalists Those who want things to stay as they are.
(j) Utopians   Those who want the world to be a better place.
(k) Cynics   Those who have to have something to complain about.
(l) Cowboys   Those who want easy money.

You should not think of such categorisation as fixed and irrevocable. It is simply one of the tools used by advertisers to make distinctions between different sectors of audience groups. The recent proliferation of such categories is a result of the expansion of research into what is often termed 'lifestyle marketing', which claims that we all belong to a particular lifestyle group: 'strivers' and 'achievers', for instance, are categories used to describe groups of businessmen. The advertising industry increasingly employs this approach of classifying individuals. Advertisements for jeans, for example, are often aimed at 'rebels', while a famous Coca Cola campaign of the 1970s aimed at the 'utopians' with its 'I'd like to teach the world to sing...' theme song, which was sung by people of all races and ages. More recently, the Benetton campaigns of the late eighties and early nineties can be read as more sophisticated versions of the 'Utopian' variant.

It is possible for any advertisement to appeal to more than one psychographic variable. In the 'Melt her to the Coeur' advertisement, for example, insofar as fairly conventional notions of romance are being circulated, it might be argued that the advertisement is aimed at 'traditionalists'; notwithstanding this the (sanitised) Bohemian lifestyle projected might also appeal to the 'rebel'. What we might conclude is that neither the demographic nor the psychograpic approaches to the classification of audiences are precise scientific tools; it is clear, however, that they must work sufficiently well to enable campaign planners to make successful decisions about the style of advertisements. If this were not the case such categories would very quickly be cast aside.

If you are new to media studies you are bound to find this imprecision a little disturbing. It is quite natural to think that audiences either can or cannot be broken down into precise groupings. The important thing to remember is that this whole field of audience research is an evolving one and that within it there are contrasting approaches and rival methodologies. This serves to emphasise the fact that numerous cultural and ideological factors influence the way in which advertisers and researchers think about audiences.

Having discussed what the likely target audience was for the advertisement, we now need to consider what it is that the advertisement is encouraging the audience to think and to feel about the product or about the service being offered. This is true of all media texts, but is clearly demonstrated by advertising, which manifestly sets out to direct people's feelings in a particular way. What we, as consumers of a media text, are being encouraged to do, is to take up some kind of 'position' to the text on offer – whether that is an advertisement, a novel, a TV comedy, a film, or whatever. This aspect of media use is known as **audience positioning**. And so, the next question to consider is:

2.2.2   What is the audience positioning strategy?
In discussing how the possible users are 'positioned' in relation to this service we are considering just what the audience is being encouraged to think and feel about it. You will notice that we are told relatively little about the service in the Royal Mail advertisement. This in itself gives us an indication of the audience positioning strategy employed. The Royal Mail advertisement is '**soft sell**', which means that information is being given by implication only: rather than pointing explicitly to the service's benefits, the advertisement chooses instead to show the service in a context with which the audience can feel comfortable (the relaxed informality of our Parisian scene), an approach which relies less on communicating hard information in a forceful way to the audience. '**Hard sell**', on the other hand, tells us directly about the virtues of the product or service being offered. For example, if the advertisement consisted solely of metre-high bold black lettering telling us about the relative inexpense and speed of the

service compared with any other similar modes of transcontinental communication (the telephone, for instance), then it would come under the category of 'hard sell' advertising. So the first question to ask under the category audience positioning strategy is whether the media product is hard sell or soft sell.

The Royal Mail advertisement is a soft-sell media text because it communicates its information in an implied way: the airmail is given a 'human face' – you do not have to have a pen-friend in Australia or a relative working for the armed forces overseas to use this service, it is for everyone, and all of the normal sorts of letter (here presumably a love letter) can be sent using it. The service is being simultaneously 'positioned' as similar to the normal mail services (this positioning will encourage us to use it because it is like the normal postal services), but it is also, we feel, being positioned as something a little special – the recipient of an airmail letter feels she has got something a little out of the ordinary and that the sender cares just that little bit more.

We can also return to some of the issues covered above in Construction mise-en-scène and technical codes of construction, since these also help to establish our position in regard to the Royal Mail advertisement. As onlookers we are compelled to occupy the physical position at which the photographer placed the camera; the placing of the camera is not at all neutral, since it affects how we feel about the events shown.

While the positioning of the camera in front of the mise-en-scène determines our response to the subject matter in one way, the actual contents of the mise-en-scène determine our response in another. For example, many advertisements contain both stereotypes and stock social situations: old people are shown as quirky and cantankerous; young people as exuberant, boisterous or rebellious; fathers act the 'silly daddy' with the children while mothers are frequently 'long-suffering'. The locations themselves, the homes of 'professional' people, cheery locals, rolling English countryside and so on all position us within the social space of the *status quo*. Codes of mise-en-scène and technical codes of construction therefore play a significant part in audience positioning.

Several important issues arise from this. The first is that it is always important to remember that the five key areas we are using in this book do not stand in isolation to each other: Audience is related to Construction, and also to Narrative, Agency and Categories. But, second, it is always worth remembering that, just as we give meaning to the Royal Mail advertisement, so it gives a particular 'meaning' to us: like any other media text it constructs a 'space of communication' in which we, as the audience, can create certain meanings. The very 'naturalness' of the space of communication in the Royal Mail advertisement is in fact a good indication that key social values are at work – the innocence of youth, romance and femininity are here 'naturalised'. The advertisement seems to say to us 'look how natural and innocent all this is', and we are clearly expected to agree with this view of reality.

This notion of some kind of agreement taking place between producer and consumer (the audience) is fundamental to all media texts, as we can see in the Royal Mail advertisement. In positioning its audience in particular ways the Royal Mail advertisement is attempting to facilitate what is sometimes referred to as a 'preferred reading' of the advertisement. The term 'preferred' is used here because it relates to the interpretation that the advertisers wish us to make and is thus related to the values and beliefs that form a defining focus for the campaign (the freedom of youth, romance, and so on). Because of this only a limited number of 'positions' are available to the viewer: we can only find in it images of freedom, romance, youth, a natural and carefree attitude, etc. It might therefore be argued that it is impossible to make a positive feminist reading of the 'Melt her to the Coeur' advertisement, given the representations it contains.

This leads us to the mode of address. The issue of mode of address is an extremely important one in media studies in general and in the study of advertising in particular. Just as your lecturers address you as a student, your parents as their son or daughter, your children as their parent and so on, nearly all media texts address their audience in a particular way, although you (as an audience) may often be unaware of the fact that they are doing this. It is important, however, that you (as a student or critic of a media text) are aware just how the text addresses its audience, and so you need to ask:

2.2.3 How is the audience addressed? (Mode of address)

In the space of one commercial break a man can be positioned at one moment as a concerned father making sure that his insurance is sufficient to provide adequate money for his family, and as 'one of the lads' by a beer commercial at the next. A variety of modes of address can be found in the advertisements that take place over any one evening. Some seem to talk down to us whilst others acknowledge our sophistication; some are aggressively pushy, others warm and intimate. Naturally we tend to make an unconscious connection between the product and the voice that tells us about it. How we are addressed and the tones used play a big part in creating the right impression.

This question can be extremely complex when we start to consider films and TV dramas, as we will see later, but in advertisements we can break the issue down into some manageable concepts. The five basic styles employed in copywriting for advertisements are:

(a) Question: 'Is it fair to put the health of others at risk?'
(b) Statement: 'The best soap powder money can buy.'
(c) Command: 'Melt her to the Coeur.'
(d) Emotional Appeal: 'Only the best dog food is good enough for your puppy.'
(e) News: 'Woolworths takes action on prices.'

In each of these the audience is obviously being addressed in a different way. A command is different from an emotional appeal and both these are different from a statement. We can say that the 'Melt her to the Coeur' advertisement is in the command style. In a TV programme, we may be addressed in many different ways at different times, but the basic concept remains true: that we, as audience members, are responsible for making sense of the media text, but that it also creates for us particular positions from which to understand it.

But it is also important to remember that any reading of a media text is itself culturally specific. For example, just consider the different responses you might have to the model in the Royal Mail advertisement, according to your own culturally specific postion. Is she the sort of person with whom you could identify, whom you might have as a friend or acquaintance? If so, it could be that the advertisement is aimed at people like yourself. The young woman looks to us to be a 'student type', and, depending upon your background, you will respond negatively or positively to such images. A retired army Colonel or local magistrate may read her as a 'scruffy student' sort and find her jeans and baggy cardigan distinctly 'unfeminine'. A feminist critic may object to the representation of women and romance here. S/he may feel that the sentiments and emotions expressed – romantic love, etc. – are of a very traditional sort, the kind of feelings more appropriate to a Mills and Boon romantic novel than to a young woman of the 1990s.

We can no longer argue, therefore, that the 'internal structure' of the Royal Mail advertisement determines the interpretations that are made of it. As a media text it is neither simply a conveyer of the advertiser's ideas nor of some abstract 'dominant ideology'; it is much more accurate to say that it is we, as audience members, who produce meanings from it given our own cultural knowledge. Media texts are not packages of fixed meaning and, further, because culture is itself constantly changing, we cannot simply extract a final definitive meaning from any text, whether it is an advertisement, television programme or a film. As society and the individuals within it change, so the meanings of the texts change also.

2.3   Narrative

(The way in which the narrative unfolds is far from natural, but is instead the result of information being manipulated and edited.)

The photograph that formed the basis for the Royal Mail advertisement captured just a moment, the fraction of a second when the photographer took the picture on a particular bridge over the Seine. And yet even this moment in time tells a story, a Narrative. This Narrative is not always obvious. But by using the basic framework which we outline in this section to organise your own thoughts about Narrative, you will be able to direct your thinking in a more purposeful way as you work gradually toward more complex issues. The secret of building a coherent analysis, if you are new to media studies, lies in this patient attention to the different levels of meaning in media texts.

There are three basic levels of analysis to think about when you analyse any advertisement or media text in terms of its Narrative. The first is a straightforwardly descriptive level, in which you describe what is happening in the story. You can then move on from a straightforward description to offer some interpretation of the explicit meanings offered by the text. And finally, you can develop your thinking to account for meanings implied by the Narrative told by the text.

2.3.1   Describe what happens in the Narrative

First, you need to be able to state, in a detailed and descriptive way, the key elements that make up this 'story'. The things that you need to consider at this first level of analysis all relate to what you actually see and to the event you witness taking place. In the Royal Mail advertisement we see a young woman standing on a bridge over the Seine reading a letter. The advertisement thus refers to places and events we recognise and which have a particular meaning and significance for us. Your sole object at this first level of analysis is to describe, as carefully as you can, these basic elements – the period, the setting, and the nature of the story that is being told.

So, what can we say about these things? The photographer's task was clearly to choose just the right moment – catching the expression on the girl's face as she starts to read the letter – in order to enable the viewer to build up a story around the image: is she French and he English (this is perhaps implied by using the the word 'Coeur' – which would make it a story of love conquering national and cultural differences)? Is this letter his first expression of true love? As the cliché has it, every picture tells a story, and many different narratives are possible. We can extend the story forwards as well as backwards by asking what will happen next – a proposal or a holiday together perhaps? Given the nature of the photograph, its construction at the level of mise-en-scène and so on, we tend to think that this is not a relationship that will end in tears, simply because of all the images of security and stability surrounding the Narrative.

It is from this that we can begin to offer an interpretation of the explicit meaning of the story. We can say, for example, that the story being told in this advertisement seems to suggest something like, 'old fashioned romance is not dead'. This readily apparent 'explicit' meaning would be clear to most people looking at the advertisement. Even complex narratives, of the sort that would be found in a full-length feature film, a play or a novel can be discussed in terms of their explicit meanings; *Othello* and *Fatal Attraction* are both about jealousy, for instance. What distinguishes them as texts is their unique presentation and exploration of jealousy through character and dramatic setting.

2.3.2   *What meanings are explicit in the Narrative?*
Moving from a basic description of the Narrative of the advertisement or still to an interpretation of the explicit themes suggested by the Narrative is an important step to take in your analysis of a text. Returning to the Royal Mail advertisement, for instance, it is fairly clear that one of the central themes suggested by the Narrative is the idea of romance, as we have suggested above. But there is much more being suggested also. The young woman in the advertisement seems

manifestly modern and yet the advertisement itself gives us a fairly traditional image of romance. This combination of old and new works together to give rise, at the second level of analysis, to the idea that there are some things that remain constant in human experience. This is sparked off by the idea of romance, but is supported by other information gleaned from the text. For example, at the first, descriptive level, the pair of jeans the young woman is wearing is just a pair of jeans; at the level of explicit meaning, however, this pair of jeans can be seen to represent other things also: freedom, youth or rebellion, depending upon your interpretation. But it would be difficult to think of the pair of jeans as representing, say, Victorian family values or technological progress.

What complicates analysis at this level of explicit meaning is that the connotations of a word or image are not fixed forever: flared jeans were once a mark of trendy sophistication, whereas now they mean just the opposite. If you think about it such connotations only arise when words or images interact with your own values and emotions. Advertisers know this and good campaigns are successful because of the way they operate on their audiences at this subjective level.

When you write about magazine or television advertisements, then, remember that nearly everything you see has been included because of its connotative meanings. In a snapshot there may be a bicycle in the background that just happened to be there by accident, but if a bicycle is included in an advertisement then it will be a certain kind of bike that carries particular associations. Further, it is not just what is shown that you need to write about but also how it is shown – a photograph of a young woman wearing jeans can be taken in many different ways, as we have seen under Construction: *mise-en-scène*, above. If the image used bright colours it could connote vitality and a picture-postcard quality; if it was a 'grainy' and 'contrasty' black-and-white picture this might connote 'arty', and if it were in sepia then it would connote the past, and so on. Clearly, then, it is important to move on from the explicit meanings suggested by the story told by the text to meanings or connotations implied by it also.

2.3.3 *What implicit meanings can we find in the Narrative?*

At this level of interpretation you will need occasionally to stick your neck out and risk making mistakes, for you can isolate these implicit meanings only by putting forward some tentative ideas. Let us turn once again to the carefree young woman of the Royal Mail advertisement. You can probably think of many other campaigns that represent young people in this way. Certainly it would be fair to say there are not many representations of angst-ridden uncertain teenagers in advertisements (except, perhaps, in those for acne creams), so what implicit or hidden meanings can we extract from this seemingly innocent Royal Mail advertisement? The first question to ask yourself before you go any further is just why young people are being represented in this way? Like many other advertisements involving young people this one paints a picture of young people as both breaking with tradition (she dresses in a fairly unisex way, seems carefree and slightly Bohemian), and yet still adhering to some of the values of earlier generations (romantic love, for example). We need, at this level of analysis, to try to account for this combination. You could suggest that by combining carefree rebelliousness with traditional values advertisers are helping to stop young people challenging the core values of society: young people do not have to overthrow 'the establishment' to express their youthful disrespect for tradition. Instead, this can be shown just by wearing a particular brand of jeans – or so some advertisements seem to suggest.

It is interesting in this respect to compare the representations of youth found in the Royal Mail advertisement with those found in American advertisements for jeans and soft drinks. We are offered in these a vision of America as a natural, open, free society which is itself an expression of humanity's basic natural needs and aspirations. You could therefore suggest that campaigns such as this, which seem to encourage young people to put aside everyday rules, are in fact working to spread deeper beliefs and values, which relate to American society and culture. This is why we have termed this level of analysis 'the search for implicit meanings'. The values in such American advertisements are presented to their young audiences as natural and universal – exuberance and self-expression are shown to be intrinsically good, human and universal qualities. Nevertheless such values, far from being universal, relate to a particular society, the USA, at a particular point in time. Although the young woman in the Royal Mail advertisement is much more reserved – indeed the whole advertisement has an air of traditional British restraint about it – the same tactic of combining the seemingly modern with the traditional is there and this, it could be argued, tells us something about the nature of contemporary British society, its values and beliefs, and about the kind of image it wishes to present about itself.

Now, although it would not be possible to point to any one thing in the advertisement that gives rise to these implicit meanings – in the way that, at the second level of analysis we could point to the letter or the Eiffel Tower and say these connoted romance and Paris respectively – this does not mean that analysis at this third level is all just guesswork. To step from the second level of analysis to the third, all you have to do is to remind yourself what key values or themes the advertisement presents in its Narrative, and then to attempt to relate those themes to society and its values more generally. Depending on the advertisement, its central theme could be the kind that we mentioned above – masculinity, the family, femininity, success, romance and so on. Each of these issues plays an important part both in contemporary society and in our own lives and it is only to be expected that advertisers will direct attention to such issues when planning advertising campaigns – just as the director of a film will be aware of similar ideas when constructing a full-length feature.

All you have to do, therefore, in order to move from the level of explicit meanings to the level of implied meanings is to relate the advertisement or media text to dominant values and beliefs within society – beliefs about the roles of men and women, about family life, about work and leisure, about success and status and so on. The story told in the 'Melt her to the Coeur' advertisement makes sense to us because we ourselves are familiar with such themes and because they are so widespread they seem natural. What could be more natural than this picture of a young woman smiling as she reads a letter from her boyfriend/partner? And yet this relies upon a naturalisation and acceptance of values that are in fact social – femininity, romance, etc. At this level of analysis you need to question why things are presented in the way they are and how this relates to dominant social values. It is this that makes analysis at this level a more critical and analytical exercise.

2.4   Categorisation

(The idea that when we watch a film or TV programme we bring to it a considerable amount of knowledge and understanding about media texts in general and that part of the enjoyment of the text involves the pleasure of seeing an artistic or fictional form take shape before us.)

It is very important in media studies and communication studies to consider just how we might begin to classify and categorise the various types of mass-media output that form the basis for these subjects. Yet as soon as we think about this in any detail we realise how difficult it is. You might, for instance, categorise a media text in terms of the medium in which you find it (radio, television, cinema, etc.), or in terms of its relation to real events (fiction or non-fiction). Alternatively, you might think that the most important category is the one that allows you to identify it as a recognisable genre type (the western, the situation comedy, the musical, the thriller, etc.).

Because of this difficulty in classifying and grouping media output, we suggest that you follow the series of points listed below, in order to direct your thinking in a purposeful way. These points are certainly not exhaustive, but they do have the advantage of being sufficiently flexible to allow you to talk about nearly all forms of media text.

2.4.1 *Identify and comment upon the medium*
Before you go on to analyse any advertisement or other media text it is important to consider, first, the medium in which it occurs. The advertisers will have planned the 'Melt her to the Coeur' advertisement for a street hoarding rather than as an eighth-of-a-page magazine placement. The message for the former must come across 'at a glance', for it is seen for just a moment by passing motorists and busy shoppers. At the outset, then, when dealing with categorisation, always remember to consider which medium – television, street hoarding, radio, film, computer software, etc. – you are trying to analyse, for you need to think about the specific qualities of that medium and how this affects the nature of the advertisement.

2.4.2 *Identify and comment upon the form of the media text*
One of the first things we all do almost instinctively when watching television, reading a magazine or newspaper or listening to the radio is to classify the various things we look at or hear in various ways, identifying some as news, others as advertisements, documentaries, light entertainment, and so on. Each of these types of media output is termed a **media form** and we shall be using this term in later chapters when we return to issues of categorization. Each, of course, has its own styles and conventions: we expect TV advertisements to be a certain length (not two seconds or twenty minutes, say), and to mention or show the product advertised. Occasionally an advertisement 'borrows' the conventions of another form – some advertisements, for instance, are shot in a pseudo-documentary manner – but

it is nevertheless clear that the media form we are dealing with here is that of advertising.

2.4.3   Identify and comment upon the genre or style

The output of any particular medium (2.4.1) can be classified in terms of recognisable types or genre. Thus with television we have such genres as the police series, and the sitcom. In the cinema there are the horror movie, sci-fi, Westerns, musicals, and many others. We will be discussing most of these genres in later chapters. But advertising is not itself a genre. It is rather a media form (2.4.2); does this mean, therefore, that there is nothing we can say about advertisements in relation to the concept of genre ?

In order to answer this question we will need to look a little closer at how different genres are defined. The subject matter and themes are clearly important – we expect Westerns to be about law and order, about men taming the Wild West, about gun-slinging and violence. There is also the issue of style: we would expect, for example, a gangster movie to have a dark gritty realistic feel, a musical to have colourful bright scenes.

Advertisers frequently make use of the audience's knowledge of genre conventions when devising a campaign. They know that as soon as we have identified a particular advertisement as relating to a known genre, then certain expectations will arise in our minds. The advertisers can then play around with these 'genre expectations' in a witty way, and many campaigns of the 1980s and 1990s have done just this.

The Royal Mail advertisement perhaps reminds us a little of a light-hearted innocent teenage romance movie although the link is far less obvious than it would be in campaigns which very clearly relate to such genres as the thriller (such as the Pirelli tyre campaign) or the sitcom (as in Maureen Lipman's advertisements for British Telecom). The Royal Mail advertisement itself is not strong on genre, however, although it is clear that it does derive its 'place' in society from the kinds of messages it puts out in other ways. If the aim of this book were to concentrate on just the analysis of advertising, it would be worth spending time thinking about the exact way that the advertisement projects these various messages. To do this, we would need to analyse the advertisement's relationship to the product being sold, the selling strategy employed, product appeal (through reinforcement of previously held values, or the desire to identify with a particular lifestyle). But this is not the aim of this book, fascinating though such analysis is. Instead, at this point, we want merely to reinforce the notion of Categorisation outlined above, since this will be necessary for you to understand when we embark on the analysis of film and TV texts, or when you start on your own analyses.

It will now be useful to summarise what we can say about the Royal Mail advertisement in terms of Categorisation. First, the medium employed is that of a street hoarding, and this means that the message has to come across more or less at a glance because it is seen for just a moment by passing motorists and busy shoppers. This in turn means that the story it tells must be clear on the level of Narrative, but allowing for development of both explicit and implicit meanings through its use of, for example, setting and props, as we saw under Construction: *mise-en-scène*. Second, the Royal Mail image conforms to the conventions we normally associate with hoarding advertisements, and uses photography and presentation (black-and-white film stock, camera angle, etc.) which fit in with these expectations. And finally, under genre or style, we can note that the Royal Mail advertisement perhaps reminds us a little of a light-hearted innocent teenage romance movie. Taken together, these three aspects of the advertisement help us not only to identify it as a media text, but allow it to function more precisely by working within the conventions of form, style and genre to reinforce its audience's expectations and the values of stability and order it is promoting.

2.5 Agency

Like most media texts the Royal Mail advertisement is the result of collaboration between a number of individuals. An advertising company will have been employed who were responsible for generating the creative idea, a photographer will have taken the shot, a typographer will have been involved in selecting the typeface and type size, a printer produced the individual sheets which were then pasted together on the billboard to form the hoarding advertisement. One of the problems that you will face as you attempt to analyse any media text in terms of these areas of agency and organisation is the difficulty of finding out the relevant facts. You know an advertising company will have been involved in its production, but the precise decision-making processes, the discussions that led up to the final campaign and the complex proceedings that led from rough idea to final poster can be very difficult to unravel. Open any magazine and you will certainly find an advertisement that you can talk about in terms of the colours used, the lighting or the ways in which the figures are posed; but to track down all the advertising companies involved in the production of the advertisements in just one magazine would be almost impossible. This does not mean, however, that it is impossible to consider the major factors involved in the text's production.

The term 'Agency' is used to discuss these aspects of the production and circulation of media text because it nicely captures the two essential dimensions which must be taken into account. First, there is Agency as 'creative activity', the work of the photographers, art directors and graphic designers involved; and second there is 'agency-as-agency' – by which we mean the way in which the media company operates, how it is organised internally, and how it is governed externally by certain rules and laws (the Advertising Standards Authority, the British Board of Film Censors and other legislation concerning the media, for instance).

This means that as well as accounting for the various inputs made by the creative team in the production of any media text, there is also the issue of external pressures governing that production. A writer of a TV drama, for example, may want to set the whole thing in the seventeenth century with 300 extras and two sea battles. The director may well agree with this, but knows that the programme producer has an extremely limited budget and is under pressure to shoot the programme in studio. This means that there is not only a specific relationship existing between the creative agency and the media organisation in which the production takes place, but another, equally significant relationship existing between these agencies and the various media technologies available and involved in the final production of the media text.

Now, while it is the case that some media technologies do come into the hands of the general public (such as cameras, sound-recorders and personal computers), it is highly unlikely that the complex technologies relating to television studios and broadcasting do so. This may seem to be stating the obvious but it is in fact an important point – the general public has little access to the key media agencies and to their technologies. More importantly, even if you happen to possess a well-equipped sound studio, video-editing facilities, and have access to excellent actors, it is most unlikely that you would be able to 'broadcast' your programme to more than just a few friends, who might watch it with you on a VTR. Even when, in programmes such as *Punters* on radio or *Open Space* on TV, individuals are granted access to media technology, this is only granted on the terms of that media organisation which is itself controlled by external legislation.

Another point to bear in mind is that each form of media production has its own quite specific internal organisation. An advertising company, for example, will be made up of many interrelating departments. Similarly, a television programme will be the result of the work of at least tens, and sometimes, hundreds of people, all working within requirements specific to the nature of their particular responsibility. And these responsibilities will themselves be mediated by the particular agency within which they operate. Our point here is that the relationship between the media text and the various agencies feeding in to its final realisation is both an extremely complex one, and one that is specific to the particular media technology being employed. This means that there is a reason why a media text looks the way it does. For example, if the Creative Department of the Royal Mail's advertising agency had suggested an image for the 'Melt her to the Coeur' advertisement which featured the young woman nude, smoking a cigarette and riding a Harley Davidson one-handed over the same bridge while reading the letter using her free hand, then the idea would not have gone through to production. Even if the technical problems of producing such an image could have been resolved, the advertisement would not have conjured up the images of order, stability and tradition which the Royal Mail, as the advertising company's customer, would have wanted.

But as well as this very important requirement – that the customer gets what s/he wants – there are also other, external, pressures on the media organisation. Because the broadcast media is such a powerful and influential medium it is understandable that it should be governed by various rules, laws and codes. All forms of printed advertisement, including our Royal Mail advertisement, come under the aegis of the Advertising Standards Authority (ASA) whose remit is to examine all complaints and say whether they have offended the British Code of Advertising Practice. If you were to find our Royal Mail advertisement distasteful or blatantly untrue (although this is, of course, unlikely given the context), you could write to the ASA who would investigate your complaints. Certainly, these are powerful enough reasons to suggest why the Royal Mail advertisement looks the way it does, and why it does not show the young woman nude, smoking a cigarette and riding a Harley Davidson. Such external Agency pressures are just as strong as the customer's brief.

When writing about Agency, then, it is important to be aware of the various pressures which all feed in to the final production of the text. This is to some extent specific to each industry (TV and advertising are not structured in identical ways, for example), but there are general principles that apply across the whole media industry. An awareness of these principles, as we have outlined here, will give your own analyses greater confidence in the way that you handle the relationship between the media text and Agency. And remember, it is just this, the relationship between text and Agency, that is the central issue: the final text looks the way it does because of the customer's requirements, the internal organisation of the media organisation concerned (including the relationship between creative and production agencies, and external governing bodies – such as the ASA), Parliament and the various Acts governing the media industry as a whole.

This brings us to the end of what has been a fairly lengthy introduction to the five central concepts of which you need to be aware if you want to produce your own readings and analyses of a media text. Some of the issues involved are no doubt easier to grasp than others: it is much easier to work out whether a shot was taken using a wide-angle lens than it is to say precisely what the relationship is between a media text and the agencies responsible for its production. But don't be worried by this. The important thing is to comment upon what you find of significance in a given media text, and to fit that in to your overall impressions. Our descriptions are there merely to help you to formalise your thinking, so that when you do spot something you will at least know what it is you have spotted, and how you can account for its significance. Don't worry if everything doesn't make equal sense just yet. It takes time, and practice at analysing media texts yourself, for a coherent picture to focus. While you gain that experience, use this chapter as a sort of reference guide until you feel familiar with the topics it raises. The same applies to the next chapter which is concerned with how to develop your analysis further.

3

Looking at aspects of a media text

IN the previous chapter we formed a general view of the Royal Mail advertisement, using our five key media aspects as a framework for analysis. Media texts, we argued, can be 'read' insofar as they are structured and organised in particular ways; in analysing the Royal Mail advertisement we were drawing attention to the ways in which the advertisement constructed its 'meaning' through its use of visual codes and conventions. This area of communications and media studies is often described as **semiotic analysis**, and it will be useful here to introduce you to some of the technical terms associated with this type of analysis.

Semiotics is the study of the ways in which **signs** communicate meaning and of the rules that govern their use. Its specialised vocabulary aims to describe just how the signs and codes to be found in all media texts work to produce meaning in particular ways. As an approach to the analysis of media texts, semiotics has been growing in influence since the 1960s. One of the main reasons for this is that it can be applied to all kinds of text from comic books, sitcoms and rock music to literature, paintings, the highway code and much more besides.

You have probably come across the phrase 'semiotic analysis' before. Even if this is the case, however, we would still suggest that you read this chapter. Semiotic theory underpins much of our analysis of television in this book, and we will be using many of the concepts associated with semiotics in later chapters, so it is important that you do understand these concepts more or less from the outset.

As we saw in the previous chapter, the Royal Mail 'Melt her to the Coeur' advertisement contains a number of sign systems on which it is possible to comment in detail using this type of semiotic analysis. The posture of the young woman and the contentment indicated by her facial expression are signs within the larger sign system of non-verbal behaviour, while her jeans and cardigan are signs within the sign system relating to dress. When you look at the advertisement you are interpreting many such signs; the model's hair, dress and posture say something about her as a person, they have a meaning, and, because of this, they can be regarded as signs within a semiotic system.

For the purpose of analysis it is useful to consider the sign as a composite entity made up of:

(i)   the physical or material thing that is perceived through the senses(the girl's hairstyle or clothes);
(ii) the meaning that this has for us (such as, for example, 'carefree').

In semiotics the former physical 'thing' is referred to as the **signifier** and the latter 'concept' or meaning, the **signified**. Any sign – whether it be putting out one's hand at a bus stop or a hairstyle – can thus be considered to be composed of these two distinct parts, one physical and one conceptual. To interpret the signs in our Royal Mail advertisement involves, therefore, isolating the signifiers that communicate the advertisement's message – gestures, facial expressions, etc. – and commenting upon what we take to be their meaning or 'signified'.

Of course, all that we actually experience is the sign, which is, as we explained above, the combination of signifier and signified. Only in semiotic analysis are these two separated. What we see are innumerable signs waiting for interpretation. For example, props play a major role as signs in most advertisements. The props that you need to identify in your own analyses are those that play an important part in what the advertisement is trying to put across. If an advert for tea shows the product being poured into a fairly ordinary teacup, then this cup is a prop only insofar as it needs to be there for tea to be poured into. As its role is clearly purely functional you need not analyse this. However, if the tea were poured into a highly decorated bone-china teacup, then the cup, since it conveys a meaning (class or sophistication) is clearly a sign to which you need to pay attention. As such, it is what is termed a **symbolic prop**, that is to say, one which symbolises particular ideas or qualities. Spectacles, for example, are often used as symbolic props. Advertisements for washing powders which have a 'scientific' laboratory-type setting will often include a scientist who talks to us. The scientist, particularly if it is a woman, will wear glasses because these connote 'intelligence', and this suggests that the product itself is one which, because it has been tried and tested by inquiring, scientific and precise minds, will appeal to the more discerning consumer.

It is important that you isolate any props in an advertisement that have this type of symbolic significance and are, therefore, important signs. If you were discussing an advertisement in which all the people were wearing green wellingtons, then you would need to comment upon their symbolic significance. For example, we tend to associate such footwear with the activities of certain classes of people – yuppies who spend their weekends in the country, or perhaps the hunting and shooting fraternity of the upper classes. In the 1980s the phrase 'the green-welly brigade' was used to christen such groups and we ought to expect to find other props in the advertisement – Range Rovers or labradors or people dressed in waxed Barbour coats – that have a similar symbolic significance to green wellingtons.

The main symbolic prop in the Royal Mail advertisement (the 'roadster' bicycle) is a sign of considerable significance insofar as its signified connotes both tradition and also the carefree quality of student life. This message is reinforced by the NVC signs used in the advertisement. We've already spent some time looking at the model's dress and pose, but the area we want to develop here has to do with the model's facial expression. It is often the facial expression of a model that captures our attention in any advertisement. Sometimes this expression is intended to emphasise the appeal of the product, so that we expect the models and actors in advertisements to look delighted, happy and contented with what the product has to offer. A move away from this rather obvious strategy took place in the 1980s when many cosmetic firms started using pictures in which the woman scowled, frowned, grimaced, pouted, glowered or sulked. By carefully using these codes of facial expression advertisers were able to sell 'the sullen look' to the audience. Before this, however, the smile was the dominant facial expression in women's advertising when women seemed to smile endlessly in baked-bean ads, advertisements for cleaners and scourers, in gravy advertisements and so on. But why did they smile, what are the connotations of this simple and universal expression? Clearly, the main one is that these women are at ease in their respective domestic worlds, their social roles as wives and mothers seem to be endlessly fulfilling. The message behind such expressions is one of reassurance – all is right with the world as it is currently organised; it could therefore be suggested that the female smile thus functions as a sign of female submission, placing women in an almost childlike state of pleasure when given a new domestic product. This, however, is not quite the type of smile found on the face of the model in the Royal Mail advertisement, which gives, instead, a feeling of shared intimacy.

However, it is always important to remember, when analysing any advertisement, that facial expressions, like all other signs, can only be properly understood when they are related to the context in which they occur. It is often difficult to say, in isolation, whether a smile signifies contempt or happiness. In the Royal Mail advertisement we can see that the smile represents the specific pleasures afforded by the communication of romantic confidences through the agency of the airmail service. This reading of the advertisement is supported by other NVC details also, including our sense of distance, contact and orientation towards the model. Some sense of physical closeness is created in the Royal Mail advertisement by having the model positioned in a medium-shot (MS) rather than a long shot (LS). However, we do not feel that we are invading the model's personal space, and this is important in the context of the advertisement as a whole. We all feel awkward if someone we do not know invades our personal space; how close we approach someone gives them in turn a message about our feelings towards them. There are, of course, all sorts of cultural differences here – the British traditionally like a lot of personal space while Latin peoples are usually thought to prefer closer contact. Research has shown that in American and English groups people rarely pat each other on the back, let alone hug or caress. In fact, a comparative survey revealed that, while, over a specific period of time, 102 touches were made between people in conversation in a Parisian coffee bar, no touches at all were made by their counterparts in a London coffee bar.

Distance and touch are not only nationally and culturally specific, they are also related to gender. Women are far more likely to be shown touching objects or caressing their surfaces in advertisements than are men. Look at the careful way in which the young woman holds the letter from her boyfriend or partner in the Royal Mail advertisement. This sort of ritualistic touching is something you will notice again and again in advertisements containing female characters. Women in advertisements seem to be far more tactile beings, forever appreciating the touch and feel of things, while men tend to be shown appreciating their structure and purpose.

Again, this is reinforced in the Royal Mail advertisement by our sense of Orientation towards the model. The young woman in the Royal Mail advertisement is turned slightly away from us, which suggests a feeling of quiet privacy. If she were facing us directly or had her back toward us, this would alter the meaning significantly. The orientation of the actors or models towards each other and towards the viewer are an important part of any media text. If two characters are in conversation but face slightly away from each other, this affects the way we see their relationship. Nevertheless, you should always remember to link orientation to context; if two people are facing each other directly then this can signify either close intimacy or hostility, depending on the context.

It is important to point out that not all the signs that we find in this advertisement are of the same type. nor do they all function in the same way. The American semiotician, C.S. Pierce claimed that it was possible to distinguish the following three categories of sign:

(i) *Icons*

Iconic signs always resemble the things that they represent. This does not mean, however, that they all exhibit the same degree of realism; a photograph and a detailed drawing are iconic but so also are the diagrammatic signs that we find in gentlemen's and ladies' lavatories.

As our advertisement is in photographic form and is, therefore iconic, it signifies that which it shows – the young woman, the Eiffel Tower, etc. – not by some arbitrary convention but by its direct resemblance to those things. In such cases the signifier (the photographic image) is described as being 'motivated' by the signified (the reality that it represents). As a result, photographs are known as **motivated signs** (maps being another example).

Of course, the signifier does not have to resemble what it represents; it can be quite independent of the signified. The words 'Ladies' and 'Gentlemen', for example, have no natural connection with that which they signify which is why, in Germany they can be replaced by the words 'Damen' and 'Herren'. Because the relationship between signifier and signified here is purely a matter of convention these are referred to as **arbitrary signs**.

Most of the signs that you will be concerned with in your analyses of advertising, or of television more generally, will be iconic simply because the media technologies involved (video and film cameras) record, either electronically or on film, 'real events'. The iconic nature of such signs explains the immediate impact that this medium makes on us. Consequently, it is often argued that it is in the areas of news and documentary that their power to convince us that reality is unfolding before our eyes is the greatest.

(ii) *Index*

Indexical signs are in some way connected with the things that they signify but they do not represent or picture them in the straightforward and direct way that iconic signs do. For example, because we associate Churchill with his cigar and Napoleon with his hat each of these historical individuals can be evoked by these objects.

It is important to note, however, that a picture of Napoleon's hat is both an iconic sign insofar as it signifies that French Emperor's hat but also an indexical sign in that it signifies the French Emperor. Clearly the same applies to the Eiffel Tower in our advertisement which functions iconically to represent the Parisian landmark and indexically to signify 'Paris'. To explain how this happens we need to look at the concept of metonymy.

Metonyms are figures of speech which refer to a particular attribute of a thing for the thing itself: 'the crown' for the Queen and 'the bottle' for alcoholic drink are examples. A second figure of speech that relies upon such replacements is **synecdoche** in which a part is substituted for the whole (as in 'wheels' or 'motor' for a car) or, more infrequently, the whole for a part (as in 'the police have arrived' instead of a policeman or policewoman has arrived).

(iii) *Symbols*

Some signs, the words in our advertisement for instance, have no logical connection with, or resemblance to, the ideas and things that they signify. The written word 'Coeur', for instance, is an arbitrary sign because it could be replaced by any other word for heart (although the pun, on 'core' would, of course, be lost in the process).

Writing is not the only type of symbolic sign, however: a red rose is a symbol of romance and love not because it resembles either of these concepts but because, over the centuries, it has come to symbolise these things. You simply need to remember that with **symbolic signs** it is not possible to guess what the signified might be from the signifier if you have not learnt the connection. It is for this reason that to understand how a sign works we need to be able to place it within a broader concept of the code.

CODES

Individual signs communicate a meaning but it is important to look at the larger collection of signs from which any individual one is chosen in order to comment more fully on the way in which meaning is produced. These collections of signs, whether the English language or techniques relating to filming, are known as **Codes**. Thus we might say that:

A sign   =   a physical thing (signifer) which carries a meaning (signified) for a group of people.

A code   =   a recognized system of signs (the English language, the highway code, etc.)

A message   =   a particular combination of signs that follows established rules (those of grammar, say) and which communicates a meaning.

Codes are to be found in all social life: to dress in the morning is to 'encode' a message, for in doing so we choose certain elements to combine (trousers, shirts, sweaters, dresses, blouses, jackets, etc.) in order to say something about ourselves. Nevertheless, it is important to point out that it is already socially agreed what the signs that make up the dress code mean: you cannot individually make them communicate anything else. And, of course, the meanings of such signs will differ from culture to culture: in China white is worn at funerals, while in the West black is normally associated with death.

In any media text a whole host of codes relating to lighting, composition and so forth will be in operation and it is to these technical codes that we now return. Students often make the mistake, when they first start to analyse an advertisement in terms of its technical codes, of approaching this in a mechanical way by simply listing the type of film stock or lens that was used. It is important to remember that you are engaged in analysing an advertisement rather than writing a technical account for a specialist photographic magazine. The reason why you need to take these technical codes into account is because they are extremely important in creating the meaning of the image as a whole, since they have been used in a creative, rather than simply a technical way, to create an overall meaning. For the director, lighting focus, camera angle and composition are the very building blocks of his or her practice. We will now comment on these codes in greater detail.

(a) Shot size

Shot size is clearly significant in the Royal Mail advertisement As we said earlier, the advertisement is a medium shot (MS). In the medium shot we do not feel as if we are invading the subject's personal space, so that, if, for example, the subject were speaking to us, then the MS helps to maintain a certain social distance. This choice of shot-size in the Royal Mail advertisement is effective because not only does it enable us to see a fair amount of detail in the young woman's face (the smile), but we do not lose sight of the setting, which is of equal importance in establishing the overall meaning.

But there are many other shot-sizes available to the film-maker, and it will probably be worthwhile to run through these here, particularly as we will be using shot-size as part of our analyses in later chapters of this book. We are including photographs alongside these, just to make the differences clearer still.

In Figure 3.1, the **extreme long shot (ELS)**, the subject takes up only a small part of the frame; the setting itself is the main thing that we see. Because of this such a shot is often known as an **establishing shot** because it establishes what scene or location we are looking at. In Figure 3.2, the **long shot (LS)**, the camera has come a little closer to the subject. Nevertheless we can still see all of the standing subject within the frame, neither feet nor head being cut off. The subject is no longer quite so lost in the setting as in the ELS but the setting still takes up most of the frame. Figure 3.3, the **medium shot (MS)**, is one of the most commonly used shots. The MS is obtained when the subject is cut off just below the waist by the bottom of the frame. In such shots the subject and the setting normally occupy approximately the same area of the frame. This shot is frequently used in film and TV work as a transition shot between long shots and close-ups, because to jump suddenly from one to the other would be far too abrupt and disorientating. Taking the medium shot in closer still produces Figure 3.4, the **close-up (CU)**. This is sometimes known as, **head-and-shoulders shot**. The subject now fills most of the frame and we can see little of the setting. The close-up is really at the limit of intimate space and is usually reserved for particular occasions, news items relating sudden or grave news, for instance. The close-up allows

Figure 3.1   Extreme long shot (ELS)

Figure 3.2   Long shot (LS)

Figure 3.3   Medium shot (MS)

Figure 3.4   Close-up (CU)

Figure 3.5 Big close-up (BCU)

you to study the subject in detail; on a large cinema screen every flicker of emotion will be registered on the face of the subject which may be 12 or 15 feet high when shown in close-up. Take the close-up in any further and we have a shot that is reserved largely for special occasions, Figure 3.5, the **big close up (BCU)**. This is obtained when only a part of the full face is shown, such as tear filled eyes or a smiling mouth. Such shots are usually reserved for drama and you will see them used frequently in melodrama to reveal the inner states of characters to us.

(b) Camera angle

Alongside shot size we can consider camera angle. Again we are illustrating these with photographs, just to make clear exactly what we mean. Figure 3.6, the **high angle shot**, is probably the easiest to identify. Here the camera looks down at the subject which inevitably makes the viewer feel more powerful than the subject being shown; we feel like an adult who is looking down on a child. We may also feel pity for the subject depending on the nature of the context. With Figure 3.7, the **eye-level shot**, we are at the same level as the subject. If the subject talks to us directly we feel as if we are taking

Figure 3.6   High-angle shot

Figure 3.7   Eye-level shot

Figure 3.8   Low-angle shot

part in a communication between equals. If a TV advertisement cuts between various figures in a room, all in conversation and all of whom are shot at eye level, then it almost feels as if we are in the room ourselves taking part in the discussion. Figure 3.8, **low-angle shot**, is as easy to identify as a high-angle shot, but in a low-angle shot the subject looms above the viewer and, because of this, appears powerful and dominating. The audience is now in the position of the child and the on-screen subject in the position of the parent. Such shots may occasionally be reassuring, but, because of the spatial disorientation involved in such a shot, normally they make us feel uneasy.

It is often quite difficult, if you have had no artistic or photographic training, to work out what camera angle is being used. Obviously it is easy if the shot is very high or very low, but it is rare for directors or camera operators to use such shots. You might have thought the Royal Mail advertisement was an eye-level shot whereas in fact it is a relatively low camera angle. There is a very easy way of ascertaining this since the laws of perspective dictate that the horizon, if it is included in the shot, reveals the height from which the shot was taken. We know that in the Royal Mail advertisement the camera was placed a little below the model's hands and at about the height of the bridge in the background because the bridge is the approximate horizon line in the still. The shot is therefore a relatively low-angle one.

But why did the photographer choose this angle for the Royal Mail advertisement? Bear in mind what has just been said about the horizon and the camera level. If this shot had been taken at eye level then the Parisian scene in the background would also have risen up the frame (with most of the Eiffel Tower disappearing out of shot). The model is more effectively framed in a relatively low angle shot because we see her against the background of a clear open sky and such a sky tends to connote open horizons and future possibilities. This fits in well with the general theme of a romance about to blossom in the future. You will perhaps see now why we state so emphatically that we are dealing with a visual language here, a language of codes and choices. The photographer who took this shot was clearly 'visually literate' in this sense, insofar as he or she knew exactly what they wished to communicate.

(c) Lens type

The photographer can add to the effect of camera angle through the choice of lens. S/he has a choice between three main types of lens: **wide angle**, **standard** and **telephoto**. Figures 3.9, 3.10 and 3.11 were all taken from the same point using each of these three lenses. Notice how these different lenses change not only the size of distant objects, but how they also affect what we are shown. For example, the perspective effect of a wide angle shot is much more dramatic than that achieved with a normal lens. See how the railway lines vanish towards the horizon much more quickly in Figure 3.9. If you used such a lens to film two characters in conversation in a pub and one was closer to you than the other, then the wide-angle lens would seem to increase the distance between them. This can be useful if you want to communicate a feeling of remoteness rather than intimacy between the two characters.

The standard lens gives the various objects and people in a shot approximately the same proportions in relation to their distance from us as you would get in real life. The sense of perspective in Figure 3.10 seems quite 'natural'. Objects do not suddenly seem to vanish towards the horizon as they did in the wide angle shot and the effect is to produce a sense of everydayness and normality: things are as they are supposed to be, and there is no sense of drama or disorientation.

Figure 3.9   Wide-angle shot

Figure 3.10   Standard-lens shot

Figure 3.11   Telephoto-lens shot

The telephoto lens, however, can produce some dramatic and even alarming effects. As you will see from Figure 3.11, the telephoto brings distant objects much closer to us. For this reason such lenses are often used for wild-life documentaries, sports photography and news-gathering. The use of the telephoto lens sometimes makes us feel that we are spying on the subjects, for, with such a long lens, people are often unaware of the photographer's presence. Also, it is worth noticing that telephoto lenses are highly selective and exclude much of the setting. Here, this 400mm lens is used to take us close in to the distant railway station. We see neither the bridge that crosses it nearer to us nor the factories that were revealed on the right-hand side in the wide-angle shot. The station now seems to be no more than a couple of hundred yards away and the railway lines certainly do not converge as quickly as they did in earlier shots. Because of this selectivity, the telephoto lens can draw us close to subjects, creating what often seems to be a more intimate relation between us and the subject.

(d) Composition

In terms of codes of composition, you will recall that we pointed out that the Royal Mail advertisement was an asymmetrical composition. Most professional photographers avoid placing the subject in the centre of the picture unless there is a good reason, for this tends to divide the image in half. It is a mistake often made by the amateur photographer who thinks that because the subject of the picture is the most important part, then it should be placed in the centre. In fact it is much better to compose pictures according to what has come to be known as the '**rule of thirds**'. The rule of thirds states that the main subject – a person, say – should be placed one-third of the way across the picture from either edge and that the horizon (if it is an outside shot) should be placed one-third or two-thirds of the way up the picture. You can see that the Royal Mail advertisement conforms to this rule: the Eiffel Tower is positioned one-third of the way across from the left-hand side and the letter that the young woman is holding is positioned almost one-third from the right-hand side; the horizon established by the block of buildings on the left is also about one-third of the way up from the bottom of the picture. This has the effect of creating certain key areas of interest (sometimes referred to as '**hot spots**') within the picture at the points where the vertical and horizontal 'thirds' lines cross – here where the young woman is holding the envelope.

In Table 3.1 we have utilised the semiotic concepts of signifer and signified to clarify the meaning of each of the choices relating to the technical codes. This is useful because it helps you to isolate the significant aspects of the visual image.

Table 3.1   Choices offered under technical codes

Signifier	*Signified*
Shot size	
Big close-up	Emotion, a vital moment, drama
Close up	Intimacy
Medium-shot	A personal relation to the subject
Long shot	Context, public distance
Camera angle	
High	Domination, power, authority
Eye-level	Equality
Low	Weakness, powerlessness
Lens type	
Wide angle	Dramatic
Normal	Everydayness, normality
Telephoto	Voyeurism
Composition	
Symmetrical	Posed, calm, religiosity
Asymmetrical	Natural everyday
Static	Lack of conflict
Dynamic	Disturbance, disorientation
Focus	
Selective focus	Draws the attention – 'look at this'
Soft focus	Romance, nostalgia
Deep focus	All elements are important – 'look at everything'
Lighting	
High key	Happiness
Low key	Sombre
High contrast	Theatrical, dramatic
Low contrast	Realistic, documentary
Film stock	
Grainy	Documentary realism, authenticity
Smooth 'fine' grain	Natural everydayness
Colour	
Warm (yellow, orange, red, brown)	Optimism, passion, agitation
Cool (blue, green, purple, grey)	Pessimism, calmness, reason
Black and white	Realism, fact, actuality.

Table 3.1 continues over

Table 3.1 cont.

Signifier	Signified
Cinematic codes	
Zoom in	Observation
Zoom out	Context
Pan (left or right)	Survey, follow
Tilt (up or down)	Survey, follow
Fade in	Beginning
Fade out	Ending
Dissolve	Passage of time, a link between scenes
Wipe	An imposed conclusion
Iris out	Old movies
Cut	Simultaneity of time, attention

Using a table like this is a very productive way of organising your thinking about any visual text, and it is a method we suggest you adopt when dealing with two more concepts frequently used in the analysis of a visual text: **paradigmatic** and **syntagmatic**. These two terms, derived originally from linguistic theory, refer to the two fundamental choices that face the maker of a visual work: first, what things to select to go in the scene (the paradigmatic); and second, how to combine these together (the syntagmatic). The syntagmatic axis describes the choices that actually were made (combination); and the paradigmatic axis describes the choices that could have been made (selection).

Obviously, a lot of thought went into selecting all the various details that go to make up the scene in the Royal Mail advertisement. Indeed, the idea of selection is an important one to consider when you start to develop your analysis of any media text. Always remember that meaning arises not only from what is in the text, but also from what may have been there but now is not. This may sound a little tricky, but is actually quite simple.

For instance, in our Royal Mail advertisement the advertiser has selected Paris for the **setting**. Now Paris is, of course, a European capital city and it has been chosen rather than Rome or London. As soon as the advertiser starts to consider codes of mise-en-scène s/he has to make a selection. If the advertisement is to be set in a European capital city then which one will it be? Likewise, the creators of the advertisement decided that a bicycle should be included, but this could have been a mountain bike or a racing bike or an old boneshaker, or whatever. But not only have a setting (Paris) and some **props** (the bicycle) been chosen, we also have a host of choices at the level of technical codes and codes of non-verbal communication (NVC), all of which affect the overall meaning. This process of selection is absolutely fundamental to the effect of the text; if, for instance, soft focus had been used the picture may have seemed slushy and sentimental rather than romantic.

Okay, you might be saying, I can see it is an important area, but the number of possible choices is massive, so where do I start? A good way to deal with this whole area of selection, once you've completed a preliminary analysis, is to write out a page of possible choices that could have been made in the creation of the image (whether an advertisement, television still, or whatever) and compare these with the choices that were actually made. All you have to do is to look at any element that makes up your advertisement and try exchanging it for another. If the short straight hair of the young woman were replaced by a 'Mohican' cut, then this exchange would obviously change the meaning we derive from the advertisement, and it would be hard for us to think of her as coy and demure.

This way of dealing with the idea of selection will very easily take you on to **combination** (the **syntagmatic** axis). Images are not only the result of selecting some things and leaving out others, but are also the result of combining things in a certain way. So, across the top of the page you should describe the final Combination – 'Paris + Young white woman + Casual dress + etc.' Then down the page under each of these elements you can then list some of the alternative selections that could have been made. Remember, the horizontal axis describes the combinations that actually occur, the vertical axis describes the selections that could have been made. So, if you are talking about the **paradigmatic** choices available in the Royal Mail advertisement under, say, 'props' (the roadster bicycle), then these would include a racing bicycle, mountain bike, skateboard etc. See Table 3.2.

Whether you are analysing a still from a television programme or a picture in a newspaper, using a chart of this kind will help you to make sense of the way in which selections have been made across the range of codes in terms of the mise-en-scène. It is then just a small step to go from considering the reasons behind any one selection – the woman's hairstyle, say – to discussing the meaning of these elements. For example, let us take the paradigmatic set of possible hairstyles. The straight, short hair of our model, cut in a fashionable imitation of

Table 3.2 Syntagmatic and paradigmatic axis

SYNTAGMATIC AXIS					
Paris	Young white woman	Casual dress	Roadster bicycle	Straight short hair	**P** **A** **R**
London	Middle-aged white woman	High fashion	Racing cycle	Bouffant	**A** **D** **I**
Rome	Older white woman	Punk	Mountain bike	Plaits	**G** **M**
Berlin	Young white man	Gothic	Skateboard	Pony tail	**A** **T** **I**
Madrid	Older white man	Twin set	Roller skates	Mohican	**C**
New York	Young black woman	Working overall	Motor cycle	Crew cut	**A** **X**
Delhi	Young black man	Tracksuit	Scooter	Perm	**I** **S**
Peking	Middle-aged black woman	Surfer fashion	Moped	Spiked	

a 1960s style, conjures up a feeling of youthful innocence and optimism. If you look down the column relating to hairstyles (the paradigmatic set) you will notice that some of the styles, such as a pony tail, connote similar things, whilst others, the Mohican cut for instance, invoke a rebellious disrespect for all traditions. The young woman's hairstyle therefore not only says something about her personality but it also says something about what she is not: (i) flamboyant (the bouffant), (ii) plain and homely (plaits), (iii) tomboyish or asexual (the crew cut) and so on. In this way, you can move rapidly and easily from identifying the various elements in any visual text (hairstyle, dress, etc.) to discussing the meaning of these elements.

In fact, the paradigmatic and syntagmatic dimensions of any visual text can help you to isolate those signs which play an important part in establishing its meaning. To find out exactly which signs are significant in establishing meaning and why, you can use a simple method known as the **commutation test** which makes use of the paradigmatic and syntagmatic dimensions discussed above. First, choose a particular sign which you might feel is significant – in our case here, the hairstyle. Then substitute any other related element (the other hair-cuts in the paradigmatic set) and consider whether this changes the overall meaning of the advertisement. If it does, then you can be sure that it carries a particular meaning (as we saw when we substituted the Mohican cut for the straight, short haircut of the model). As our grid above shows, each of the key units of meaning – Setting, Codes of dress, hairstyle, etc. – can be made the subject of a commutation test, and it is this that assures us that they are meaningful elements within the advertisement.

The elements we have chosen to isolate in the above grid have largely to do with setting. Setting is of prime importance in the creation of any media image, and, of the many aspects of television that you might want to discuss, is probably the one with which we are all most familiar. If you try to remember any Levi jean advertisement you will probably find it relatively easy to conjure up images of a laundrette, a pool hall or a fishing boat, but you are unlikely to remember the complex cutting and editing or the camera angles that were used. Similarly, the Parisian setting plays a very important part in establishing an overall meaning for the Royal Mail advertisement.

In semiotics, as you have probably realised by now, many of the concepts come in pairs – signifier and signified, paradigm and syntagm, etc. We shall now look at two more, **synchronic** and **diachronic**, which relate to the dimension of time – an important issue in the study of television, for obvious reasons. Synchronic analysis proceeds by isolating a set of signs within a media text and discussing these independently of the part that they will play in the unfolding story. If we turn from this to discussing how it functions in the advertisement itself then we are considering it from a diachronic perspective. This should alert us to the fact that there are some useful connections between these two pairs of terms, paradigmatic and synchronic; syntagmatic and diachronic. The paradigmatic axis of selection is a synchronic one: it is simply the set of signs from which the sign has been chosen, since there are no temporal relations between them. The syntagmatic axis of combination is a diachronic one and therefore involves time – whether the thirty seconds of a TV advertisement or the two hours of a feature film.

To interpret the signs that you isolate within the advertising image – the Eiffel Tower or the young woman's hair – you need to move from describing what is in the image (denotative) to accounting for how it creates its meaning (connotative analysis), remembering, as you do so, that the meanings to which the sign gives rise are generated by the interaction that takes place when you, as a 'reader', interpret the sign in a particular way. Given this fact it is tempting to conclude that anything you write about the connotative dimension of a sign must be correct because it is based on your personal response. However, as we pointed out earlier, all signification is first and foremost a social phenomenon: if signs are to communicate anything at all they must be understood by a community of sign-users (of which you are, of course, a member). Because of this, such connotative meanings might more accurately be described as intersubjective, rather than as subjective or personal.

The whole 'Melt her to the Coeur' advertisement is referred to in semiotics as a syntagm in which the signifiers at the first level of denotation (the things that we see in the advertisement) function as signs, at the second level of connotation, of 'young love'. However, it is important to remember that such connotations derive not from the signs themselves – the young woman, the Eiffel Tower (signifying 'Paris') but from their use in society and the cultural meaning that they carry. The advertisement is successful because it manages to condense, into a single image, the range of values and beliefs with which it is concerned.

Once you have got to grips with the connotative dimensions of meaning within any still you will be in a good position to refine and extend your analysis by looking at the way in which various social 'myths' relate to, and develop out of, these connotative levels. Whereas connotations, as we pointed out above, arise from the form of the signifier (the camera angle, composition, etc.) **myths** are connected with signifieds. You need, therefore, to think about the ideas and concepts – gender, age, romance, and so on – that the Royal Mail advertisement inspires. These signifieds still relate to the signs that we find in the advertisement, but this relation is now at one remove, for this image of a young woman on a Paris bridge itself now serves as a signifier for the wider range of cultural meanings (myths) that the advertisement serves to conjure up. It is as if it loses its particularity in order to serve as a conduit for more general themes and values. The first point to grasp, when considering any advertisement from this perspective is that the key signs work to activate these social myths in us as we look at them. It is important to remember this because, all too often, students write about myths as if they were 'in' the image itself. But myths only come alive when we appropriate them, when they resonate with our own values and beliefs.

In our society such myths and values are relatively independent. There are no obvious or natural connections between myths relating to, say, motherhood, masculinity, nation, work or romance. Each of these has its own identity and, perhaps more importantly, its own history. Our ideas of romantic love differ markedly from those of the middle ages or even of the Victorian period.

In today's society advertisements such as our Royal Mail one are amongst the most significant carriers of contemporary myths – ideas about glamour, romance, success, sophistication. Such representations have important social effects. Communication can only take place because encoders (such as advertising creative teams) and decoders (audiences) draw upon certain key social myths: myths about work and leisure, men and women, about the young and old. Indeed, the terms communication and community both derive from the Latin, '*communis*', meaning 'having in common'; to communicate is therefore, in one very important sense, to share meanings and experiences. This aspect of myth-creation is obviously particularly important to advertisers, simply because they are concerned to attract people to a particular view of themselves and of their position in society in order to encourage them to buy the goods the advertisers want to sell. The influence of such myths does not stop at advertising, however, as we will see in the following chapters, in our analyses of television output: the whole concept of social myth fundamentally underpins not only how we respond to certain TV programmes, but also the way in which we watch the types of TV programmes we choose to watch.

This is one of the things that makes the study of television so worthwhile: it forces us to make explicit the connections between what we know and how we come to know it. The tools of semiotic analysis described in this chapter should have added to your understanding of the analysis we carried out in Chapter 2 and, taken together, these two chapters should enable you to carry out your own analysis of any media text. In the next chapter we will show you how, by working at a text using the five key media aspects in a series of steps, to build an analysis of a television programme.

4

The police series:
The Bill

THE previous two chapters have, we hope, provided a full
introduction to the key concepts used in media studies – they are
meant to help you see what to look for when you start to analyse a
visual text. But you also need to be able to talk about a TV
programme as a whole, and to do this successfully you need a method
of analysis that will enable you to build your own views on any
programme that you have chosen to study. This is what this chapter
is about: it shows you how to use a sequence of steps to build up a
critical view of a television programme, drawing on the ideas outlined
in Chapters 2 and 3.

I   CONSTRUCTING AN OVERALL ANALYSIS

The Bill developed out of a play written for Thames TV by Geoff
McQueen, the series originator. The play was called *Woodentop* (the
nickname that the CID have for the uniform branch), and was
directed by Peter Cregeen. Cregeen had worked on a number of
British television police series throughout the 1960s and 1970s,
including *Z Cars*, *Softly Softly*, *Juliet Bravo* and *The Gentle Touch*.
Woodentop received good reviews in the media, and a month after its
transmission in the autumn of 1983, Thames decided to produce a
series of twelve sixty-minute episodes to be called *The Bill*. This was to
be built around policing in a busy London East End station, Sunhill.
With a cast of over twenty main characters it was to deal with the
whole range of contemporary crime faced by the Metropolitan police.
Also – and unlike other police series previously made in the UK – its
narrative focus was specifically on the job of policing, avoiding home

64

life and off-duty activities. Its other main characteristic was to be its documentary realism: a complete police station was constructed in a converted warehouse in which there was no studio space as such, and lightweight cameras were to be used to follow the rapidly unfolding action.

In fact three series were produced in this format and, after the success of the third, Thames TV decided that *The Bill* should have a more permanent place in the weekly schedule. The fourth series, which began in July 1988, had a twice-weekly all-year-round thirty-minute format, making it as much a regular feature of the week's viewing as soaps such as *Coronation Street* or *EastEnders*, although Thames TV has always been keen to play down *The Bill*'s 'soapiness'. However, in its new format – now three times a week – broadcast before the 9.00p.m. watershed and in a peak family viewing slot, there is no doubt that the programme has started to look much more like a soap than not: the strong language and violence of the earlier series had to be toned down considerably, and, in the new thirty-minute slot, the programme's audience changed from the male one traditionally attracted to the police series to a largely family audience.

There is no doubt that one of the factors that made *The Bill* different from other British police series was Geoff McQueen's decision to show everything through the eyes of the police personnel at Sunhill police station. This meant that viewers could not, for instance, witness a crime being committed if no police officer were present to witness it. Instead, viewers are shown only how the police cope with the crime. Also, the audience is told nothing about the characters' home environments; the intention from the outset was that the programme should stick resolutely to the settings of the Sunhill police station and its 'patch'. Such decisions played a major part in giving the programme its distinctive brand of a type of documentary realism. Peter Cregeen had been greatly impressed by the 1982 BBC documentary series *The Police*, a fly-on-the-wall look at the Thames Valley force, and its influence is clearly apparent in *The Bill*. In order to give the programme this raw 'as it happens' feeling, outside broadcast (OB) camera crews are used for the filming, using a filming technique closely related to what is often called 'ENG' (electronic news gathering). Because ENG crews are trained to cover real, actuality events for news, current affairs and documentary programmes, they tend to develop a speedy responsiveness to the unpredictability of rapidly unfolding action. To enhance the feeling of immediacy further, many of the scenes in *The Bill* are shot without the actors having first gone through the traditional camera rehearsal and this, it is claimed, gives their acting a more spontaneous feel. And finally, for the moment, the absence of any non-diegetic music or sound effects (SFX) tends to separate *The Bill* from the type of police series in which we find action centring on car chases and the sound of racing engines and screeching tyres. The overall intention of the programme is, therefore, to avoid the polished look of a staged drama in favour of the re-creation of apparently real-life events. As such, it could be argued that, while *The Bill* does partake of many of the characteristics of earlier, documentary-style police series, such as *Z Cars*, it also attempts to increase the fly-on-the-wall atmosphere associated with that tradition.

By making such choices (all of which relate to the area of Construction) the director was able to ensure that the programme's style was very different from that of most television drama, and also very different from most television police series. In the past, TV drama was filmed using three cameras in a studio set. You can best imagine this as a room from which the fourth wall has been removed, with the cameras occupying the space of the fourth wall. Although this practice enhances the professional look of the production, the predictability of the shots can make it look staged and undynamic. The Sunhill station has no such sets, which means that each of the rooms appears to us exactly as it would in reality. This, as we mentioned above, is made possible by the use of lightweight ENG cameras rather than the much-more-cumbersome studio ones, and again reinforces the distinctive style of the programme, as well as introducing various constraints on the production team, as we will see later.

What should be clear already is that *The Bill* is a programme built around a very definite format, and with a highly distinctive style of production. These are some of the areas you will need to consider in your own analysis, as we will be doing in the rest of this chapter. But first, we want to establish something about the programme's broad structure and recurrent patterns or interests, since this will allow us to think about its particular episodes in a full context. Then we will move on to examine one of the opening sequences from an episode of *The Bill*, 'A Woman Scorned', by Victoria Taylor, first broadcast (TX) on 19 December 1991.[1] And then, with the information gleaned from this analysis, we will move on to look closely at several sequences from the rest of this particular episode to establish the way in which the programme's major concerns and interests are developed. Finally, in the second part of this chapter, 'aspects of the text', we will develop the concept of Agency in the context of the programme, including an interview with John Foster, who has written for many TV police series and serials, including *The Bill*. At the end of the chapter, we include a fairly detailed sequence synopsis,[2] to give you a better idea of the episode's narrative. You will need to refer to this synopsis, when we start on analysis of the particular episode we are going to examine here.

As you read this chapter, try to remember that we are primarily concerned to illustrate the step-by-step method by which you can work on an episode of a police series yourself. The method itself falls into two stages: the first stage consists of six steps which enable you to construct a basic analysis; the second stage is where you develop your analysis, taking things further, as you might, for example, in a project. It is not always necessary to pursue your analysis as far as this, but often you will find you want to explore a particular aspect of the text, and this is what this second stage is about. The steps themselves, as you will see later in this chapter, are very straightforward to use and will help you to think through your responses in an ordered way.

The first step is an important one because it encourages you to look at the overall narrative shape of a television programme in a broad way. It is an enormous help to begin in this way, for it is not until you have a grasp of the overall organisation of a media text that you can satisfactorily proceed to a more detailed analysis. The main point to remember here is that you are not, at this stage, attempting to produce a complicated, sequence-by-sequence analysis of the narrative but rather aiming to establish the programme's main themes and to outline its basic narrative organisation.

Having looked at these factors you can then move on to a more detailed analysis by examining an opening sequence. We suggest that you start with a sequence from fairly near the beginning of the programme because very often an important issue, conflict or enigma will be introduced in the programme's opening few sequences. This close analysis helps to strengthen your broad overview of the programme's central tensions, conflicts or interests, and enables you to move on to analyse other sequences in the light of your first responses. In this chapter and the ones which follow, we will be analysing four sequences from each programme, focusing on a different media aspect each time in order to produce a full interpretation. Of course, the choice of four sequences is, to an extent, an arbitrary one, and we are certainly not saying that you should limit yourself to this number. We have chosen four because a detailed analysis of every sequence in each of the TV programmes we examine would be impossible in a book of this length. Nevertheless, our analysis of four sequences is certainly enough to show you how to structure your response to a media text.

At first, you may find it very difficult to know which media aspect to choose when commenting upon a particular sequence. We feel, however, that as you work your way through the book you will see just why we have made certain choices. For instance, if a sequence in a television soap seems to be sitcom in style then you clearly have some points to make about genre. If, on the other hand, you find yourself emotionally moved by a sequence, then the aspect of Audience is one you might consider. Remember that learning is a cumulative process and that nothing comes easily in the early stages of analysis. There really is no substitute for your own attempts to tackle a media text using these aspects. It is far better to struggle to produce an original interpretation than simply to repeat some standard points from media-studies books, and this is because you will inevitably come to the point in your studies when you will be asked to respond first-hand to televisual texts. And this is what we are enabling you to accomplish in this book.

After looking at four sequences in a detailed way we then move on to the last step in the method of analysis where we ask: 'Have we achieved a sufficiently complex sense of the media text?' Here we encourage you to probe a little deeper into the structure and organisation of the programme as a whole. We make this suggestion because we have found from experience that students who have examined a number of sequences in a detailed way, often feel that they begin to want to focus in on some specific quality of the programme which interests them in some way. Usually this will relate to one of the key aspects – Narrative or Audience, for example. The choice of aspect depends very much on the type of programme you are analysing and what you want to say about it. You should, at all costs, get away from the idea that the five aspects are to be used in a rigid way: think of the aspects as flexible tools that enable you to think through your own response. This is a very important point, for, in nearly all media studies work, you are required to do more than simply list basic points about audience or agency in a mechanical way. This leads us in to the second stage of our analysis: **Aspects of**

the media text. In this we again focus on a particular aspect – Categorisation or Narrative, say – but this time in order to introduce some more advanced debates. Often these discussions take us beyond the media text itself, prompting a consideration of the social and cultural context of its production.

You may be wondering why, given the complexity of the contemporary mass media, we use only five key media aspects in this book. Certainly, it would be possible to think of possible additions to this list, and you are bound to come across some slightly different suggestions in other textbooks. For example, one important area in media studies that we have not included in our list of five is **representation**, which deals with the way in which the media present particular social groups – women, black people, the working class, etc. This does not mean that we do not tackle representation; in fact we deal with it, and with the related issue of stereotyping, many times in the course of this book. We have, however, chosen to discuss it in relation to our five key aspects, rather than separately; thus in a section in which we consider Audience we are also likely to discuss gender, race or class. We feel that by approaching the task in this way we have shown you how to avoid discussing issues of representation in too general a way. Far too often students submit essays which deal with, for example, the representation of women in police series, in which the discussion soon becomes a much broader consideration of sexism in society. Of course, some background comment on this issue is essential to any discussion of representation, but it is also important to remember that you are dealing, first and foremost, with media texts. Any analysis of such important contemporary concerns as sexism or racism should therefore be carried out bearing this in mind. We have, for similar reasons, decided to deal with the technical side of production in an integrated way, discussing the various media technologies only when such a consideration is directly relevant to our analysis. This is the case in this chapter, where we look at the way in which the use of ENG cameras in *The Bill* helps to give the programme a documentary feel.

As you read this chapter, then, try to remember that we are primarily concerned to illustrate the step-by-step method we have outlined here. Our whole intention is to give you the tools and the confidence to work on a media text yourself, and how to move from some simple ideas towards a more complex analysis. The moment you do this you should discover how enjoyable and rewarding working on a media text on your own can be.

Step 1

After watching the programme, see if you can identify any kind of pattern or structure at work.

One of the things you will notice as soon as you watch any episode of *The Bill* is the number of story strands running alongside and feeding into each other. Although this may make the programme appear fairly complex, it is important that you establish from the outset something about the basic pattern or story that emerges from the episode you want to study.

In '*A Woman Scorned*', the story revolves around the discovery of a skeleton in Mrs Jacobus's garden. There is also a subplot involving the tension between DCI Kim Reid and DI Burnside. The skeleton turns out to be that of Arthur Cruikshank, who was murdered about twelve years previously by his lover, Sally Josephs, who was then a student and is now a local teacher. The skeleton is discovered in the garden of Mrs Jacobus, who is also 'scorned' by her daughter, who, although living nearby, never visits her. In the subplot, Kim Reid is fighting a running battle with the surly and insolent Frank Burnside, who resents the fact that a woman is his boss. Reid is invited to give a paper at Scotland Yard, and is fully involved in both management and the development of her career. While Burnside is coping with a murder investigation, Reid is trying to manipulate her superiors into moving Burnside out of Sunhill, where his insolence is causing her problems.

What emerges from this story is a series of tensions, all revolving around the episode's title, '*A Woman Scorned*'. This means that the relationship between men and women is at the centre of the episode, and this is developed in several ways, bringing in questions of rank and management style and of how women cope with emotional rejection: Sally Josephs took a spanner to the back of her lover's head; Kim Reid suggests that she has 'more subtle weapons' to deal with men. But both are 'women scorned' – just as is Mrs Jacobus, whose daughter fails to visit her. These issues are everywhere we look in the episode and are developed in each of the episode's various story strands.

The notion of the various story strands employed in any media product is a significant one. Whenever you analyse any film or television programme, you always need to identify the different narrative strands it uses, and to see how the broad issues fit within these. In '*A Woman Scorned*' there are three main story strands:

1. The riddle of the skeleton discovered in Mrs Jacobus's garden;
2. DCI Kim Reid's trip to Scotland Yard to present a paper;
3. Reid's and Burnside's arguments about the attitude of the CID officers at Sunhill.

Within these three narrative threads, the episode develops its unique concerns and interests. This is what you need to get at in your own analysis: the unique quality of this individual episode and how it develops its interests within the broader scope of the programme as a whole.

As we have said, the central tension or conflict that has emerged from our synopsis is the nature of the relationship between men and women and how women cope with emotional rejection: do they 'take a spanner' to the situation (as Sally Josephs does), or are there 'more subtle weapons' at their disposal, as Reid suggests? To comment meaningfully upon this relationship, you need to start analysing separate sequences from the episode. This is the way to deal with any media text: start with a few controlling ideas, a simple tension between two sides, then focus on a few scenes or sequences to see how these ideas are developed. The best way to divide the programme up into what seem to you to be identifiable short sequences is to watch the programme several times and then to write your own programme synopsis, sequence by sequence. We have done this on pp. 91–2 where you will see we have divided it into 24 segments or passages. You may also want to produce a story-board of the sequences you want to study, to analyse, say, shot-size or edits. If you do want to do this, use the blank story-board in Figure 4.1 as a model. But in this chapter, we are going to work from our prose synopsis on pp. 91–2.

Step 2

Analyse the opening sequence, or, if this proves unilluminating, a sequence from fairly near the beginning, featuring one or two of the major characters.

It is always a good idea to begin by looking at the opening sequence because this often provides us with an insight into the central issues and conflicts that will structure the episode. However, because the first sequence of '*A Woman Scorned*' is a very short 'establishing' scene, merely involving two officers turning up at the scene of the crime, the second sequence can be more appropriately considered as a rather more interesting opening to analyse.

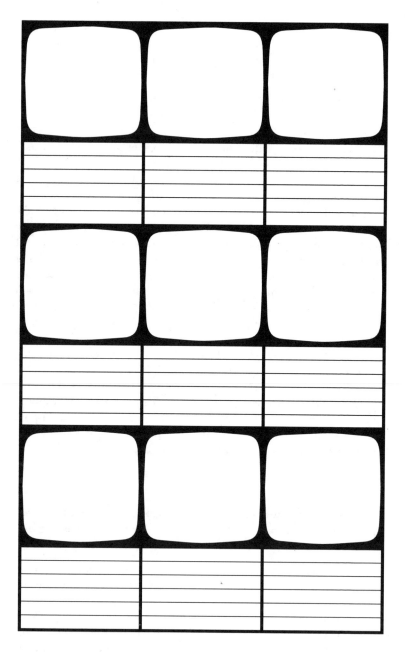

Figure 4.1   Blank storyboard

Sequence 2   DCI Kim Reid's Office. Sunhill
DCI Reid and DI Burnside are discussing the low morale of the CID team at
Sunhill. Burnside claims that this is due to the fact that his team are overworked
and underpaid. Reid on the other hand thinks that if the CID team had more
pride in their work this would improve their performance. Burnside suggests
giving some of the officers more overtime as a financial incentive but Reid thinks
this a bad idea. She then goes on to criticise a report submitted by 'Tosh' Lines of
CID. The dialogue is particularly significant here, so we are including a
transcript. This is not 'in format', but is instead a straight transcription of the
dialogue as it occurs on screen.

> DCI KIM REID: [about the report submitted by Tosh Lines] This isn't
> good enough, Frank. Grease marks, dried food stuck to it. What's
> the CPS meant to do: read it, or try and work out what Tosh Lines
> had for lunch?
> FRANK BURNSIDE: Right, well I'll wave a big stick in the CID office,
> then, shall I?
> REID: Yes, if you would. Oh, and as you're interested, Frank, the
> memo's about the street crime initiative meeting at the Yard. I'll be
> there most of the afternoon. I'm meeting AC [Assistant Commis-
> sioner] Renshaw.
> BURNSIDE: Oh yes. Well, don't worry, ma'am, I'll hold the fort for
> you.
> REID: And I'd like to see you at six o'clock if that's possible Frank, to
> go through our policy.
> BURNSIDE: Ma'am?
> REID: Before the Jasmin Allen community leaders arrive tomorrow I'd
> like to try and make sure we don't contradict each other.
> BURNSIDE: [With apparent irony] Good idea ma'am.

You now have a sequence to talk about, but what should you say
about it? Sometimes you might feel that you know exactly what you
want to write about such a sequence, but if you are unsure it is always
a good idea to tackle the sequence systematically using the five
controlling concepts we have identified earlier: Construction,
Audience, Narrative, Categorisation and Agency. It is not,
however, absolutely necessary to say something about each of these:
sometimes there simply may not be anything particularly interesting
to say about a sequence in terms of, for example, Agency. The area
that interests us here is Narrative, the way in which the sequence
unfolds several layers of story, one upon another. You may often find
that you want to start building your analysis in this way, by
developing the idea of Narrative further since it helps to pinpoint the
tensions informing the text. The response of the characters to each

other, for example, and to the situation, reveals several things: the issues about which Reid is serious (paperwork, street crime initiative, AC Renshaw, policy, the Jasmin Allen community meeting) are treated with disdain by Burnside, who appears dismissive and even openly ironic. These things are simply of little interest to him, he implies.

This first, impressionistic response to the sequence feeds into the episode's concerns more generally. For example, Reid and Burnside's parting exchange about the memo on street crime and her meeting at Scotland Yard marks the differences between the two officers that are at the heart of this story. Burnside, committed to sorting things out on the streets of the Sunhill patch, does not move in DCI Reid's world of important memos and meetings at the Yard: it is clear that he cares little about resolving a common policy for the meeting with the Jasmin Allen community centre residents.

The difference between these two characters' approaches is often introduced into the stories through the use of a simple narrative motif, involving a discussion about 'paperwork'. In this sequence, Reid points out to Burnside the unsatisfactory nature of Tosh Lines's report. Burnside's abhorrence of paperwork is linked to the way in which his own masculinity is defined in the series: because paperwork is deskbound, it is, for him, symbolic of feminine domesticity since it is a part of the internal day-to-day, domestic running of the police station (and therefore by implication feminised). Burnside's view of police work is one which rests upon its intrinsic masculine nature, defined essentially in terms of fighting crime on the streets.

It may be worth noting here the centrality of the female character in the series. The strategy of having a central female figure around whom the narrative is organised is one frequently employed within the genres of melodrama and *film noir*. In these, the woman is something of a mystery to the other characters, and similarly, in episodes of *The Bill* featuring DCI Reid, she is often presented in this way. In the episode which introduced her in 1990 the audience saw Reid interrupt her first journey to Sunhill to apprehend a criminal. Her cool arrival at the station with sandwiches purchased on the journey in one hand and a villain in the other immediately made her a challenge for the male officers of Sunhill.

One final important point to remember is that you must always try to say how the sequence relates to the episode as a whole. The assumption you have to make in looking at a sequence is that it will reflect the larger tensions of the episode and the series. When you look

at an extract, therefore, you must step back and relate it to the
episode as a whole, trying to sum up what the sequence has added to
your overall impression. Here, we can note how this sequence
establishes one of the episode's central conflicts or tensions: the
relationships between men and women and how these relationships
involve issues such as authority, against the backdrop of a
traditionally patriarchal structure. Reid is struggling to assert her
authority within the structure of the police hierarchy. Similarly, it
could be argued that the murder of Arthur Cruikshank by Sally
Josephs was the ultimate response to a patriarchal society, in which
women may feel undervalued ('scorned'), dominated and abused.
Working at a sequence in this way allows us to fill out and develop
our ideas about the characters and about the programme as a whole.

Step 3

Select a second sequence for discussion.

We shall now look at a sequence involving our second story strand –
Reid's trip to the Yard. Contemporary police series usually involve
story strands that are not only related to solving crimes: enigmas and
riddles apart from 'who dun it' are frequently featured. One that is
often used in *The Bill* relates to the career of DCI Reid. The following
sequence deals with the issue of whether or not she will make
promotion.

   *Sequence 11   AC Renshaw and DCI Reid in conversation over lunch in a
Chinese restaurant.*

   *Reid suggests to Renshaw in a serious but confiding tone that Burnside's
career would benefit if he were to move from Sunhill, pointing out that he has
been there for some time and that he has obvious leadership qualities. Renshaw
reminds her that Burnside has made no formal application for promotion. After
pointing out that a new opportunity would present a challenge to Burnside,
Renshaw replies as follows:*

   RENSHAW: If you remember you complained about him [Burnside]
      to me yourself a couple of months ago. Let's just get this problem
      into the right context, Kim.
   REID: It hasn't been easy for me but there are genuine reasons for my
      suggesting that he be promoted.
   RENSHAW: Yes, I'm sure there are. But I've never believed in solving a
      problem by shunting it somewhere else. If this is your way of
      telling me you can't cope with Frank Burnside then it's something

I'd really rather not be hearing. At least not in any official capacity.
Unofficially well . . .
REID: I'd be grateful for your advice then, Sir.
RENSHAW: Don't let him exclude you, if that's what you think he's
doing. He's your DI. Use him, sort him out. It'll do you more good
than trying to remove him. You're too senior and considered too
promising to get into personality battles, Kim, especially now.

This sequence raises once again issues relating to rank. There is a
tension between the informality of the Chinese restaurant in which
the scene takes place and the formal distance in terms of rank
between the Assistant Commissioner and DCI Reid. This in turn
suggests that while Reid wants to succeed in a traditionally male-
dominated world, she is willing to use her feminity in an informal
situation to get her own way. Notice, for example, how her dialogue
changes from the confiding 'It hasn't been easy for me . . .' to the
much more formal 'I'd be grateful for your advice then, Sir', after her
mild ticking-off from Renshaw. There is a hint here that Reid is
adopting an approach more characteristic of Burnside in trying to
solve her problems by establishing something of a nepotistic
relationship with Renshaw. It is not until she accepts the telling-off
and asks Renshaw what she should do in the situation that things are
smoothed over. As Renshaw speaks we get a string of big close-up
(BCU) reaction shots of Reid, who now looks much less the self-
confident woman she appeared at the Yard and in her earlier
confrontation with Burnside.

This sequence also serves to develop further one of the key
narrative enigmas of the episode: is DCI Reid cut out for a high-
flying career in senior management? Renshaw's criticisms of the way
in which she is trying to deal with Burnside places a question mark
over her own career and, although the episode as a whole seems to
foreshadow a potentially upwardly mobile police career, this
conversation makes us speculate about her future. The fact that
this sequence emphasises this tension between Reid as a woman in a
traditionally patriarchal hierarchy ('I'd be grateful for your advice
then, Sir'), and Reid as the little girl lost ('It hasn't been easy for
me . . .'), makes it an interesting sequence to consider in the context
of Audience, since it presents one of the tensions facing many women
and men in contemporary society. It is clear, for example, that
although the sequence appears to be presenting a woman's
perspective, the world-view being offered is one which quickly
reverts to conventional, stereotypical beliefs about the role of women

in society, and, since the programme has to maintain its audience in order to continue to be made, just how it presents issues which may be even mildly contentious is of considerable importance.

This relationship between the economic factors underlying media production and the audience served can have a particular effect on the aesthetics of the programme itself. As you can see from the following chart, *The Bill*, as the fifth most popular programme for the week 1–7 June 1992, was beaten only by the regular soaps. The fact that it attracted more viewers than gameshows and sitcoms is significant, for it establishes that the police series, as a television genre, can be a big attractor of advertising revenue.

Table 4.1   Programme ratings, 1–7 June 1992

	Programme	*Channel*	*Audience (Millions)*
1.	*Coronation Street* Fri/Sun	ITV	18.28
2.	*Eastenders* Thu/Sun	BBC1	16.99
3.	*Neighbours* Fri	BBC1	15.45
4.	*Home and Away* Fri	ITV	13.83
5.	*The Bill* Thu	ITV	12.53
6.	*Through the Keyhole*	ITV	12.00
7.	*Heartbeat*	ITV	11.77
8.	*Wheel of Fortune*	ITV	11.23
9.	*A Small Dance*	ITV	11.11
10.	*Cluedo*	ITV	11.03

Source: Broadcasters' Audience Research Board (BARB) for 1-7 June 1992. When more than one episode is broadcast in a week the highest figure is given. If a programme is repeated the audiences for the first and repeat broadcast are added together.

In the year 1991/92 *The Bill* earned £53.8 million in advertising revenue for ITV. At that time, Thames produced 104 episodes a year, and these were sold to ITV for £12 million (£150 000 per episode). Now that the programme has been changed to a tri-weekly format, 156 a year, it is to be expected that Thames has negotiated a significant increase, while ITV can expect to earn more in advertising and spin-offs from the programme. It could therefore be argued that these kinds of economic pressures will severely restrict or limit any kind of change in the programme's format: it attracts its audience because of the kinds of conventional world-view it provides, and any alteration to that may lose it the very audience it sets out to attract, and which the advertisers pay to access. And this, in turn, may have serious implications for the aesthetics of the programme itself, as we will see later.

Step 4

Select a third sequence for discussion.

The sequence that we now examine relates to the first story strand concerning the skeleton discovered in the garden of Mrs Jacobus. In sequence 3 we see a shot of the human skeleton that the dog had unearthed. This sequence, as well as advancing the story, serves to stress also the unpleasant side of police work. In sequence 21 we see DC 'Tosh' Lines and WPC Martella dealing with a woman who has murdered her former lover as a result of his violence towards her. As a story strand it actually gives us information about the day-to-day nature of police work, and about the kinds of skills required by the police to deal with what are quite often unpleasant situations. It is important to notice how each story strand develops various aspects like this, outside the straight development of story and plot: we are always being told much more than just a simple story. Keeping this in mind will help you to write more fully and more confidently about any sequence you aim to analyse.

Sequence 21   DC Tosh Lines and WPC Martella arrive at Sally Joseph's house and are shown inside.
Sally Joseph, a teacher, is a single woman living in a large well-furnished house. The modern prints, sculpture and books suggest she is a woman of culture and taste. Although somewhat shy and reticent she is cooperative and polite. In response to Tosh Lines's questioning she at first admits to having known the dead man slightly, then to the fact that they were lovers and eventually that she had killed him. Her confession comes almost unsolicited, with Lines just asking a few strategic questions. The impression is that Sally Joseph is to some extent pleased to tell the police, as if she is now clearing her conscience. She goes on to explain what happened.

SALLY JOSEPH: He used to hit me and . . . um. . . . I was miserable
and it annoyed him and um . . . on Sunday we were at home
because the others had all gone away for the summer and we
fought . . . over. . . I can't even remember what it was about . . .
he shouted as usual and he pushed me around. . . . and I . . . I
thought, no, he's not going to hit me . . . I'm going to hit
him. . . . so I picked up a spanner and um . . . after I hit him once
I had to do it again and again because there was no going back
was there?

This speech gives the impression that Sally Joseph had gone over the
scene many times in her mind previously, trying to explain her
emotions to herself. We notice, for example, that details are forgotten,
while the overriding impression of an emotional response is very
powerfully recreated. The police officers are silent and serve as
background to this confessional moment, which further increases our
sense that Sally Joseph is almost talking to herself, as if to try to
explain to herself how she felt at the time.

The area we want to concentrate on in our analysis of this sequence
is Construction, since the long speech, and the way in which the
camera is used in this sequence immediately draws attention to its
own artifice, the fact that it has been 'made' in a particular way to
create a particular effect. The sequence is filmed in one continuous
'take', with the camera taking a minute and a half to go from a MLS
to a BCU of Sally Joseph. This makes the sequence nearly eight times
the length of the average sequence and the longest single shot in the
episode. Many sequences in *The Bill* are shot in 'real time' in this way.
For example, in one particular episode, *They Also Serve* (TX, 5
September 1991, writer Russell Lewis, directed by David Hayman),
the entire first half of the episode was one continuous take of fifteen
minutes. This strategy tends to increase the programme's attempts at
documentary realism, by making us feel that we are watching real
events unfold as they happen.

In this sequence, also, we are given a strong impression of
respectability, which is strangely at odds with what is being
confessed: a violent murder. This is established through the codes of
mise-en-scène – this is a 'nice' woman in a 'nice' neighbourhood from
which villains are noticeably absent. Because the codes relating to
Construction (settings, props, NVC and dress codes) are handled in the
way that they are, we read the situation as one in which an otherwise
normal and respectable woman has been driven beyond the bounds of
civilised behaviour because of the way that she was treated by her

lover. Once again, working at a brief extract has enabled us to build on previous ideas and to develop our view of the programme's issues.

Step 5

Select a fourth sequence for discussion.

Sequence 24   DCI Reid and DC Martella in the women's toilets, Sunhill. Martella is putting on lipstick (shot in BCU, showing only her lips). Reid enters and starts to discuss the case and what form of punishment, if any, is appropriate given the circumstances.

REID: How is she?

MARTELLA: Oh all right, considering. I couldn't really tell her what I thought would happen. Anything from two years suspended to life if they could convince the jury it was premeditated.

REID: Any other mitigating circumstances? Sexual abuse?

MARTELLA: Oh naturally. Tosh reckons they'll put her away 'cos she's got an education so she ought to have known better.

REID: She did kill someone, Viv.

MARTELLA: I sort of know how she felt.

REID: Taking a spanner to the back of a man's head?

MARTELLA: Haven't you ever thought like that?

REID: You want to know how often? Every day of the working week. But there are more subtle weapons.

What is interesting here is that we see Reid with Martella in the act of putting on make-up. This establishes the link of their femininity, irrespective of formal distinctions of rank. Martella's suggestion that 'she sort of knew how she felt' perhaps hints at some failed relationship of her own outside Sunhill, while it is quite clear that Reid's plans for dealing with men will employ 'more subtle weapons' – such as her own ambitions for promotion by using her position with Assistant Commissioner Renshaw, as hinted at earlier.

The questioning of the law in relation to issues of domestic violence implicit in this sequence would not have been found in such earlier British series as *Dixon of Dock Green* or *Z Cars*. In those series the law was always represented as inviolable, and, further, because they had male characters at their centre, it could be argued that the perspectives they presented reflected more entrenched patriarchal values. It will be interesting, therefore, to consider this sequence against the backdrop of other police series. This takes us into the area of Categorisation.

The development of feminist perspectives since the 1960s presents a challenge to patriarchal values and the increase in the number of police series in which women play the central roles, such as *The Gentle Touch* (TX 1979), *Juliet Bravo* (TX 1980), *Cagney and Lacey* (TX 1981) and *Prime Suspect* (TX 1991) reflects this social change. We are certainly not arguing that these programmes offer a sharp feminist perspective, but they do address issues of gender in a way that the more 'macho' police series of the 1970s such as *Starsky and Hutch* or *The Sweeney* did not.

The Gentle Touch, *Juliet Bravo*, *Cagney and Lacey* and *Prime Suspect* all had women playing the central role/s. This enabled a shift in the thematic concerns of the genre away from violence and harsh justice towards the areas of social conscience and guardianship. It is tempting to conclude that such representations of women are positive ones because the qualities involved, such as care, concern, social conscience and so on, are themselves positive. While it is certainly true that such images of successful career women provide a female audience with positive role models, there are other factors relating to the structure of such series that need to be borne in mind if you wish to write about these issues in a more analytical way.

For example, while it cannot be denied that the introduction of central women characters into a traditionally all-male genre was, in many ways, a positive and progressive step (contemporary police-women are less likely to be shown solely as ministering angels providing tea and sympathy), it might be argued that their presence simply returned the genre to its roots with the representation of policing as 'caring guardianship' (as in *Dixon of Dock Green*), which was, indeed, the dominant representation of the police during the 1950s and early 1960s. You need to look to outside pressures in an attempt to answer why police series of the 1980s tended to return to the heart of their narrative problematic. You may want to argue from this evidence that because during the 1980s the police were called upon to act as political agencies of repression (through their increasing use to quell inner-city riots and industrial disputes), it was therefore made very difficult for scriptwriters to deal with the increasing politicisation of the police. And so, it seems, the police series returned to its original, core-narrative problematic. *Juliet Bravo* is just one example of such a retreat.

What you should notice here is that we are moving from issues to do with straight Categorisation into issues to do with Audience and Agency and areas related to this. This merely emphasises the point we have been making all along: that each aspect of any media text is intimately related to another. While it is possible to treat these aspects as discrete units for the purposes of analysis, it is always necessary to be aware of the way in which they function as parts of an interrelated whole. To do this, as we have just suggested, you need to set the extract, and the programme you are analysing, in its wider cultural context. *The Bill*, in common with other output, both mirrors and creates the ideology of its time: because the political role of the police was changed during the 1980s, so the narrative problematic at the centre of the police series was changed also.

By this stage, having looked at four sequences, you should have pieced together a view of the episode as a whole. If you are still puzzled, look at more sequences until you feel you have worked out a coherent reading. Your ideas might well develop in a very different direction from ours, but this is the whole point about this method of looking at a media text – that it allows you, as you move from sequence to sequence, systematically to develop your own interpretation. At this stage, however, stop and ask yourself whether you feel you have got to grips with the episode. Try to be precise: what else can be said about the episode? One big gap that we are aware of in our analysis so far of '*A Woman Scorned*' is the need to identify how *The Bill* develops its narratives within the constraints of the police-series genre. This is what we want to do now: to consider the episode in relation to the key aspect of Narrative.

Step 6

Have I achieved a sufficiently complex sense of the media text?

In this step we are going to look at issues relating to the key media aspect of Narrative, since when you analyse an episode of a series it is important that you identify the type of narrative structure it uses. It is possible to distinguish two different types of narrative structure in the majority of police series. In the first the narrative is focused on a central character or characters (certainly rarely more than three), whose name provides the title for the series – *Dixon of Dock Green, Spender, Starsky and Hutch, Kojak, Taggart, Ironside, Cagney and Lacey,* and many others. Because these individuals are at the centre of the action we tend to see the problems that crime presents through their eyes.

In the second type of narrative structure commonly employed by the police series, much more emphasis is placed on the work of the police team as a whole. The first of these types is usually described as a **centred biography** and the second as a **decentred biography**. *The Bill*, with its cast of twenty-five or so regular characters, clearly conforms to the decentred biography model. In this, the usual method of story construction is to choose particular characters of the team on whom to focus in each episode. This is the case in '*A Woman Scorned*', which centres on Burnside and Reid.

Decentred biography police series such as *The Bill*, *Z Cars* or *Hill Street Blues* characteristically present the team as one big 'extended family', although there may be some long-running 'family feuds' such as in the conflict between Burnside and Reid. The centred biographical form of *The Sweeney*, *The Professionals*, and *Starsky and Hutch*, on the other hand, focuses upon the closer and more intense relationship between the two or three key characters who form its 'nuclear family'. It is this, in part, which helps us to identify the police series as a narrative genre. This is supported by the type of action sequence commonly employed.

There are many recognisable action sequences to be found in episodes of *The Bill*. Search and chase, secret rendezvous with 'grasses', and complex missions involving coordination between uniformed and CID police are just some of the generic categories of action sequences in any police series. It is interesting to note that in such police series a murder is actually a rare event; instead, small lives are filled with small crimes. In '*A Woman Scorned*', for example, the murder took place years before the action we see in the programme, and there is a continual tension between the drastic event of the murder itself, and the domesticity of the characters' present. Such sequences and tensions, together with the various enigmas posed in the narrative, are responsible for maintaining the impetus of the unfolding story. However, the apparently fragmentary nature of the series as a form, in which many apparently unrelated narrative strands are operating simultaneously, may make you feel that any essay you write on a television series will itself be similarly fragmentary, as it reflects the shifts and changes between the various story threads contained within it. It is, though, important that you avoid the fragmentation to which a straightforward description of events in the episode would lead. The best way to avoid this is to do as we have done in our analysis of short sequences, that is draw out the major themes, concerns and recurring interests of the programme as you go along. This will allow you to isolate some of the key oppositions to be found within the episode, for these tensions and conflicts are central to the whole concept of the programme itself. What might concern you is that by using this approach you may limit your interpretation. This should not be the case, however, because once you have completed your initial analysis you can go on to develop it in your own distinctive way. How to do this is something we consider in the following section.

Remember, though, that you can only really develop your ideas if you have got a sound basic analysis of the text. Certainly it is on this that you should concentrate at first, using the six steps we have described to build a clear sense of what the text is about and how its details work and fit into its overall meaning. In the case of 'A Woman Scorned' look at the way we identified its central concern with the relationship between men and women and then went on to examine and refine this idea, using our five key areas and focusing on the idea of domestic violence. At the same time, of course, we have tried to provide you with information about how police series fit into television and society as a whole. This is also true of the next stage of our analysis where we wish to develop further the key area of Agency. But all the time governing our analysis and shaping our argument is the simple idea of a tension in the text.

II ASPECTS OF THE TEXT: AGENCY

THE first point to grasp when considering a police series such as *The Bill* in terms of the media aspect of Agency is that it is above all a media product and, as such, something produced by and within the media industries. The ITV company involved, Thames, was concerned with making the right product, because, like any other industry, it has to sell its products to a market. This means that most new programmes will be commissioned on the basis of their similarity to already existing programmes. There is a simple reason for this: in order to market any media product, a company's audiences must be familiar with the qualities and characteristics of the product. This does not mean that change does not take place, just that new media forms evolve from pre-existing programmes. The police series must therefore conform to the existing expectations of the genre, even though it will also need to establish its own identity. It is these two factors, (i) repetition of recognisable genre characteristics; and (ii) difference from other series within the genre, that are central to the success of any new series.

The decision had been reached at ITV in 1987 to axe the soap opera, Crossroads. This programme had, by then, run for some twenty-three years (only four years less than *Coronation Street*) and, although it had acquired something of a reputation for its creaking plots and wooden acting, these were not the main factors influencing the ITV Network Board responsible for its axing. *Crossroads*, along with other programmes such as *3-2-1*, *Play Your Cards Right* and *The Price is Right*, did not appeal to the audience that advertisers were interested in reaching.

As we pointed out in Chapter 2 the commercial television stations have to be able to convince potential advertising clients – who are their sole source of revenue – that the target audience they wish to reach will be watching a particular programme. In the late 1980s the advertising industry was mainly interested in reaching the relatively affluent A/B/C1 social group, none of whom tended to watch the programmes mentioned above. It is for this reason, rather than any aesthetic ones, that these programmes were replaced by programmes designed to appeal to a younger more affluent audience, particularly those living in the South-East of England. It is important to remember that the media industry is an industry. The product it sells is a media product, and it is packaged in a particular format. It is these two areas – the tightness of *The Bill*'s format, and the need for a large number of episodes a year to be made within that format – that we wanted to discuss with John Foster, a writer for *The Bill*, in an attempt to come to some understanding of the relationship between Agency and the final broadcast product.

A word of caution, however. Do not think that what a scriptwriter or producer or director of a programme says is the final, definitive reading of any media text: the perspective such professionals may offer on a text will certainly be interesting and informative, but remember that it is only one more perspective on a complex situation. Use the information you glean from such contacts with professional media practitioners to extend your own reading of a text, not to replace it. What we wanted to explore with John Foster were the two areas we have mentioned already: the programme's format and its mode of production. It may have been possible to have interviewed a member of the production team involved in the episode of *The Bill* we analysed earlier, but we felt that, because John Foster has such a broad experience of the police- series genre, ranging from *Z Cars* right through to *The Bill*, he would be well-situated to give us some insight into the areas in which we are interested here. Also, when John Foster was writing for the programme, it was then in its bi-weekly, 104-episodes-a-year, format, so his comments refer to his experiences writing for that time. We started by asking him how he felt about the programme's strong format requirements.

US: Can you say something about how the 'Bible' [series format] is used, how it influences the writer?

JF: The thing is, with *The Bill*, it's all about the format. I mean, basically, there just has to be a copper, a police officer in every scene, and this is a major problem. I mean sometimes you might want to cut away to a robbery, say, some event, in the process of its happening, or even before. And, you can't do that with *The Bill*. So everything happens after the event. You never get any of the build-up to the event, because there just has to be a copper there all the time. And that, really, although it's a nice clear format, makes it very difficult. But it's a serious drawback, really.

This took us on to a more specific question concerning John Foster's relation, as a scriptwriter, with the production team of *The Bill*.

US: What about the production schedule? Does the fact that *The Bill* uses two or even three production units working simultaneously, does that restrict how you use characters, are you aware of which characters you can use and which you can't?

JF: No, that's up to the producer and so forth . . .you just go for the characters you want and if there is a problem of some kind . . . you just sort of work around that, if you need to, on the basis of the information you get from the script editor. The script editor would be the contact, if you needed to know any more. And because, of course, the script has to be up and finished, because they virtually shoot once. That is, the actors go in front of the cameras and they shoot without much rehearsal because they want to achieve what they feel is a sort of gritty realism. They don't like to over-rehearse anyway, or in fact they don't really rehearse at all. The actors simply go in front of the cameras and virtually say the lines. And the results are quite good, in fact, in those terms. But I do feel that, in the shows they've made of mine, if I had had a discussion with a director, in the way that one is used to having on other shows, then there are certain things that may have been better about them. I mean the final performance. You don't feel it's sort of a final performance with *The Bill*. I mean, a certain interpretation of lines which would have been more understandable to an audience, if those discussions had occurred in the normal way. And I do think we might have ended up with slightly better shows, even though I was very pleased with the end result of those shows.

US: So it seems, then, that the writer on *The Bill* doesn't experience a very intimate relationship with the director or with the production at all.

JF: That's true, yes. You don't experience any relationship with the director on *The Bill*, and yes, that is unusual. You don't even talk to the director on the phone.

US: What about the producer?

JF: No, you don't have any involvement with the producer at all. The only person that you have any involvement with is the script editor, who in this case was Tim Vaughan, who was extremely good.

US: So really, the script editor was the lynch-pin?

JF: Yes. Absolutely. Yes.

US: So no contact with lighting, designers?

JF: No. None at all, absolutely none. That is unusual. But no. Absolutely none at all.

Before we made any interpretation of this lack of involvement of the writer with the rest of the production team, and how far this is a result of the programme's format and mode of production, we needed to know how this compared with other police series.

US: You've mentioned your work on other series, like, for example, *Z Cars*. Would you say you felt less restricted by the format and by the way the programme went into production when you were writing for *Z Cars*?

JF: Oh, absolutely, yes. Absolutely. Yes, I really would . . . I mean, you could go on to *Z Cars* and write a drama. It just happened to be within a particular police format. But it could be a totally individual piece of work. You could use the regular characters in whatever way you wished. You could make a character, like, say, Bert Lynch, do whatever you wanted. You weren't at all constrained by what other writers had done with that character, as long as it wasn't totally inconsistent. The producers and script editors welcomed a different perspective, a different attack upon the format and the characters, to ring the changes, to change things, to shake up the cosiness. But in *The Bill*, it's just a production unit. A very effective production unit, but limited by the fact that it is really geared up to produce . . . You see, with, say *Z Cars*, you were just able to go on to that programme and be totally creative, and to write very much what you wanted to write, within the obvious parameters of weekly series, television going out at peak time. But, you didn't, for instance, rather slavishly have to have a police officer in every scene. You could build up a story over a week, and a lead character of the week, and really have police involvement to the minimum.

> Or you could take one of the regular characters and write a play entirely around that one character. It was a much more creative vehicle than the one experienced on *The Bill*.

What is clear in this view of things from John Foster is that the representation of policing seems to be much more important on *The Bill* than the nature of the television drama itself. Certainly, the programme has to be dramatic also, but its production schedule appears to take precedence over its dramatic content, and this pressure can only have been increased in the switch from a bi-weekly to a tri-weekly schedule. Keeping *The Bill* production line flowing is the main task of the unit producer. Every effort is made, no matter what problem presents itself, to shoot an episode within a five-day schedule; any hold-ups will obviously interfere with the shooting of the next batch of episodes. Each episode is sold to ITV for £150 000 (1991–2 figures), and unless programmes stay consistently within budget the programme could price itself off the air. This then takes us into the next area of interest to us here: the question of *The Bill's* production-line style, and what effect this may have on the programme's aesthetics.

> US: So do you feel that you're more constrained by the format in the 1980s than you were in the 1970s? Because of the production and factory ethos, the idea that the accountants have taken over, or what?
>
> JF: Well I think that there are even more restrictions coming . . . I think that the accountants have to some extent taken over television. I think that's true to some extent, yes. But I think that the problem with *The Bill* is that they just have to make so many shows . . . they are trying to maintain a creative front, they are trying to make it a creative show, and largely I think they succeed. And it is, very often, a very strong programme. But, you know, they have to produce an enormous number of shows a year. And that's the simple fact of the matter. And if you're producing that number of shows, then you can't really have a system, of people, writers, veering off from the format . . . I think it really comes down to the fact that *The Bill* is making too many programmes. I mean, there are 104 thirty-minute episodes of *The Bill* to be made a year and there just aren't 104 good scripts to be written about those characters that are going to be good, creative scripts. So, there's going to be a lot of dross, inevitably, in such a series.

Again, it is significant to note here the emphasis put on the sheer demand for production, which, arguably, takes precedence over its creation of quality drama. Such a tension is not new in television drama production: there has traditionally been something of a conflict between the writer, who wishes to communicate a unique and individual view of the world, and the media industry's demand for a commodity of a certain type. We wanted to explore the dilemma that the creative writer faces in any media institution.

US: And what about this, the tension between what the writer wants and what the Agency, the company, the means of production wants?

JF: There's always a tension between what a writer, or director, or producer and programme unit will want and what the company want . . . You always want more space than they will give you, and that's quite a creative conflict. I think that . . . with the rising costs and the problems the medium's been through in recent years, there's a tendency to go for cheaper programming and cut-backs on all kinds of things that cost money, and that you can get away with not having. But . . . it's not a good thing to do. Not in the long term. It really isn't. I think television already suffers enough from a certain conveyor-belt mentality in its programming, and I think directors should want to go against that as much as they can, by involving writers in the whole production . . . The BBC have always been good at involving writers in their programmes, they've always brought writers together in story conferences, on a series . . . Granada, also, are another company that have done this, consistently. It just gives you all a bit of time where you can really think it out and you want to make the best you can. And it pays off at the end of the day . . . You just get better scripts and better programmes and a greater sense of loyalty, and it's noticeable that the BBC and Granada have consistently produced the best programmes and that these are the two organisations which give writers the best deal.

US: From what you're saying, it sounds to me that the format and the factory system in which *The Bill* operates had the effect of distancing you both from the final interpretation or production of your work, and, perhaps, even closed down some of the avenues that you, as a writer, might have wanted to explore. Do you feel that is an accurate interpretation of the situation?

JF: Well, certainly, yes. You're right in a way . . . But of course, I think it's a very creative programme, too. I think they maintain a very high standard, for what it is. I don't think, for instance, that it compares at all with things like early *Z Cars*, but I do think it's a quite strong police series. I think it's quite a creative programme in its way, with its very strictly defined sense of format definition. But I felt that from my point of view, I'm not that interested in the police. I'm interested in the police drama, as a vehicle to explore certain dramatic situations. But *The Bill* doesn't really allow you to do that, except in its own terms of the police perspective, and I think that's very limited . . . And I think that's a pity, because I think that the dynamic of the programme could be, say, much more like *Hill Street Blues* . . . but *Hill Street Blues* was a much more powerful programme, much more, a much braver programme, a much more controversial programme, and *The Bill* is very much watered down from that. And I think the best police series ever was early *Z Cars*, which took a documentary approach, but was a much braver programme, much angrier, much more ferocious. And, again, you didn't have to stick with these rather boring regulars all the time. There's not a lot more to say about the police, there have been a lot of police programmes, and there's not a lot more of interest to say about them any more. The police may be having a hard time, we're all having a hard time, but there's not really that much more to say. Its lack of interest is I think, for me, a real problem with *The Bill*.

What John Foster has to say here is very significant, drawing attention to the fact that *The Bill* is first and foremost a media, and not necessarily an artistic, product – even if such a distinction can be drawn in the first place. However, as we saw in our analysis of '*A Woman Scorned*', the writer's individual and unique view of the world, and the writer's development and exploration of certain ideas, still comes through, despite, and perhaps even because of the various production pressures within which the script is finally produced. There is, then, a very real and identifiable tension between what the writer wants to write and what pressures of Agency are brought to bear on that.

It is important, however, that you do not run away with the idea that this tension between the writer and the means of production is unique to television. It is not. The writer, who imagines or creates, and the reader (in the broadest sense) of the text, have always communicated through some process of media production – whether that was oral story telling or reciting of poetry, or even through the production system of *The Bill*. As John Foster has pointed out here, any writer has to work within a whole Agency of production values, including many people with whom the writer may have little personal contact, but all of whom may have some impact on the final production of the writer's creation. Whatever a writer wants to say will always have to be accommodated within the means of production and the socio-economic context of the day. The concept of Agency thus helps us to begin to understand the various processes involved in producing and broadcasting media texts. An understanding of the importance of Agency also serves to tell us something about the nature of television as a medium, and underlines the need to relate the particular episode you are analysing to issues that inform the series, and the programme, as a whole.

Notes

1. Details of the programme discussed in this chapter are as follows: *The Bill*, Series 4, Thames TV plc; Episode title: '*A Woman Scorned*'; TX: 19.12.91; Writer: Victoria Taylor; Production Manager: Derek Cotty; Script Editor: Gina Cronk; Director: Nigel Payn; Design: Philip Blowers, Jan Chaney; Executive Producer: Michael Chapman; Producer: Peter Wolfes.

2. Sequence synopsis of '*A Woman Scorned*':

    Sequence 1 A 'respectable' residential area with tree-lined roads and semi-detached houses. Ackland and Smollet at Mrs Jacobus's front door.

    Sequence 2 DCI Kim Reid's Office. Reid and Burnside discussing the low morale of the CID team at Sunhill. They have differing views.

    Sequence 3 The interior of Mrs Jacobus's house.

    Sequence 4 CID room, Sunhill. General discussion of various cases in progress.

    Sequence 5 Mrs Jacobus's back garden where a human skeleton is being unearthed.

    Sequence 6 Scotland Yard. Reid presenting a paper on community policing to various high ranking officers.

    Sequence 7 Mrs Jacobus's back garden, where a police incident tent has been set up.

    Sequence 8 A corridor in Sunhill. Discussion between Cryer and Carver on station politics.

    Sequence 9 Scotland Yard. Reid, Brownlow and Renshaw discuss the issues relating to community policing following Reid's presentation.

    Sequence 10 Interior of the Jacobus House. Discussion between Ackland and Mrs Jacobus.

    Sequence 11 AC Renshaw and DCI Reid in conversation over a working lunch at a Chinese restaurant.

    Sequence 12 The Jacobus's back garden. Garfield unearths a plastic bag containing various documents identifying the dead man.

    Advertising break.

Sequence 13   Murder Incident Room, Sunhill. Discussion identifying the murder victim as Robin Arthur Cruikshank.

Sequence 14   Smollet on house-to-house enquiries in the Jacobus neighbourhood.

Sequence 15   Murder Incident room, Sunhill. Discussion filling in more of the background of the murder victim.

Sequence 16   The Jacobus Street. Smollet on house-to-house enquiries.

Sequence 17   Murder Incident room. Sunhill. More information on the identity and background of the murder victim.

Sequence 18   Corridor in Sunhill. Reid and Burnside in discussion about the case and about Reid's visit to Scotland Yard.

Sequence 19   Interior, local library. Lines and Martella interview the librarian, who gives them a list of the former occupants of Mrs Jacobus's house. It turns out that the only one still living in the area is a teacher, Sally Joseph.

Sequence 20   The CID office. Burnside and Roach finishing work.

Sequence 21   Lines and Martella at Sally Joseph's large, well-furnished house. Josephs eventually admits to the murder.

Sequence 22   Monroe at Mrs Jacobus's. He is informed, over his police radio, that the search of the house can end as the crime is now solved.

Sequence 23   Murder Incident room, Sunhill. Reid congratulates Brooks on the successful completion of the case.

Sequence 24   Reid and Martella in the women's toilets, Sunhill, discussing the case and what form of punishment, if any, is appropriate given the circumstances.

5

The TV sitcom: *Fawlty Towers*

I CONSTRUCTING AN OVERALL ANALYSIS

WHAT we aim to do in this chapter is to look at TV sitcoms, concentrating our analysis on the episode '*Gourmet Night*' (TX 17 October 1975, BBC2), from the *Fawlty Towers* series, written by John Cleese and Connie Booth. There are several reasons why we have chosen to study this programme. The first and most obvious reason is that we feel *Fawlty Towers* is excellent television, supported by superb scripts and some brilliant acting. Second, the scripts have been published as *The Complete Fawlty Towers* (Mandarin, 1988) so you should be able to get hold of the script fairly easily if you want to develop your analysis of this or of any other episode from the series. And third, recordings of the programme are available through video libraries and from the BBC. All in all this programme seems, therefore, a good place to start looking at the TV sitcom.

As a media form, *Fawlty Towers* follows a simple format: it tells the story of a couple, Basil and Sybil Fawlty, running a hotel where everything that can go wrong, does – not least because of the class pretensions of Basil Fawlty, and because of Manuel, a Spanish waiter with a weak grasp of English.

It is worthwhile, before we start on our formal analysis, to spend a little time tracing the history of the sitcom as a genre. The arrival of ITV in 1955 brought to British screens the immmensely popular American sitcom, *I Love Lucy*. Until that time, comedy and light entertainment at the BBC had consisted mainly of rather tame comedy and polite variety shows, but the popularity of the imported and relatively outspoken and raucous *I Love Lucy* soon convinced the BBC that it would have to introduce its own sitcoms to win back its audience share from ITV. So began the 'great tradition' of BBC sitcoms of which *Fawlty Towers* is a part, a tradition which includes *Hancock's Half Hour*, *Steptoe and Son*, *Till Death Us Do Part*, *Dad's Army*, *Porridge*, *Yes, Minister* and *Blackadder*.

The BBC's *Hancock's Half Hour* was to be as influential in the development of the sitcom form as *I Love Lucy* had been in jolting the TV sitcom into life in the first place. Like many other sitcoms of the period it transferred in 1956 to television from radio (where it was first broadcast in 1954). The arrogance, pomposity and pettiness of the Hancock character soon attracted huge audiences – between 12 and 13 million in 1960 – and over the years the sitcom has come to play an increasingly important part in BBC scheduling. Between 1980 and 1982, for example, over 120 sitcom series (including repeats) were broadcast by the BBC alone. *Fawlty Towers* itself was repeated twice on BBC2 in this period.

It is generally agreed that writing great comedy is exceptionally difficult, so it is quite natural that you may feel rather daunted by the idea of writing critically about it. Further, you are bound to feel that to analyse humour at all is to risk destroying it, for surely comedy is one of the most natural things. But this need not be the case. We would agree that to dissect a programme such as *Fawlty Towers* in a cold and mechanical way, without making any mention of the pleasures that it gives you, is a counter-productive exercise. As fans of sitcom in general and *Fawlty Towers* in particular, we certainly do not wish to give an impersonal reading of it in this chapter, and we are sure that the method we use, and which we are suggesting you adopt, helps in building an informed, critical and appreciative analysis to any media text.

Step 1

After watching the programme, see if you can identify any kind of pattern or structure at work.

The story in the episode of *Fawlty Towers*, 'Gourmet Night', which we want to analyse in this chapter, is simple enough, even though there are several strands operating within it. Baldly stated, the episode tells the story of the snobbish Basil Fawlty, who is determined to try to break into the gourmet high-life by setting an evening aside for his new chef, Kurt, to provide the best food in town. Unfortunately for Basil, Kurt falls in love with Manuel, and, when his affection is unreturned, he becomes hopelessly drunk. Basil's hopes for a gourmet night fall apart rapidly, and the evening degenerates into disorder and chaos.

Working inside this broad story outline, we find, in common with other episodes of *Fawlty Towers*, a very tightly organised plot, and you will need to watch the video or read the script several times to appreciate fully the episode's many twists and turns. Nevertheless, there is much more to *Fawlty Towers* than the pulling together of story strands in a rather contrived way. One of the things that distinguishes this programme from other, rather pedestrian farces in which people lose their trousers or get caught in a cupboard with the maid, is the way in which thematic structure, character, plot and technical production work together to create the programme's unique quality. Before going any further, therefore, it will be useful to spend some time looking at the two types of plot commonly employed by the sitcom. In media and communications studies these are referred to as (i) **the organic plot**, and (ii) **the structured plot**. The first thing you need to do with any TV sitcom, therefore, is to identify which plot type it uses.

Of course, all plots are structured, as you will be aware, but the first of these two plot types, (i) the organic plot, is structured in such a way that it attempts to hide its own processes of structuration. In such plots there does not seem to be any strict logic to the ordering of the sequences, and, because of this, these sitcoms have what is often referred to as a 'slice-of-life' quality; in *Roseanne*, for example, we drop in each week to see how the members of the Connor house are coping with the pressures of work or family life. What actually happens in the episode is not the main concern, since we are more interested in the response of characters to the various events that seem to grow and develop in a natural ('organic') way around them. The impression given is that these characters are there all the time and we just happen to drop in on an unedited and unstructured part of their lives to watch how they attempt to cope with the situation in which fate has placed them. This is clearly not the type of plot we encounter in *Fawlty Towers*, which is much more obviously patterned and structured.

The second type of plot commonly employed by the TV sitcom is the structured plot. This is often ostentatious in its structuring, so that we are aware that we are in the presence of a 'made' and edited account. Such plots are artfully and carefully arranged and depend upon characters making sudden discoveries, or upon the story being resolved by what might otherwise appear to be somewhat unlikely coincidences. This complexity is further compounded by the introduction of numerous shifts of scene and/or of time, which is not what we encounter in the 'slice-of-life' organic plot. *Fawlty Towers* quite obviously uses the structured plot form. One thing that is important to grasp here, however, is that although we talk about the structured plot as being highly contrived and patterned, this does not reflect negatively upon it; indeed, much of the pleasure we get from watching such plots unfold comes precisely from our delight in their artifice.

In the structured plot, we tend to find a narrative line which depends upon a central character who schemes to fool those around him or her. *Sgt. Bilko, Hancock's Half Hour, Blackadder* and *Steptoe and Son* are all good examples here. Such 'scheming' plots are invariably highly structured – Bilko will think up a complex scheme to dupe the men of the motor pool out of their money, just as Blackadder attempts to manipulate other characters for his personal advantage.

Such a structured and scheming plot is characteristic of *Fawlty Towers*: most of Basil's schemes in the series revolve around his snobbish desire to improve the quality of the clientèle at *Fawlty Towers* and '*Gourmet Night*' is no exception to this basic rule. In this programme, the whole aim of the evening is to attract what Basil calls 'the right sort of person' to his hotel. He is therefore extremely pleased that Colonel and Mrs Hall ('both JPs') and Lionel Twitchen ('one of Torquay's leading Rotarians') will be at the 'Gourmet Night'. The plot here works to achieve several ends, which link in to the thematic development of the programme: Basil's plan is frustrated when his dreams of grandeur are confronted by the real world. This is important thematically because we can see this basic conflict between Basil's scheming dreams and the inanimate real world at work everywhere we look in the programme: the opening sequence figures Basil talking to his car which will not start, and which he later thrashes with a branch torn from a tree. We can see, therefore, that one of the basic conflicts or tensions in this programme (the tension between Basil's snobbish dreams and the reality of life for the small-town hotelier) is actually underpinned by the very nature of the plot and narrative development of the programme itself. It is thematic linking of this type which underlies the programme's genius and brilliance.

It is important, when you analyse any TV sitcom, or, indeed, any media text, that you stand back from the programme's details a little and try to think about the broad patterns or structures at work. What becomes clear when we think about the programme in this broad way is that this relationship between the plot structure and the general thematic concerns of the programme is to a large extent dependent upon failings in the central character's personality. '*Gourmet Night*' is actually about Basil's snobbishness more than it is about the events which unfold before us, simply because these events would never have happened if Basil were not motivated by his own snobbishness. Consequently, we can predict that the central character's scheming will always fail, because his scheming tells us something about a failing in his own character: *Fawlty Towers* will never become a hotel for the refined upper classes, just as *Bilko* will never become rich. It is this basic conflict which shapes to a greater or lesser extent all of the *Fawlty Towers* episodes, and you could use this basic conflict or tension as a springboard into an analysis not only of any one of the *Fawlty Towers* episodes, but also as a springboard into your own analysis of any other sitcom which makes use of such a structured and 'scheming' plot. Once you have identified this basic conflict or tension at work, as we have here, you can begin to turn your attention to close analysis of short sequences from the programme itself, just as we did in the previous chapter.

Step 2

Analyse the opening sequence, or, if this proves unilluminating, a sequence from fairly near the begining, featuring one or two of the major characters.

Having looked at the basic dramatic tension in the narrative of the programme as a whole in step 1, that is, how Basil's schemes always fail, what we want to do here is to work from a storyboard of the opening sequence, since we want to concentrate on some of the technical codes of Construction involved. The area in which we are particularly interested is the area of editing, because we have found in our own teaching that one of the things that most puzzles students is just how the many thousands of frames which make up the programme can be combined to produce a smooth and coherent end product.

Certainly, as we watch '*Gourmet Night*' we are hardly ever aware of the many decisions made by the director, the camera operators and the editor to achieve this smooth end result. It is important that you understand, as a media student, the nature of some of these decisions, although you certainly do not need to know about all the technical terms or technology employed in the industry. There are many technical textbooks that you can consult to find out about the technical details of editing or camera work. If you have ever used a video camcorder to shoot a simple sequence you have probably noticed how different your results were from broadcast television programmes. The main factor separating the professional product from the amateur video is neither the camera technology (most directors and camera operators could make professional quality programmes using quite simple video cameras) nor the lack of access to editing facilities, since it is possible to shoot a sequence by editing 'in-camera' or by planning your shots carefully in advance. Instead, what separates the amateur from the professional product is the understanding of the principles of narrative and pictorial continuity. As we watch *'Gourmet Night'* we are generally unaware, for example, of the many changes of camera position in the sequence, because its pictorial continuity is so successful. However, when we view most home videos the changes of scene and camera angle destroy any real sense of pictorial continuity, and it is this which tends to make most home videos very difficult to follow.

In classic continuity editing, as it is sometimes called, the editing process becomes largely invisible, as in this opening sequence to *Fawlty Towers*.

'Gourmet Night': the opening sequence

Before you read the rest of this section, either watch the opening minute of the episode, or look carefully at our storyboard of the sequence. The sequence breaks down as follows:

Shot 0: Figure 5.1 Long Shot (LS)   This is the programme's establishing title shot. A dissolve is used between this opening title shot of Fawlty Towers Hotel (which establishes the programme) and the first shot of this episode to establish the relationship between the programme and the episode.

Shot 1: Figure 5.2 Mid Long Shot (MLS)   Eye-level camera angle. Basil Fawlty is attempting to repair his car engine. This is the establishing shot of this particular episode, and in it we see all the main elements required to set the scene – Basil, the car and the corner of Fawlty Towers in the background. This is enough to let us know that Basil is at home trying to fix his car in his car park.

Figure 5.2

Figure 5.4

WARTY TOWELS

Figure 5.1

Figure 5.3

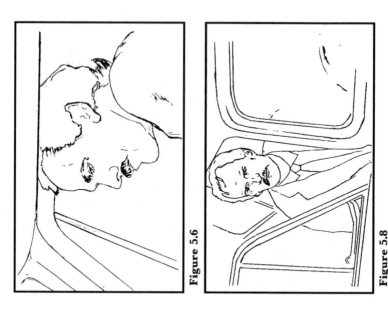

Figure 5.6

Figure 5.8

Figure 5.5

Figure 5.7

Shot 2: Figure 5.3 Mid Shot (MS)   Eye-level camera angle. Basil inside the car trying to start the engine.

Shot 3: Figure 5.4 Mid Long Shot (MLS)   Eye-level camera angle. Basil takes a piece of food from what looks like a rag on the front of the engine compartment. He eats the food while still poking about under the bonnet.

Shot 4: Figure 5.5 Mid Long Shot (MLS)   Low camera angle. The car's horn is sounding. Basil reprimands the car by talking to it and by waving an admonishing finger at it.

Shot 5: Figure 5.6 Close Up (CU)   Low camera angle. Basil trying to start the car. Again, he is complaining to the car. He looks down as he fiddles with the controls.

Shot 6: Figure 5.7 Mid Close Up (MCU)   Low camera angle. Manuel arrives telling Basil that there has been a telephone call. He mimes the activity of making a phone call to compensate for his imperfect English. This is a point of view (POV) shot (from Basil's viewpoint).

Shot 7: Figure 5.8 Mid Close Up (MCU)   High camera angle. Basil, still seated in the car, leans out of the open door and stares at Manuel in incomprehension.

Table 5.1 summarises the various technical codes employed in the sequence and the effects that they have on us.

It is important, when analysing the technicalities of a scene like this, that you resist the temptation merely to list the various technical codes employed. Instead, you should always try to show how the technicalities of production feed in to and reinforce the underlying tensions or conflicts of the drama. For example, as you can see from this breakdown of the technical codes employed in the editing of this sequence, the major impression given is that of everyday naturalness with the audience engaged in watching the scene unfold before us. Also, through codes of shot-size and camera angle it is clear that this sequence wants to give us some impression of Basil's psychological state, and this means that, although the scene is made to seem very natural, everything we see carries significance.

Technically, this is achieved through the use of deep focus, so that we see everything in focus, whether it is in the foreground or the background. Because the sequence is shot in deep focus we can see

Table 5.1 Technical codes and their effects on viewers

Technical Code	Effect
1 Choice of shot size	
Close up (shot 5)	We see Basil's psychological state
Mid shot (shot 2)	A closer relation to the subject
Mid Long shot (shots 1, 3, 4)	Establishing/re-establishing the scene
Mid Close Up (shot 6, 7)	Establishing the relationship between Basil and Manuel
2 Choice of camera angle.	
Eye level (shots 1, 2, 3)	We witness the action and do not feel either dominated by, or superior to, the subject
Low (shots 4, 5, 6)	Basil rises above us and seems more dominant
3 Choice of composition	
Symmetrical (shot 6, 7)	It feels as if we are being directly spoken to by the subjects
Asymmetrical (shots 1, 3, 4)	A natural, everyday feeling
4 Choice of focus	
Deep focus (all shots)	All elements are important – 'look at everything'
5 Choice of lighting	
Low contrast	Realistic, everyday feeling
6 Choice of colours	
Cool (brown, green, grey)	Realistic everyday feeling
7 Choice of cinematic codes	
Pan (end of shot 1)	We survey/follow Basil
Dissolve (start of shot 1)	A link with opening titles
Cut (all shots)	Simultaneity of time

very clearly that Basil takes a piece of food from the rag on the front of the engine compartment. Having a piece of rag on the engine ties in well with the everyday naturalness of the scene: it is what we would expect to see there if we were watching somebody tinkering with their car engine. But the fact that the rag has food resting on it creates a thematic link between the car and food, and informs our sense of Basil's psychological state also: Basil Fawlty is hardly a gourmet himself, and appears to know nothing about the tasks he is attempting. The idea that he can run a 'gourmet night' is as ridiculous as his attempts to fix the car. And yet he persists, driven by his own particular psychological failings. As he says at the end of this sequence: 'Right, leave it to me, I'll do it! I'll mend the car, I'll answer the telephone, then you can all handcuff and blindfold me and I'll clean the windows. . .' The problem is, Basil is ironically ill-equipped to cope with the world, which he seems unable to understand (he obviously does not know what he is fiddling with under the bonnet) and which seems to assault him physically (note that the car blows its horn at him). It is clear that he should really take the car to a mechanic to have it mended. This is just what Sybil tells him to do, and his refusal to do this is what leads to the final catastrophe and the failure of his 'Gourmet Night'. Basil's 'Gourmet Night' fails not only because the car fails him, but also because there is something in his own psychological state which causes him to fail also. We can see, therefore, that there is a specific link between the way this scene is constructed technically, and how it fits in with the artistic and thematic interests of the programme as a whole: the food and the rag upon the car engine creates a thematic link between the two subjects. This is what you must always remember: that there is a specific link between each individual sequence and the programme's broader conflicts and tensions.

Step 3

Select a second sequence for discussion.

As we have seen, the opening few shots of '*Gourmet Night*' work to establish much about character, narrative and theme, and all this information is presented to us through the use of various technical codes of Construction. What we want to do in this section is to develop our analysis of the opening sequence by looking at the way it links in with just the first minutes of the programme (*The Complete Fawlty Towers Scripts*, pp. 107–10). These first few minutes seem to work almost as a self-contained piece of drama: we see the hotel, and Basil poking about under the bonnet of the car; we are introduced to the new chef, Kurt, receive hints about Kurt's liking for alcohol, see Sybil insisting that Basil should take the car to a mechanic to have it mended, and then see Basil drive away from the hotel, apparently to take the car to the garage. In fact, he stops just outside the hotel and opens the bonnet. The screen then fades to black, marking off the end of the sequence. The viewer is being told, by the fade to black, that this is the end of the prologue, which has served to establish the programme's central dramatic tensions. It is important to establish the relationship between this sequence and the opening few shots of the episode.

The best way to do this is by looking at the other branch of Construction, *mise-en-scène*. Codes of setting play a very important part in sitcoms because they establish the general mood of the programme, providing an appropriate background against which the characters can be developed.

Codes of mise-en-scène

Setting
In both the title and opening sequences of '*Gourmet Night*' we get a clear picture of the hotel. Probably the first thing that we would want to say about the building itself is that it conjures up a feeling of polite gentility. This is further enhanced by the title music which evokes the tea dances of palm-court quartets. The hotel lobby with its barometer, umbrella stand, and rather basic reception desk help us to categorise Fawlty Towers as a small family concern. It is clearly not a part of a thriving hotel chain.

Frequent mention is made in '*Gourmet Night*' of the fact that Fawlty Towers is in Torquay. This is done for two reasons. First, to locate the programme in a known place and milieu makes it more realistic and is usual sitcom strategy: *The Good Life* was set in Surbiton, *Till Death Us Do Part* in West Ham, *Birds of a Feather* in Chigwell and *Only Fools and Horses* in Peckham. Second, and more importantly, each of these locations carries particular associations that permit the exploration of particular class themes; Surbiton signifies 'middle class' and West Ham or Peckham 'working class', while in Chigwell the class aspirations of two working-class 'Essex girls', Sharon and Tracy, are contrasted with the middle-class outlook of the other residents.

As a seaside resort Torquay markets itself as being relatively refined and genteel in comparison with, say, the brasher more working-class Blackpool. If we carried out a commutation test, replacing Torquay with Blackpool, it would become clear that its selection is not arbitrary. It could, for example, possibly be exchanged with any of the resorts in the left-hand column below but not with those in the right-hand column, if the meaning is to stay the same.

Bournemouth	Southend
Eastbourne	Blackpool
Brighton	Skegness

Because situation comedies return to the same setting week after week, mise-en-scène is clearly of prime importance. The cluttered chaos of the living room in *Steptoe and Son*, the muddy army camp in *M.A.S.H.*, and the seedy bedsits in *Rising Damp* are amongst the most memorable aspects of the programmes. It is important to remember, therefore, when writing about codes of setting in the sitcom, that these play a vital part in establishing a general mood that prevails throughout the series and which even the characters themselves seem to share. Settings are thus not merely the background against which the action takes place, they are used to deliver key themes that are central both to the narrative problematic of the series as a whole, and to the characters.

As we pointed out above, nearly all sitcoms are based in either work-based or home-based settings. You would expect them, therefore, to deal with the values and beliefs normally associated with these two fundamental aspects of all our lives. One of the reasons we have chosen to look at *Fawlty Towers* is that, like *Steptoe and Son*, it represents a fusion of the two forms – because the hotel is a small family firm themes related to both the family and the workplace can be introduced. It was probably to some extent because its narrative problematic or configuration had these two dimensions that *Fawlty Towers* was such a successful sitcom.

This narrative problematic is certainly at the centre of the sequence we are considering here, which deals with issues of authority and domination against a background of domestic conflict; the struggles for control between Basil and his wife, Sybil. Such power struggles exist in both the traditional settings for the situation comedy – work and the home. One of the questions we have to ask ourselves, therefore, is whether this sequence illustrates Sybil's superiority in the hotel or in their marriage. Much of the comedy of *Fawlty Towers* comes from just this overlap between the home and work situations in the Torquay family business, and the way in which this generates role ambiguity – Sybil as wife/boss, Basil as husband/boss.

In most work-based sitcoms the hierarchical relationship between bosses and subordinates is central to the comic interchange and this is clearly what is going on in this sequence. Basil bullies and punishes Manuel but is stopped in his tracks by his wife Sybil who is trying to get him to take the car to the garage for servicing. Again, the strategy of having a pompous, ineffectual or incompetent boss alongside a shrewd, capable or wily assistant or subordinate is a common pattern in the sitcom. In *Yes, Minister* (later to become *Yes, Prime Minister*), for example, the honest but gullible MP, Jim Hacker, is continually outwitted by his civil servant assistant, Sir Humphry. In *Dad's Army*, the leader of the Home Guard of Warmington-on-Sea, Captain Mainwaring, is pompous and officious; his assistant, Sergeant Wilson, is far more level-headed, calm and practical, quietly offering advice to Mainwaring that prevents his often misguided schemes from collapsing. In just the same way, Basil tries to give us the impression that he is the efficient, competent manager of Fawlty Towers. In fact, both the other characters and the audience recognise that it is Sybil who gets things done and solves the problems.

In most sequences Sybil emerges as sane and as the more practical character, the organiser and 'doer', and Basil as the nominal boss, given to reflecting on cruel fate and the inadequacies of the rest of humankind (philosophical ponderings which have little to do with the practicalities of hotel management). Relations of power clearly affect both Basil's interaction with inanimate objects (he scolds his car for its inefficiency) and with people (he dominates and bullies Manuel). By developing this theme in the sequence, we are given a clear insight into Basil's character: he confronts a world which he simply cannot either understand or control, and his attempts to do so lead us to much of the comic and dramatic core of the series.

Props

In the lobby of Fawlty Towers there are a number of props selected from paradigms – the grandfather clock, for instance, is selected from a paradigmatic set which includes cuckoo clocks, digital display clocks and so on. Each of these props, selected from their respective paradigms, are combined together (such combination relates, as you will remember, to the syntagmatic dimension) to convey a message about the lobby at Fawlty Towers. Had other props from other paradigms been selected – fishtanks or murals of the Rocky mountains say – then a different message would have been communicated. Clearly these particular props have been chosen in order that the setting helps to establish the broader thematic setting of the series, suggesting polite gentility but also rather old-fashioned inefficiency.

NVC

The effectiveness of '*Gourmet Night*' depends largely on the comic ability of Cleese, who creates for us this particularly monstrous Torquay hotelier from the script written by himself and Connie Booth. If we watch the opening sequence from '*Gourmet Night*' without the sound we can see just how extensively Cleese draws upon the full repertoire of NVC to express his domination of Manuel and his submissive relation to Sybil. Later, his fawning subservience towards what he considers to be his prestige guests at the gourmet evening, and his aggressive bullying of both Manuel and Polly, come to the fore. Basil's excessive bowing and scraping moves rapidly through deference and flattery to servile, almost slavish, obsequiousness; likewise, as the Gourmet Night proceeds, the guests' earlier feelings of unease and apprehension give way to anger and disbelief.

Dress codes
These play an important part in Fawlty Towers. Although we frequently see Basil sporting cravats and bow ties, and dressed in the suits and sports jackets that we would associate with middle-class dress codes, these are never quite so well-tailored or stylish enough to give him the elegance we might associate with the clothes themselves. Similarly, in this sequence, Sybil's twin-set, pearls and frilly blouses have a flamboyance that prevents us from reading them as refined. In consequence, there is a slight hint of vulgarity in her dress sense. Clearly codes of dress are being used to establish the class status of the key characters in this opening sequence.

We can now see how the non-technical codes of Construction are being used in this sequence to develop issues established in the opening few shots: issues to do with class and snobbery, the fact that Fawlty Towers, for all its pretensions, does not quite make it. The concept of a 'Gourmet Night' draws upon Basil's desire to attract prestige guests to his hotel, but the hotel itself, as a reflection of Basil's own failings and snobbish desires, will let him down just as effectively as the car lets him down by failing to start. Again, broader issues and tensions can be seen to be intimately related to the details of the final production, and it is the closeness of this relationship which ensures that the programme works so effectively as both drama and comedy.

Step 4

Select a third sequence for discussion.

The sequence we want to look at now is one which raises issues of stereotyping. Stereotypes are ways of conveying to audiences recognisable cultural images of certain individuals or groups, and because of this, the media concept on which we want to concentrate in our analysis of this sequence, involving Kurt's unrequited love for Manuel (*Complete Fawlty Towers Scripts*, pp. 120–2), is Audience.

In sitcoms the audience is generally presented with two different types of characters. The first are recognisable social types: the efficient secretary or the domineering boss, for example. The second are identifiable stereotypes: the gay man (interestingly, as far as we know, no sitcom has ever featured a lesbian character), the domineering wife, the henpecked husband and so on. When writing about a sitcom in terms of the key central aspect of Audience you will need to pay close attention to these two forms of characters: the social type and the stereotype. This is what we want to concentrate on here: the stereotyping of the chef, Kurt, as a homosexual, and how this stereotyping functions in the programme. Although Kurt's love for Manuel comes as something of a comic surprise, it is nevertheless effectively foreshadowed in the narrative by the fact that Kurt buys Polly's drawing of Manuel in an early sequence, and by a cryptic conversation between Kurt and André (ibid., p. 113) which suggests some dark mystery in Kurt's character or background.

Gay or camp characters are often included in sitcoms. Mr Humphries in *Are You Being Served?* and Gloria in *It Ain't Half Hot, Mum*, are typical examples of the way in which gay or effeminate men are represented in the genre. One of the difficulties with which we have to deal in looking at such stereotypes is seeing how stereotyping operates in the programme. Kurt, for example, becomes the subject of some fairly standard homophobic remarks from Basil (ibid., pp. 120–122) But what do you make of this? It may be possible to argue that Cleese is criticising the narrow-minded social type he is playing in the same way that Johnny Speight was attempting to disparage the bigotry of Alf Garnett. There are, however, some serious problems with this argument. As many people have pointed out, Garnet's racism and sexism were interpreted by racist and sexist members of the audience as confirming their own beliefs rather than representing a criticism of them (which was of course the intention). That is, it could be argued that any sitcom which contains stereotypical gay characters will fuel homophobia even if those characters are given a very positive role in the narratives.

Clearly, there are no easy answers here, since there is much to be said for both points of view. What is important is not necessarily that you adopt either interpretation but that you are aware of the roles that such stereotyped characters play in the plots of a sitcom. In a sitcom such as *Agony* (which starred Maureen Lipman), for instance, the audience were asked to laugh along with the gay couple (who were, none the less, stereotypically represented) at the attitudes and prejudices of the 'straight' characters that surround them. This is why it is important to examine the place of the stereotype in the structure of the sitcom itself; if we were to judge the two gay characters in *Agony* as negative representations because they conform to dominant media portrayals of male homosexuals we would miss the positive aspects just discussed.

It is often argued that any use of character stereotypes must in itself be harmful insofar as they confirm conventional or negative views of particular social groups – the working class, women, ethnic minorities and so on. Although there is possibly much truth in this it is important to look at these issues in more depth: it is not enough simply to conclude that the stereotypes that populate the sitcom genre function merely to keep people in their place and maintain relations of power. The character of Sybil, for instance, not only conforms to the domineering wife and the self-indulgent woman stereotypes but also offers something of a positive representation to a female audience, insofar as she generally manages to organise and run the hotel, despite the incompetence of her husband. It is important, therefore, to ask how the programme uses the stereotype, since some comedies will shock or challenge our prejudices while others will draw upon cultural stereotypes to amuse us. If we now consider the differences between these two types of comedy a little more we may be able to clarify the complex set of relations that exist between comedy, the audience and the issue of stereotyping, since this can tell us something of the nature of the comedy itself.

Broadly speaking, TV sitcom divides into two types: (a) comedy which reinforces the audience's prejudices or expectations, and (b) comedy which disrupts the audience's expectations or challenges their preconceptions. A sitcom such as *'Allo, 'Allo*, which is set in a cafe in wartime occupied France, is a good example of the first type: comedy which reinforces the audience's prejudices or expectations. In this programme, the comedy is built around the repetition of stereotypical situations which the audience either finds funny or does not, as the case may be. In consequence, each scene relies on what the writers consider to be its own intrinsic humour (which is usually of a saucy seaside-postcard kind). Because of this such sitcoms are sometimes described as '**closed media texts**', since they simply offer audiences stock humorous situations and dialogue, depending to a large extent upon the representation of stereotypes which will fit in with the accepted prejudices of its audience.

If the sitcom you are analysing is of this closed type, then you could go on to argue that the programme to some extent serves merely to replicate dominant social views. The fact that the majority of sitcoms are set either in the home or the work-place would clearly endorse such an argument, because these are the two social institutions most concerned with the reproduction of key attitudes and myths within society. Genres such as sitcoms could be said, if such a view is correct, to package existing norms and beliefs for audiences, and such values and beliefs sometimes appear to hang on despite radical changes in the society reflected by the sitcom; it was not until the late 1980s that the BBC eventually decided to jettison its ageing sitcom *Terry and June*, with its cosy pre-1960s' value system. This, again, can be seen to be intimately related to the notion of stereotyping and Audience response. The stereotyping of recognisable social types – mothers-in-law, gay men, ethnic minorities and so on – is often aggressively cruel. The main purpose of such stereotyping is clearly to make the audience feel part of a cohesive social group, an 'us' that 'they', as a 'minority' group, are outside of. However, it can be difficult to understand and comment more fully upon the effect that stereotypes have on the audience if you go no further than arguing that they merely serve to maintain the *status quo*. This is why it is useful when writing about the sitcom as a genre to balance your analysis by considering sitcoms which are less 'closed' and conventional.

This brings us to the second type of sitcom we identified above: comedy which disrupts the audience's expectations or challenges their preconceptions. With Cleese's comic performance we are never quite sure of the direction his reaction to situations will take him. Whereas in *'Allo,'Allo* the comedy rarely challenges our expectations, since characters respond to stock situations in a stock way, with *Fawlty Towers* we can never quite be sure whether Basil's response will be violence or sarcasm or a philosophical acceptance. Comedy like this, which allows the audience to do some creative work or which punctures pretence and preconceived ideas, is therefore often described as being '**open**', insofar as it encourages active interpretation and involvement. *The Young Ones*, *Blackadder* and some of the work of Victoria Wood are good examples of comedy of this kind. In this sequence, for example, Basil tries momentarily to persuade Manuel to become Kurt's lover, purely to satisfy his own desire that his gourmet evening should be a success. While his initial response satisfies standard social prejudices, Basil's curious and eccentric psychological state allows him to adopt a position which seriously challenges those very prejudices. It is from this conflict or tension between the audience's expectations and Basil's reaction to the situation, that, arguably, much of the programme's comedy arises. It is important, therefore, to concentrate not just on the fact that the sitcom contains stereotypes, but to look in detail at the way that the sitcom uses stereotypes to create its unique brand of humour.

Step 5

Select a fourth sequence for discussion.

We can now turn to what is, for the moment, our final sequence for analysis. So far we have seen how technical codes of Construction are used alongside non-technical codes of *mise-en-scène* to establish the episode's dramatic core, and also how the issue of stereotyping in the sitcom can be understood in terms of the key media aspect of Audience. What we now need to do is to spend some time considering how these aspects can themselves be brought into even sharper focus by looking further at the aspect of Narrative. A useful sequence to analyse here is the final one, for in it many of the episode's themes and story strands are drawn together into a chaotic finale. As we said at the beginning of this chapter, the examination of the narrative organisation of *Fawlty Towers* forms the first step in analysis. This makes sense because sitcoms are, like most other types of TV output, narrational. Even factual programmes such as the News, sport and documentaries impose narrative organisation on their material: there will still be conflicts and resolutions, heroes and villains, and some sense of an imposed plot.

Fawlty Towers uses a classic form of the structured plot, the *reductio ad absurdum* (literally, reduction to the absurd). In *reductio* plots a simple human error or character fault is magnified so that problems multiply and everything ends in chaos. Usually we are made aware of this error or mistake in the opening scenes, just as we are in '*Gourmet Night*': despite Sybil's wishes Basil refuses to take the car to the garage, mistakenly thinking that he can fix it himself. This simple error in the opening minutes leads to all kinds of problems and culminates in the riotously funny scenes at the close of the episode.

In some comedies the *reductio* is built up around a mistake that anyone might make: on Basil's second visit to André's he inadvertently picks up the wrong entrée dish. This is not, however, the core to the comedy, as it is in most *reductio*-based plots. Instead, much of the success of '*Gourmet Night*' stems from the way in which the mistakes that Basil makes are linked to his own character faults: his refusal to return the car to the garage betrays his belief that he is burdened with the responsibility for running the hotel single-handedly, and the fact that he eats while attempting to fix the engine shows his inability to follow through any one task to completion. The *reductio* plot is perfect for showing these ridiculous aspects of human nature – pride, jealousy, ambition and so on. This is what makes it the ideal form for *Fawlty Towers*, given the nature of Basil's character.

The *reductio* plot is a highly schematic and structured one, and we find its basic patterns repeated time and again in TV sitcoms. However, differences in plot structure are not the only area on which we can comment. Sitcoms also make use of what are sometimes termed **comic strategies**. These strategies, which we outline below, are found across all comic forms, from sitcoms to romantic comedies, and it is important that you take them into account when writing about any comic form. We shall now consider the closing sequence of '*Gourmet Night*' (ibid., pp. 127–31) to see how these four comic strategies are employed here.

1.   The ludicrous
In the final incident Basil removes the cloche and reveals not the duck he was expecting, but a trifle. This is an example of the ludicrous, a comic form that involves the central character(s) being caught up in circumstances beyond their control. This clearly ties in with much of the overall motivation of '*Gourmet Night*', an episode in which Basil is shown to be unable either to understand or to cope with the world, given the failings in his own character. The ludicrous is reinforced here by the fact that the audience is aware that Basil picked up the wrong tray at André's. Basil, of course, is unaware of this.

2.   The ridiculous
A good example of the ridiculous is to be found in the scene in which Basil's car breaks down and he proceeds to thrash it with a tree branch; it is Basil himself who is at fault for not taking the car to the garage to be fixed. In writing about sitcoms in particular, or comedy in general, it is useful if you bear this distinction between the *ludicrous*

and *ridiculous* comic forms in mind; the central difference relates to whether or not the character involved was to blame for the situation which has arisen. This scene, in which Basil thrashes the car, is the culmination of the conflict between Basil and the inanimate world, a conflict or tension established at the opening of the episode and continued throughout. If you watch the scene again, you will see how the camera is being used to reinforce this tension between Basil and the inanimate world, and how this ties in with the use of the strategy of the ridiculous in this *reductio* plot. You will notice, for example, that the camera frames the car centrally, and that Basil, in his rage, runs out of shot, leaving the car sitting there, still framed perfectly in the centre of the image. This reinforces the notion of the inanimate, since the camera is merely perceiving an unmoving and unfeeling object, which is, ironically, the subject of Basil's fury. Had the camera cut away to follow Basil ripping the branch from the tree then the effect would have been totally different.

3. Slapstick

The thrashing of the car is also closely related to the slapstick. Certainly, in '*Gourmet Night*' Basil is frequently involved in highly visual slapstick-type sequences like this. The thrashing of the car and of Manuel in the opening sequence ('This Basil's wife. This . . . Basil . . . This smack on head') are both slapstick in style. Similarly, when Basil hurls the crumpled duck at the unconscious Kurt it is highly reminiscent of the custard pie fights of the classic silent movies.

It is also worth noting how the scene with the trifle relies on this visual slapstick strategy for its comedy. Having discovered that it is not duck we would perhaps expect Basil (given what we know about him), to launch into an inept cover-up, probably apportioning the blame to Manuel or to Sybil. In such an innovative comedy as *Fawlty Towers*, however, we can always expect the unexpected in terms of its comic strategies. The sequence perfectly underlines Basil's manic ineptitude, and his self-image as the perfect hotelier and restaurateur for the refined classes of Torquay is wonderfully punctured as he plunges both arms into the wobbling trifle.

4. Verbal wit

Also to the fore in the closing sequences is Basil's sharply sarcastic wit. Verbal wit of this type clearly ties in with Basil's frustration with the real world, and so he resorts to a highly imaginative and disruptive use of language in an attempt to stave off this frustration and claim the imaginative as his own and within his control. You need to be sure, however, when talking about verbal wit of this kind, that you do not confuse it with the humorous. Certainly, it is humorous, but verbal wit is wit which the character intends to be funny. Humorous remarks, on the other hand, are ones which are funny without the characters themselves being aware of this. When the Major makes the remark about the fresh mushrooms causing the soup to taste off, for instance, this is a humorous remark but the Major is certainly not being intentionally witty.

We can see, then, how the closing sequences use these four comic strategies of the classic *reductio* plot. What is particularly significant to note, however, is the way in which these sequences use these strategies to underline the central tensions and conflicts in the episode as a whole: Basil's inability to deal with an inanimate world which seems almost to assault him physically, and the depth of frustration and rage that this creates in his flawed psychology.

Step 6

Have I achieved a sufficiently complex sense of the media text?

We have now looked at four sequences from '*Gourmet Night*', commenting in detail on the various key media aspects of Audience, Narrative and Construction. One of the things that strikes us is that we have not said much about the concept of Agency, the institutions within which the programme itself was created. Since *Fawlty Towers* revolves so firmly around its central character of Basil Fawlty, an interesting way in which we can explore Agency is to spend some time considering John Cleese himself as a comedy star or personality. It is worth remembering that to comment satisfactorily on any television personality or film star their status as performers can only be properly understood if it is considered within the context of the media industries in which they work. This means, of course, that it is important to introduce the key aspect of Agency into your analysis.

TV producers and sitcom script-writers know that the presence of a famous television personality in the key role can play a vital part in a sitcom's success. Many sitcom classics have starred comedy performers such as Ronnie Barker, Penelope Keith, Rowan Atkinson, Maureen Lipman, Richard Briers and Bill Cosby, whose reputations have already been established either within the genre or in other areas of comedy. Certainly, much of the publicity and promotion that surrounds the launch of a new sitcom series will centre on the presence in it of a well-known television personality. Their faces will feature on the front of the TV guides (*Radio Times* and *TV Times*, etc.) and trailers will show them in their new role. Consequently, the marketing of sitcoms as media products whose 'unique selling proposition' is the presence in them of a personality or star is another issue that can be looked at more fully in terms of the key media aspect of Agency.

Stars and personalities, as media commodities, have to have specific qualities that transcend the qualities of the characters they play. Richard Briers, for instance, has played dithery, whimsical, boyish husbands in *The Marriage Lines* (in the 1960s), the *Good Life* (the 1970s) and *Ever Decreasing Circles* (the 1980s). Similarly, James Bolam has played likeable down-to-earth characters in *The Likely Lads* (the 1960s), *Whatever Happened to the Likely Lads* (the 1970s), *Only When I Laugh* (the 1980s), and *Second Thoughts* (the 1990s). However, John Cleese's rise to the status of television personality differs markedly from that of these male sitcom stars. Nevertheless, and despite the comic subversiveness of many of his performances, it is possible to point to the existence of a 'John-Cleese-type' character in a number of his comic roles.

In *Monty Python*, Cleese often played abusive, authoritarian figures. In one episode of *Monty Python* he plays an architect in a pin-striped suit who has been refused permission for an apartment-cum-abbatoir block. He explodes:

> this is just the kind of blinkered, philistine pig ignorance I've come to expect from you non-creative garbage. You sit there on your loathsome, spotty behinds, squeezing blackheads, not caring a tinker's cuss for the struggling artist, you excrement. . .

The similarity between this type of dialogue and Basil's classic outbursts in '*Gourmet Night*' is immediately apparent:

> Come on, start, will you!? Start you vicious bastard!! Come on! Oh my God! I'm warning you – if you don't start. . . [screams with rage] I'll count to three. (he presses the starter without success) One. . . two. . . three. . .!! Right! That's it! [he jumps out of the car and addresses it] You've tried it on just once too often! Right! Well, don't say I didn't warn you! I've laid it on the line to you time and time again! Right! Well. . . this is it ! I'm going to give you a damn good

thrashing! [he rushes and comes back with a large branch; he beats the car without mercy].

The repetition of certain phrases, sentences and patterns which draw attention to themselves simply by virtue of their very repetition is characteristic of the sitcom. Insofar as these phrases stick in our minds they function in a way similar to advertising slogans which remind us of a particular product. More and more scriptwriters use this device to ensure that their 'product' stays in the audience's mind, or, even better, enters into everyday conversation. The huge success of *The Darling Buds of May* in the early nineties was certainly made more secure by David Jason's catchphrase 'Perfick!'. One of the functions of such catchphrases (as well as ensuring the product a place in the media market) is to remind us of the relations that exist between the characters. The catchphrase works as a shorthand way of restating a relationship between characters which has been built up and developed over many previous episodes.

Without this relationship between central characters there would be no way in which the attitudes and values that they stand for could be given form. Basil is narrow-minded, self-important, backward-looking and reactionary. He is also a mysogynist (most clearly in relation to Sybil but also in relation to the other female characters), a xenophobe (he derides Manuel and Spanish culture), a classist (he despises the 'riff raff' element), homophobic (witness his remarks about his gay chef Kurt) and an ageist (he is condescending towards the elderly guests). All of these elements in Basil's character can therefore be realised through recurrent phrases which establish and draw upon this broad range of prejudices, and you need only to watch a few episodes of the programme to note what these catchphrases are, and how they operate.

This is not to say, however, that Cleese's performance as Basil is at all stock or stereotypical; instead, his virtuoso comic performance is a combination of many elements and the manic physical mannerisms together with the vitriolic verbal delivery create a vivid impression. Even so, it is possible to identify two quite different kinds of comic performance in *'Gourmet Night'* and it is important to distinguish between these when writing about sitcom generally. These are (i) the actorly performance, in which Cleese's comic acting skills come to the fore in developing Basil as a highly memorable character who is basically unaware of the humour of his own situation; and (ii) the funny performance, as seen, for example, in the character of Manuel.

Andrew Sachs, in his performance as Manuel, strives to produce the consistently funny character. His main role is to make seemingly straightforward tasks – answering a phone, taking cases to a room – seem complicated and difficult. Such characters, because they introduce complications, are often referred to as '**catalytic**'; they differ from '**cardinal**' characters whose function is to drive the main elements of the story forward. This does not, however, make such characters subordinate to the humour, since much of the comic business is organised around them. Indeed, the comedy itself normally revolves around the barriers and complications rather than the goal of the narrative itself (i.e. the unsuccessful gourmet meal).

It is within such a complex situation that Cleese's performance functions to draw together the various elements of plot, character and situation to create the unique nature of the humour to be found in the programme generally. The presence of a particular personality in a sitcom is often central to its success. If you look through the weekly schedule of any TV station you will realise just how important characters are to television programming: the publicity surrounding a series will centre on the main personality involved. Thus, if the scheduler can succeed in making a particular evening of the week '*Fawlty Towers* night' then the ratings battle has been won. The presence of John Cleese at the centre of the comic mayhem is not only an essential aspect of the programme's comic success, but is also fundamental to the success of the programme as a media 'product'.

Obviously we have tried, in looking at '*Gourmet Night*', to provide you with information about sitcoms in general as well as discussing technical aspects of the programme's structure and the features which made it such a successful media product. But underlying our discussion is the same basic method that we used in our analysis of *The Bill*: begin by looking for a basic tension in the work – here the conflict between Basil's snobbish dreams and the reality of ordinary life; then look for four or five extracts from the programme to build up your analysis, showing how the basic tension informs the details and how the details bring the tension to life. All the time you are seeking to explore the meanings of the text and how those meanings are achieved. Use the five key media concepts to help you to focus your discussion so that you do not have to rely on impressions. Then, at the end of your analysis, try to pull things together by highlighting

what seems central to you, as we did by looking at John Cleese's comic style. All the time try to be conscious of moving your analysis forward; at every stage say to yourself, 'What can I say now that I could not say before? What new point can I add to my ideas?' This way you will generate material that does reflect your own response and your own thinking.

II ASPECTS OF THE MEDIA TEXT: CATEGORISATION

So far in our analysis we have seen how '*Gourmet Night*', with its highly structured *reductio* plot and its classic solo performance by Cleese, successfully utilises and manipulates many of the conventions of the sitcom genre. What we now want to do in this further stage of discussion, is to consider in rather more detail the key media aspect of categorisation. As we pointed out in chapter 2, there are many ways of categorising media texts. For example, if you look through the weekly schedules of the different channels you will find that many seemingly different types of programme are described as situation comedies and, to add to the confusion, other titles are used by the different networks to describe programmes of this type: *The Wonder Years* is described by schedulers as comedy drama, *May to December* as romantic comedy, and *The Golden Girls* as a comedy series. Such terminological diversity can be bewildering for the newcomer to television studies. Each of these sub-genres or media forms is the result, however, of the work of programmers and schedulers rather than the products of media studies theory, and we need to think a little more analytically if we are to discuss *Fawlty Towers* in relation to the media aspect of categorisation.

Whatever media schedulers choose to call the sitcom, there is a set of features which appears to characterise this particular media product. In broad terms the TV sitcom may be seen to share in some of the following:

1. the half-hour format;
2. the use of common situations such as home and family or work;
3. the limited cast of characters;
4. the weekly 'problem' that causes a humorous situation;
5. the episodic nature of the stories;
6. their basis in common experience.

However, we can probably all think of a sitcom that appears to fit very few of the criteria in this list, even though we can all probably think of many that do fit the list perfectly.

This apparent resistance of the sitcom genre to categorisation helps to draw attention to a distinction that we introduced in chapter 2 between media forms and media genre: although many comedy programmes can be categorised as light entertainment (which is a media form), relatively few of these can be categorised as genres in their own right. Programmes such as *Monty Python*, *Not the Nine o'Clock News*, *Victoria Wood – As Seen On TV*, which are composed of comedy sketches and routines intended to be humorous, do not have the necessary structures characteristic of a genre. Although they may make us laugh they have no definite nor extended narrative in the way that, say, *'Gourmet Night'* does. So, although we all have a common-sense understanding of the genre conventions associated with the sitcom, there is nevertheless no one ideal model for the sitcom genre. New forms of sitcom are continually arising – the recent development of the melodramatic sitcom is a case in point – and because of this no yardstick can be employed that will apply to all present and future forms of the genre. If, then, it is difficult to provide any specific and unchanging list of identifying characteristics for the sitcom as a genre, perhaps a better way forward is to attempt to identify the genre through the recurrent thematic concerns and interests it exhibits in the stories it tells.

One frequent and recurring issue in British sitcoms revolves around the class system. In the history of sitcom in this country there are many examples of series in which the class aspirations and pretensions of the central character provide the focal point of the narrative. *Hancock*'s famous monologues reveal his pretensions, his social aspirations and his own view of his intellectual superiority, and this petulant pomposity is punctured by the resolutely working-class character played by Sid James. Similarly, *Steptoe and Son* to a large extent centred upon Harold's (the son) desire to escape from both the rag-and-bone yard where he lives with his father, and from his class roots. He never achieves this and it falls to the father to point out that Harold's alternative middle-class career aspirations – doctor, actor, writer – are unattainable. Harold is not only unable to break out of his physical situation, but he also knows that he is trapped in his relationship with his father and by the class system itself. Even in Fawlty Towers, it is this struggle with class that underpins many of Basil's attitudes and prejudices and forms the basis for many of the stories themselves. If we look at the sitcom more generally, we can see that this theme of class entrapment has been a recurrent feature of the genre.

Another way in which we can classify sitcoms is by looking at the relations between the characters in the series. The following types have evolved:

1   The character interplay sitcom
In *Steptoe and Son*, *The Likely Lads*, *Kate and Allie* and *Birds of a Feather*, the humour is developed around the relations that exist between the two main characters. The writers therefore have to put much thought into developing both conflicts and personality clashes between the characters while also providing a rationale that explains why they stay together. Even if the two characters in an interplay sitcom are both male there is still a tendency to employ the bickering husband and wife scenario. *Hancock* (in the early scripts, with Sid James), *Steptoe and Son* and *The Likely Lads* are classic examples of this.

2   The solo performance sitcom
Although '*Gourmet Night*' does have some classic exchanges between Basil and Sybil it cannot be described as a character interplay sitcom, for we cannot really say that Sybil has the same status in the series as Basil. Despite the significance of such catalytic characters in this series, Cleese's performance as Basil Fawlty takes centre stage in just the same way as does Phil Silvers' Bilko, Hancock's later Hancock, Ronnie Barker's Fletcher, Leonard Rossiter's Rigsby, and David Jason's Del-boy.

3   The ensemble sitcom
There are, of course, many sitcoms which have neither a central protagonist nor are based upon the interplay between two characters. In *Hi-di-Hi!* and *You Rang, M'Lord?*, for instance, there is a large ensemble of characters each playing an important part in the comic fun. This points to the virtual impossibility of identifying the sitcom as a single genre. Even so, it is possible to map similarities between examples of the genre, as we have done in Table 5.2 opposite, which gives some indication of just how successfully each of these forms has been exploited over the years.

What you need to remember when using such a chart in your own analysis of the sitcom in terms of Categorisation, is that although any sitcom series will, of course, exhibit most of the characteristics of the

Table 5.2   Examples of different types of sitcom

Solo Performance	Character Interplay	Ensemble Playing
I Love Lucy	Steptoe and Son	The Army Game
The Phil Silvers Show (Sgt. Bilko)	Likely Lads	The Rag Trade
Hancock	Liver Birds	Dad's Army
Till Death Us Do Part	Whatever Happened to the Likely Lads?	Please Sir
Porridge	George and Mildred	Doctor in the House
Some Mothers Do 'Ave 'Em	Terry and June	It Ain't Half Hot Mum
Butterflies	The Good Life	On the Buses
Fawlty Towers	Kate and Allie	Are You Being Served?
Open all Hours	A Fine Romance	Hi-De-Hi
Rising Damp	Never the Twain	Taxi
Shelley	My Two Dads	Cheers
Only Fools and Horses	Men Behaving Badly	Bread
Roseanne	Birds of a Feather	
One Foot in the Grave	Second Thoughts	

genre, it might also include some of the characteristics of other genres. *Fawlty Towers* makes use of the tightly plotted narrative structure of the dramatic farce, for example, while sitcoms such as *Butterflies*, which portray marriage and domestic life as a trap for women rather than for men, share the concerns of other family-based genres such as the melodrama and the soap. Also, some comedy programmes seem to overlap even within their own genre: *Only Fools and Horses*, for example, while being predominantly a solo performance comedy, does in some episodes veer towards a character interplay comedy. It is therefore important that you note what type of comedy performance is being used in the particular episode you want to analyse.

This underlines the fact that, like any truly creative art form, the sitcom is in a process of continual flux, forever changing, through parody, through reactions to social prejudices and stereotypes, through political comment and through the psychological insights of its writers. It is this diversity, range of reference and ability to change and to surprise the viewer that makes serious study and analysis of the sitcom so rewarding.

6

Analysing a TV news broadcast: *News at Ten*

I CONSTRUCTING AN OVERALL ANALYSIS

OUR aim in this chapter is to analyse television news, concentrating our analysis on a single *News at Ten* broadcast (TX: 7 July 1992). A few months after this broadcast there were a number of changes to the format of the programme which we will be discussing later in this chapter. The nature of these changes served to highlight one of the key issues that we will return to again and again in this chapter; that the news is not simply a summation of the day's events but is, like any other media text, a constructed product. In consequence, the format and scheduling of news programmes tend to change fairly rapidly, to meet the changing nature of the news itself.

There are of course many other types of news output at which we could look: newspapers, news magazines, national local and independent radio, and so on. In confining our attention to television news we are not, however, restricting our analysis of the nature of news production as a whole: although the technical aspects of the various news media differ in many ways, the underlying decision-making processes that lead to the final media product remain fundamentally similar.

The main point to remember as you work through this chapter is that a news programme is, like any other media text, the result of processes of selection and construction. The news is not, therefore, a 'window on the world', however much it may seem to be a neutral and impartial account of daily events. This is just one of the myths that news programmes tend to generate about themselves: that they are simple, objective accounts of reality. Such a myth side-steps many important issues, and it is therefore your task as a media student to try to 'demythologise' the news by analysing its signs, codes and conventions.

As ever, our five controlling key media concepts help to identify the areas we need to consider. The place to start, therefore, when analysing any piece of news media, is to ask yourself the following questions, all relating to our five key concepts:

1. *Construction*   What techniques and codes are employed in news programmes to convince us that we are being shown 'the truth'?
2. *Audience*   How are these constructions interpreted or 'read' by their audiences?
3. *Narrative*   What stories are being told in the particular news item?
4. *Categorisation*   How does the news differ from other actuality forms, such as current affairs and documentary?
5. *Agency*   What are the institutional sources and determinants of broadcast news?

If some of the above questions seem a little abstract to you at the moment, don't worry. We will be devoting considerable space in this chapter to explaining just what is meant by each key term, and the different ways in which you can use them. We begin our analysis of TV news, though, in the same way as before, following a series of clear steps:

Step 1

After watching the news programme, see if you can identify any broad pattern or structure at work.

It is, as always, a good idea to produce a brief synopsis of the programme you want to study, noting the content and running order of the broadcast. This will give you an indication of the relative importance attached to each news item. The running order of the *News at Ten* broadcast we will be analysing in this chapter was as follows:

News at Ten title sequence
News headlines: the first five news items of this broadcast (see below) are used in the headline sequence.
Item 1   The world leaders' G7 summit and their response to the war in Sarajevo
Item 2   The French lorry drivers' dispute

Item 3   Fishermen delivering a petition to Downing Street
Item 4   Lack of provision of training places for 16–18-year-olds
Summary of Part Two News Items
Commercial Break
Item 5   A report on a man savaged by two pit bull terriers the year before which deals with his attempt to overcome the trauma of disfigurement
Item 6   News of the Government's confirmation of its fourth *Trident* nuclear submarine order
Item 7   British Telecom's announcement that it is to conduct a new campaign against obscene phone calls
Item 8   A report on ITV's ratings battle with the BBC's new soap, *Eldorado*
Item 9   A report on wartime documents released by the Government concerning the Suffolk coastal village of Shingle Street, where locals had spoken of burned bodies on the beaches.
Item 10   The refusal of Pakistan's cricket manager to apologise after accusing the English umpire of insulting his players
Summary of news headlines.
Item 11   An extended final and lighter item concerning the restoration of Hampton Court Palace

When you first begin to analyse any news programme you may feel daunted by the task of writing about items that deal – as many of these do here – with major national and international affairs. Students often mistakenly think that if they know little about these, then they will be unable to write intelligently about a broadcast. Admittedly, some background knowledge of relevant contemporary issues will help you, and any time spent finding out about these will not be wasted. Nevertheless, you should always remember that, in Media and Communications studies, you are chiefly concerned with how news programmes are produced and interpreted, not with the political or economic issues with which they deal.

To do this here we can use one of our key media concepts Categorisation, as this will enable us to examine the structure of the news generally, and of this programme in particular. There are three basic types of news stories, and an example of each can be identified in the *News at Ten* broadcast which we are analysing here. These are:

(A) *Political and economic news* Political issues such as Government policy or events in Whitehall (items 1, 3, 4 and 6 are political) and economic issues highlighting business performance or trade figures (item 4 is economic) are found in most *News At Ten* broadcasts. Often news items have both a political and an economic aspect – as is the case with item 4.

(B)   *Domestic and foreign news* Foreign affairs stories typically deal with famines, natural disasters and conflicts between foreign Governments (items 1, 2 and 3 are foreign affairs stories). Domestic news items tend to be concerned with issues such as crime, education or the health service (items 3, 4, 5, 7, 9, 10 and 11 are concerned with domestic issues). Although most domestic news deals with 'hard' stories of this kind, a 'soft', humorous or human-interest domestic story – such as the clever pet or a pools-winning pensioner – is nearly always used for the final item.

(C)   *Occasional and sports stories* Occasional stories tend to focus on the activities of celebrities while sports stories usually focus on competitive male sports. Such news items are normally given a less solemn treatment and are less likely to be the lead story in a broadcast. For example, item 8 is an occasional story and item 10 a sports one.

Simply breaking the programme down like this in terms of its categories is a useful first step to take, since it helps you to see the broader structuring principles of the programme as a whole. However, it is also important that you then move on from this level of categories to look at the way these stories are treated. This will ensure that your work remains analytical, rather than purely descriptive, and it is to this analytical level that we will now turn.

Step 2

Analyse the opening sequence.

A good way to start, when you analyse any news programme, is to spend some time analysing its style of presentation. This is often best achieved by concentrating on the key media aspect of Construction. In order to focus your impressions from the outset, it is a good idea to take photographs of the opening sequence (see our later chapter on writing an essay for information on how to do this), or to use a video recorder with a pause button in order to study the key images in detail. Whichever way you choose, it is important that you work from close analysis both of the images used to tell the story, and of the supporting sound and text. This will enable you to examine the key elements in a more detailed way, as we do here.

The opening titles sequence of our *News at Ten* broadcast plays a very important part in establishing, at the outset, a feeling of authority. The whole introductory piece is essentially a computer-animated rapid zoom which starts from the ITN logo, moves to the European part of the globe and then into London, travelling down the Thames to the Houses of Parliament. The sequence ends with the clock face of Big Ben filling the screen. The title, *News at Ten*, appears one word at a time. The symbolism, although straightforward, is effective: the globe suggests 'news from around the world', the Thames the 'heart of the nation', the Houses of Parliament the 'centre of power'. Also, the word-at-a-time title suggests news ticker-tape and the rhythmic orchestral crescendo culminates in the strikes of Big Ben offering the nation 'up-to-the-minute news'.

The ITN newsroom itself plays an important part in creating and maintaining this feeling of authority and objectivity. Over the years a number of changes have been made to the newsroom. If we consider the 1976 *News at Ten* studio (Figure 6.1) it strikes us as remarkably plain. A fairly basic desk, a telephone to keep up with unfolding events and the mandatory newsreader's paperwork are all that we have. The background is similarly stark, featuring the simple graphic title of a world map with the programme name superimposed in a bold *sans-serif* typeface. The image itself is bright and high key. The overall impression given by this is that here we are being presented with the plain facts, unembellished truth brought to us through the aegis of the sober-suited newsreaders, Alastair Burnet and Reginald Bosanquet. The *News at Ten* studio of 1992 (Figure 6.2), which is when our broadcast was transmitted, is considerably changed; an elaborate curved desk complete with inbuilt monitors and the image of the night skyline of London in the background which situates the newsreaders in both place (they are at the heart of the nation) and time (it is evening). In addition, the fact that they rise above the city appears to give them an air of omniscience and power. All this gives the impression that the presenters, Sandy Gall and Julia Somerville, are almost like angels hovering over the world and that we have just dropped in to learn from these omniscient creatures who are in control of the unfolding events: reality may be messy and unpredictable but in the ITN studio all this untidy human messiness is under control.

Figure 6.1   *News at Ten* studio, 1976

Figure 6.2   *News at Ten* studio, 1992

Figure 6.3   *News at Ten* studio, 1993

Figure 6.4   Close-up of clock over *News at Ten* title

Recent changes to the *News at Ten* studio (Figure 6.3) have been equally dramatic. The News at Ten title is made much more prominent and a single newsreader, Trevor McDonald, is used. A bank of monitors showing Big Ben in close-up predominate. Whereas the 1976 studio seemed to connote impartiality through its very starkness the 1993 version seems to achieve this by stressing the fact that the news is being brought to you by the well-established, dependable, trustworthy *News at Ten* team.

What we have seen, in this brief discussion of the introductory sequence and the evolution of the *News at Ten* newsroom, is how the various technical codes associated with our key aspect of Construction operate to convince us that we are being presented with the truth, a fair account of the day's events. As we progress through this chapter we will look in more detail at the way that news broadcasters try to convince their audiences that what they see is an unbiased representation of affairs.

Step 3

Analyse the first news item.

We will now turn to the opening news item which deals with the meeting of the world's leading seven economic nations and with their response to the war between the Serbs and the Bosnians in what was formerly Yugoslavia. News stories like this, which are an amalgam of interview and commentary material, illustrate an important concept: the difference between what in media and communications studies is called **institutional voice** and **accessed voice**. Institutional voice refers to the idea that the person/presenter/interviewer speaks on behalf of the News at Ten organisation. Accessed voice, on the other hand, indicates that the person interviewed has been 'accessed' by the news organisation. Because the item has been put together in this way, it can be usefully considered again under Construction.

The easiest way to start is to isolate some key elements that this G7 news item shares with most other news items. Like many other news items of this sort, the filmed report from Yugoslavia is held together by commentary from the *News at Ten* presenter, who in this broadcast was Julia Somerville. A good way to begin, therefore, is to look at these two components of the news item; first, the newsreader/presenter; and secondly, at the effect of the filmed report.

1. The newsreader/s

Codes of dress
In this *News at Ten* broadcast Julia Somerville, who presents the G7 item, is wearing a beige wide-shouldered jacket, knotted golden necklace and matching earrings. She projects a softer, caring and more concerned look than Fiona Armstrong, who is wearing a dark blue dress, projecting a slightly more 'business-like' image.

Non-verbal communication (NVC)
Julia Somerville's direct frontal eye-to-eye gaze and orientation toward us bridges the distance between the television newsroom and the home. Calmly yet authoritatively she guides the viewer through the turmoil of the major events of the day (the American term 'news-anchor' nicely brings out the fact that news readers provide an 'anchor' in a turbulent world).

Verbal codes
Like all other television newsreaders, Julia Somerville talks to the audience directly, establishing an 'I – you' relationship with the individual viewer, her serious measured tones signalling to the audience the appropriate reaction to the G7 story. In other items her delivery may be humorous or even mildly ironic, encouraging us to interpret the events themselves in a similar way. The advantage of using two newscasters, as is now common on many news programmes, is that this makes it easier to change from a serious item – requiring an authoritative tone of presentation – to a lighter one. This was changed in *News at Ten* in April 1993 to a single presenter format – we will be saying something about these changes later.

Generally speaking the language employed on *News at Ten* tends to be more convivial than that used in, say, the BBC's *Nine O'Clock News*. This is principally because the programme is aimed at an audience looking for accessibly presented general information.

2. The filmed report

Nearly all news items will include a report from a journalist or correspondent in the field. In this item, Greg Wood (the location reporter in Munich) reports on the action and speeches at the G7 summit and Geoffrey Archer (ITN's diplomatic correspondent in Sarajevo) comments on developments there. As a reporter, Wood is not required to give a deeper evaluation of unfolding events, he simply describes what is happening. Archer, on the other hand, has the licence to pass judgement on issues that relate to his special field of diplomatic affairs.

In order to write effectively about the treatment of this report (or, indeed, any other) it is a good idea to search for some dramatic opposition, tension or conflict within it. When Julia Somerville informs us that the G7 leaders have 'warned' the Serbs, we expect the subsequent report to emphasise conflicts and antagonisms. Greg Wood's commentary does just this, bringing the following tensions and oppositions to the fore:

(a)   The G7 nations versus Serbia;
(b)   The French and Americans, with their 'tough proposals', versus the five other G7 nations;
(c)   Boris Yeltsin, the Russian President versus the G7 leaders;
(d)   The German Chancellor, Helmut Kohl, who wanted an economic summit, versus the other G7 leaders.

You will find that there will nearly always be oppositions or conflicts of this type at work in any news item, for without these there would be no story or drama to hold the audience's attention; indeed, one of the quickest ways of getting to grips with an item is by isolating its central structuring oppositions, just as we have here, and as we did in previous chapters.

We will conclude this section by looking at the way that the news item is brought to a close. At the end of most items the reporter will conclude his/her commentary while standing in front of a significant location, just as Greg Wood does in this report from Munich. These are known as 'stake-outs' and they have a profound effect on the way in which the news story is presented. Stake-outs like this serve not only to sign off the news item, but also to create a very strong impression that the reporter is talking, not to us, but to the newsreader back in the studio. It is important to notice the effect of this technique in reinforcing the news programme's claims for objectivity. The stake-out technique not only reinforces the image of the journalist/reporter as a globe-trotting newshound, reporting back to base from distant lands or important centres of power, but also serves to heighten the sense that the news story is being reported as objectively as possible, without any obvious 'filtering' of the story taking place.

Step 4

Select a second news item for discussion.

We shall now consider our second item, which concerns a dispute between French lorry drivers and the French Government over new legislation concerning motoring offences. We are going to analyse this item in terms of the key media aspect of Narrative to show you how to use this idea. The reason we think this piece is interesting in terms of Narrative is because it makes use of some of the key ingredients to be found in many stories: a basic conflict or tension between two cultural stereotypes; the French on the one hand, and the English on the other.

It may strike you as curious to suggest that the news, which deals with 'real events', can be discussed in terms of its narrative organisation at all, for the structuring of story material would seem to relate more to fictional media output. As we have seen already, however, news broadcasts try to create dramatic tension by focusing on conflicts, tragedies and spectacular events. News producers, like the producers of any other types of programme, are in the business of trying to capture as large an audience as possible. If you read carefully through the following transcription of the *News at Ten* French lorry drivers item, you should notice some of the narrative forces we have just discussed.

News at Ten. Item 2: French lorry drivers' dispute

NEWSREADER: FIONA ARMSTRONG: Sixty blockades set up by French lorry drivers came down today but tonight dozens are still in place and there is no sign of an end to the chaos. The European Commission urged the French Government to act quickly to resolve the dispute...Roads now clear include the A1 from Paris to Lille, the A6 between Paris and Beaune and the A7 from Lille to Marseille, for the towns of Le Havre, Caen and Rouen and Reims are still cut off.

FILM REPORT BY CAROLINE KERR IN MACON, FRANCE: At 6 a.m. this morning French riot police marched in on the lorry drivers who have beseiged the city of Lyon for the best part of a week. The drivers, like the rest of France, were woken up to the news that their dispute was supposed to be over. For the most part they moved on peacefully, some clearly relieved that a deal had been worked out.

FRENCH DRIVER: But now it is finished. We have to finish. One week is enough.

KERR: There are still some signs of defiance. This is the main motorway heading from the south of France towards Paris. I'm just a few miles outside Lyon where the road is still blocked and not a single car can pass. The frustrations and diversions are not over yet because the settlement does not answer the drivers' main demand for a more lenient penalty system. With the motorways closed tiny villages are struggling to cope with the huge volume of traffic, but in some cases the lorry drivers have blockaded the B roads too to the exasperation of motorists.

ENGLISH DRIVER 1: It's getting me down. I've had enough of it. I want to get home.

ENGLISH DRIVER 2: I'm loaded with peaches for Holland. In two days' time it should be ready for marmalade.

KERR: Some have already started to dump their loads. It's clear that the damage this dispute is causing isn't over yet. This is Caroline Kerr, ITN Macon.

As you start to analyse the Narrative of a news item such as this it is a good idea to ask yourself the following questions:

1. *What, centrally, is the story about?* We feel that the item is more concerned with the British lorry drivers stranded on the French motorways than with the nature of the French drivers' dispute. There is, for example, more in the item about fruit, mess, waste and confusion than about the real reasons for the dispute.

2. *How is the story 'made real'?* In terms of the narrative analysis of broadcast news it is often helpful to think of the accessed individuals – here the French and English lorry drivers – as the key players in an unfolding 'real life drama'. In this item the drama centres upon the attack by the police on the motorway blockades and on the frustrations in the small villages. The French action is made real by including the perceptions and actions of the central characters involved and situating it in a clearly defined context.

3. *What does the story 'mean'?* You now need to stop and ask if there is any more implicit message contained in the news item. It would be possible to argue, for instance, that the news story is implying that British drivers and holidaymakers are losing time and money and that food is being needlessly wasted. Certainly, the impression given is that the French drivers are the initiators of the disruption. This is reinforced by the fact that the French authorities have disappeared from the bulletin altogether, their views being outlined by the presenter. The item constructs a clear villain/victim conflict: the French lorry drivers are the 'villains' and the stranded English lorry drivers the 'innocent victims' caught up in events beyond their control.

As we have mentioned already, it is always a good idea, when you analyse a news item in this way, to try to identify what the tension, conflict or opposition boils down to. The following conflicts and oppositions play a central role in the item we are analysing here and, indeed, in all the news items that make up the programme:

Positive : Negative

Victims : Villains

Us : Them

Legality : Illegality

Moderation : Extremism

Government : Unions

Order : Chaos

Rationality : Irrationality

Peacefulness : Violence

Important issues are often simplified in this way in order to provide the audience with a clear moral framework of right and wrong in which it is clear who are the virtuous and who are the villains.

The impression which the audience forms of the dispute as a whole will be made largely on the basis of the pictures that they see on their screens. The fact that the news item showed lorry drivers struggling with gendarmes reinforces the implied message that the French lorry drivers' action was a violent and chaotic one. Had the *News at Ten* team decided to show pictures which presented the drivers in, say, studio discussion with the French Transport Minister, a more positive impression may have been presented.

Once again, we can notice how important the processes of selection are to the creation of any media text. This is because when we watch any news item we take the images that we see to stand for the whole event, even though those events may be only a partial and selective view of the whole. Because of this it is often argued that all news is intrinsically **metonymic**. A **metonym** is a rhetorical figure of speech in which the name of an attribute or thing is substituted for the thing itself (e.g. 'the crown' for the monarchy). The applicability of this concept to TV news is immediately apparent for, when we watch any news item, we construct the rest of the story from the elements with which we have been presented. Therefore, if we see a protesting striker hit a policeman with a placard we will tend to assume all of the other strikers were behaving in a similarly violent way even if many of them were in fact behaving peacefully. This, once again, should alert us to the idea that the news is a result of the various processes of selection that go to make up the news story as a whole.

Step 4

Select a third item for discussion

The news item we want to look at next deals with a protest staged by fishermen against Government legislation that would cut their incomes by 30 percent by limiting the number of days that they can go to sea. This is an interesting news story to analyse because it raises the issue of what, in media and communication studies, is termed **news values**. As always, it is useful to produce a brief synopsis of the story being told.

The item opens with striking images of the fishermen's bunting-festooned boats passing under Tower Bridge. We then learn that their mission is to deliver a case of whiting to 10 Downing Street. Vernon Mann, the ITN's West of England correspondent, explains, from a trawler, that 'This was no French-style blockade' (referring to the previous item) but rather a protest aginst the Government's new proposals. A spokeperson for the fishermen, Nigel Atkins, then informs us that the fishermen's anger stemmed from the fact that the legislation was introduced in the middle of a consultative process and that it did not apply to other countries in the European Community.

The fishermen are next seen delivering their petition and a box of whiting to 10 Downing Street and this is followed by shots of the protest rally in London. Then, in a studio interview, David Curry MP, the Conservative Government's fisheries minister, argues that if the restrictions are not implemented both the fishing industry and fishing stocks will be condemned to death.

We then cut to Brixham harbour, where a local fisherman, Russell Passmore, is preparing to set sail in his trawler. Vernon Mann tells us that Russell's father led the last protest on the Thames and Russell informs us that his two sons will not be following him into the industry. Vernon Mann then signs off, telling us, in parting, that Russell Passmore has put his trawler up for sale.

In writing about news in any medium, you will need to comment upon the various values which govern the selection and organisation of material. These news values relate, in many important ways, to the key media aspect of Audience. When deciding what makes a good story news producers have to take into account what audiences themselves regard as significant and this, in turn, will be influenced in important ways by values and beliefs to be found in society.

Simply stated, the issue of news value has to do with the practicalities of deciding what makes a good news story, and whether the money spent in following up a story will be repaid by Audience response. When you analyse any news item in the context of these news values, what we suggest you do is to work your way through them just making a few notes on each issue as you go. Clearly, you will have more to say on some of these areas than on others, simply because some will be more apparent or more significant in the context of the particular news story you want to analyse. These are the areas we suggest you concentrate on, followed by our notes on each issue as we work through the item:

1. Magnitude
2. Clarity
3. Ethnocentricity
4. Consonance
5. Surprise
6. Elite centredness
7. Negativity
8. Human Interest
9. Composition and balance
10. Location reporting
11. Actuality reporting

News producers are involved, for much of their time, in making evaluative judgements about content. The most straightforward of these assessments relates to our first news value, 1, **magnitude** (or threshold value), which refers to the relative significance of the event. Although the fishermen's action was not an event of great magnitude, the flotilla on the Thames and the delivery of whiting to Downing Street was sufficient to attract the attention of the media.

However, if the aims of the fishermen's protest had been less clear, the magnitude alone would not have ensured the story's inclusion. Because the meaning of the fishermen's action was unambiguous (i.e. that Government legislation was threatening fishermen's livelihoods) its news value was higher than it would have been if its significance had been subtle or obscure. The next news value we can identify is, then, 2, **clarity** (or lack of ambiguity), which is high in this particular item.

It is generally recognised in news production that the more remote an event is, either geographically or from the cultural experience of the Audience, then the greater its magnitude has to be if it is to become news. It is doubtful, for example, whether a protest by Spanish fishermen over the same issue would have featured on the *News at Ten* broadcast. This brings us to our next news value 3, **ethnocentricity** (or cultural familiarity), the idea that an event needs in some way to be a part of the Audience's cultural experience for it to become newsworthy.

Our next news value, 4, **consonance**, is also directly concerned with the expectations, values and beliefs of the audience. Vernon Mann's commentary contains the line 'This was no French-style blockade' which, it might be argued, is consonant with the view that the days of violent industrial confrontation are on the wane in this country. At a slightly deeper level we might say that the decision to focus on the more non-confrontational and good-natured aspects of the protest, rather than the street demonstrations in London, was made because this made the message consonant with the view that the British are not, by natural inclination, militant or extreme. If, however, a number of potential news items are equally consonant with Audience attitudes then the more extraordinary stories are likely to be selected, which makes our next news value 5, **surprise** (or unexpectedness).

Events involving prominent members of society are, for obvious reasons, more likely to make the headlines. By delivering their petition to 10 Downing Street, and thus indirectly involving the Prime Minister, the fishermen are acknowledging, whether knowingly or not, the operation of our next news value, 6, **élite centredness**. Events in the 'élite' nations of Western Europe and in the USA are also regarded as having a higher news value for similar reasons.

7, **Negativity**. There are a number of reasons why bad news is good news for journalists and editors. First, it is more unexpected (see 5, above). Second, its time-span makes it easier for the news medium to cover – good things usually take time whereas disasters happen quickly. Finally, people are more likely to agree that an event such as a train crash is negative than they are that a rise in share prices is positive. Negative news is therefore more consensual (see 4, above), and in consequence more likely to become a news item.

You will doubtless be aware from watching television news that stories that lend themselves to a particular kind of treatment are more likely to be selected for inclusion. In many items the news value 8,

human interest, plays an important part in the treatment the story receives. The fact that the *News at Ten* team decided to focus on the way that the legislation affects one fisherman, Russell Passmore of Brixham, nicely illustrates the importance of having a human-interest angle.

In order to maintain audience ratings and interest, producers and editors have to ensure that balance is maintained both at the level of content (home and foreign news complementing political and economic news) and at the level of treatment (human interest, drama, conflict, etc.). The humorous aspect of this news story (the delivery of whiting to Number Ten) helps to ensure its inclusion, for it provides a good counter-balance to the more serious items in the programme. The next news value we can identify then, is, 9, **composition** (or **balance**).

The fact that Vernon Mann is 'on-the-spot' in Brixham increases the item's feeling of authority and objectivity, making its news value higher than it would have been if only actuality footage and studio voice-over had been used. This illustrates the significance of the next aspect of news reporting that you should consider: 10, **location reporting** (Vernon Mann in Brixham). Similarly, visuals play an important part in this news item; images of bunting-festooned trawlers passing under Tower Bridge and whiting being delivered to Downing Street increases its value considerably. This aspect of news value, 11, **actuality footage** (the filmed material of the events), works in unison with 10, location reporting, to increase the item's impression of authenticity and authority.

You may, by this stage, be feeling a little overwhelmed by all these aspects of news value, but many of them, once pointed out, do become easy to spot. In order to help you to discuss these principles more fully we shall conclude by looking a little more closely at the treatment of this news item, demonstrating how to pull the analysis together into some fairly broad and meaningful statements by connecting news values to broader cultural issues.

The *News at Ten* team have shaped and structured the item in such a way that the conflicts between the worlds of Whitehall, Brussels and Brixham are brought to the fore and the key individuals involved in these hostilities – Russell Passmore, David Curry and Nigel Atkins – clearly identified. The treatment also suggests that it is 'our' fishing industry and communities that are being threatened by the Brussels legislators. Such references to 'our' industries are bound to create, in the minds of the Audience, the thought that they are a part of some greater national or cultural unity, for it is implied that 'we' all share a set of common concerns and values (despite differences in, say, our class and economic standing). As a result, those whose actions are perceived as constituting a threat to the established order – militant strikers, for instance, but here Brussels legislators – are invariably represented as 'outsiders' or 'deviants'.

Similar political values underpin both the G7 news item on the former Yugoslavia, and the report on the French lorry drivers' dispute. For example, most coverage of conflicts in the former Yugoslavia gave the impression that these conflicts were fuelled by religious and ethnic differences and were precipitated by the political and economic irrationalities of the former communist regime. As a result it seems entirely reasonable that the G7 leaders should focus their collective attentions on the war between the Serbs and Bosnians. Interestingly, wars involving 'our' troops will not generally be given a treatment that focuses on such 'irrational' factors. In consequence, when a war is fought by an advanced Western nation its moral and political necessity is rarely questioned. Media coverage of the Gulf War, for instance, portrayed it as a supremely rational military action fought with 'SMART' weapons against an irrational megalomaniac firing equally irrational, unreliable and inefficient 'SCUD' missiles.

The political values in the French lorry drivers' dispute again depend upon an implied 'them *versus* us' conflict. The report uses particular words and pictures to encourage us to side with the UK drivers caught up in the 'chaos' created by the French lorry-drivers. When you write about these issues in your analysis of the news, it is always important that you support your views with real, analytical evidence. It is not enough to trot out a series of political slogans criticising the authorities or the producers of news. Instead, because any news item is a constructed message, composed of signs and codes organised into a statement about the events, we can always examine the explanations it offers us, and 'deconstruct' the signs and codes out of which the item has been composed.

That news producers must inevitably be involved in shaping, structuring and selecting the material with which they deal is beyond question; however, it is certainly not enough to argue that all news programmes present a biased view of events simply because these processes are involved. What we would suggest is that broadcast news in general tends to treat news stories in a highly conventionalised way, which may have more to do with the nature of the medium employed than with the actual veracity of the story being reported.

The treatment of the French lorry drivers' dispute is a good example of this idea because it typifies media coverage of industrial unrest. The French 'militants' are represented in such a way as to encourage the audience to think that they are preventing the English drivers from going about their normal, day-to-day business: the report could therefore be seen as being less about industrial unrest than about attitudes towards 'foreigners'. That there is a shared set of political values here is clear; if you can show those values at work, then you can support your interpretation of the news with your analysis.

Step 5

Select a fourth item for discussion.

The item that we will be considering in this section reports on the Government's provision of youth training places. The area we find particularly interesting in this news item has to do with the areas of bias and impartiality, issues which are of central importance in many areas of broadcasting policy. We shall also be looking at the role played by those who made decisions about the content and treatment of the item, the editors and producers who, within media studies, are known as 'gatekeepers' (because they 'open the gate' to certain information while 'closing the gate' on other information). In order to comment upon these two areas we will be focusing, in this section, on the media aspect of Agency.

It is highly likely, if you are following a course in media or communication studies, that you will at some point be asked to write an essay about media bias. This is an issue which students often find difficult to write about in a systematic way. Perhaps the main reason for this is that the term 'bias' itself is very emotive. On the one hand news producers will naturally adopt a very defensive position if the objectivity of their accounts is questioned. On the other, it is understandable that groups who are represented unfavourably in the media, such as strikers, ethnic minorities, women and young people in general, should accuse media personnel of portraying them in a negative and biased way.

In this section we will not be directly concerned with these issues of negative representation. We wish, rather, to look at the claim that all broadcast television news is biased toward the *status quo*, consensus politics and middle-class perspectives. Some left-wing critics go so far as to suggest that all news output is little more than propaganda for the ruling class. To examine such a claim we need to look very closely at the way that media texts are organised and the role that media institutions, as Agencies, play in this activity.

These are complex areas and you will need to read more widely to make full sense of the range of debates involved. Nevertheless, we will be able to consider some of the most important aspects of these issues by looking closely at the organisational structure of this item on the YT scheme.

In this item Michael Brunson, the Political Editor for ITN, reports on the plight of 18-year-old Martin Farrell, made redundant after a year on a Government training scheme at a local garage. After trying, unsuccessfully, to find other work he applied to complete his training, only to be told that, at 18, he was too old.

The item includes footage of Gillian Shephard, MP (the Conservative Government's Employment Secretary, May 1992– May 1993), informing the House that: 'I am, today, putting into place new measures to establish a national system for monitoring the numbers of young people covered by the YT guarantee and seeking a place on YT.' This is followed by an interview with Tony Blair, MP, Labour's Shadow Employment Secretary, who claims that: 'We've been pressing the Government for two years to accept that there are many thousands of young people being denied the training they need and yet it is only today that they appear to face up to the seriousness of the situation.' Finally, we hear from Edward Roberts, the national chairman of the TECs (Training and Enterprise Councils) who run YT for the Government. He argues that the school-leavers often are not up to standard: 'Of course we could fill all sorts of jobs with hairdressers, with motor mechanics. But within the cities those aren't the sorts of jobs that are available, so therefore there is a higher level of knowledge required'.

When a story with considerable social and political significance such as this one breaks, the media will normally seek to include the comments of official bodies in any coverage. In this item Gillian Shephard puts forward the Government's response to the YT figures and Tony Blair, the Shadow Employment Secretary, outlines Labour's position. Edward Roberts provides the final comment on behalf of the Training and Enterprise Council. Because the opinion of these individuals plays such an important part in establishing the initial definitions of the shortfall in training places they are described, in media and communication studies, as **primary definers**.

Socially accredited sources such as the police, professional bodies and official union spokespersons regularly appear in news broadcasts, providing 'authoritative' comment on issues with which they are directly concerned. Such 'official' primary definers help to provide an atmosphere of authority and reason to the news programme. However, although news producers are obliged, for reasons of impartiality and equal access, to include alternative or oppositional views, the agenda for debate will frequently have been established in advance by these primary definers. The contributions of these 'pro-establishment' figures, you may argue, ensures that coverage stays within the confines of the *status quo*. It is obvious, for example, that while views such as Shephard's and Blair's are given prominence, other political groups who are outside consensus politics, such as the left-wing Socialist Worker Party, or the right-wing British Party, are not given the same consideration. Because of this their view on the current YT training figures is unlikely to be given coverage. The views of the major parliamentary parties are taken to define all that can be said (or 'reasonably' said) about an issue; it could therefore be argued that the media implicitly suggests that any political positions other than those of the major political parties are either unrepresentative or extreme.

The coverage of the shortfall in training places thus replicates parliamentary debate, impartiality being achieved by ensuring that a proper balance is maintained between the views of the major parties. In choosing to cover the item in this way it might be argued that the *News at Ten* team is staying within the framework of consensus politics, for it presents each political party's account as an accurate representation of the realities of YT schemes in the UK. It is noticeable that neither Shephard nor Blair comments upon any of the underlying problems involved. In fact their comments are quite short (48 words for Shephard and 57 words for Blair). Instead, much of the time is taken up by the human-interest angle provided by Martin Farrell who claims he was 'too old at 18' to find work.

In order to comment adequately upon the final form of the broadcast in terms of Agency we need to make clear the relation between two important areas: **gathering and selection**; and **planning and presentation**.

The first of these areas, **gathering and selection**, is the area of news production of which most people are aware. It involves correspondents (Michael Brunson in this case) and camera crews following up stories and returning to the newsroom where editors cut or modify their material. **Planning and presentation**, on the other hand, has to do with the daily routine and organisation of the finished product. For example, a number of meetings and conferences will be held in the newsroom throughout the day, to discuss how this item on Government training schemes should be covered.

Within media and communication studies, journalists and correspondents are often described as the 'news-gatherers' (because they collect information) and editors as 'news-processors' or gatekeepers. If we wish to look at news production in a very general way the notion of gatekeeping can be quite useful for it focuses our attention on the processes of selection and rejection. However, like many other basic concepts and models used to explain the news process, it tends to minimise the complexities involved. First, the term 'news-gatherer' creates the false impression that correspondents such as Brunson are super-sleuths, beating their competitors to the story 'scoop', whereas in fact much of their time is spent in preparation and discussion in the News at Ten newsroom. Second, the term 'gatekeeper' suggests that the final form of a news item is determined solely by the producer and duty editor, whereas in reality a number of practical constraints (the availability of equipment or a key interviewee) and day-to-day operational routines will have influenced the kinds of decisions taken about what news can be covered.

There are various ways in which we can account for the issues we have raised so far. First, we could take the '**conspiracy theory**' approach. The conspiracy theorist points out that the mass media are owned and controlled by the dominant class, and claims that this dominant owning-class therefore uses the media to maintain the *status quo* by presenting only their way of seeing the world. This theory, since it links the areas of ownership and ideology, clearly relates in a number of important ways to our aspect of Agency. While it is probably true to say that the conspiracy theory may have little academic credibility, it has nonetheless exerted a powerful influence on the thoughts of many media critics, particularly those on the political left.

And there are certainly a number of facts that back up the conspiracy theory hypothesis. First, a small number of '**media barons**' do in fact own large parts of the media industry. Rupert Murdoch, for example, the Chairman of News International, owns Sky Channel, one third of daily newspaper sales in the UK, 60 percent of Australian newspaper sales and much much more besides. Second, these barons are close to the political establishment and use their influence to control the content of their newspapers. The British Labour Party, for instance, complained that the slurs on Neil Kinnock in Murdoch's *Sun* newspaper helped to lose them the 1992 General Election.

However, although the values and beliefs reproduced by the media may coincide with those of the dominant or ruling class, this fact does not in itself substantiate the conspiracy theory. For one thing, if such a well-coordinated conspiracy were in operation it would be difficult to hide. For another, the conspiracy theory ignores the fact that the editorial decision-making processes and news values that shape the news are also important determinants (although the editors can, of course, be sacked by the owners if the latter dislike their decisions or their politics). Nevertheless, insofar as the *News at Ten* team plays an important role in shaping public understanding of a news item (here the shortfall in places on YT schemes: 55 000 according to Labour and 25 000 according to the Conservatives), it might be argued that, like the rest of the media, the *News at Ten* team operates within the framework of the dominant value system and therefore helps to maintain the *status quo*.

You should always remember, however, when writing about these areas in terms of Agency, that ideology is all-pervasive, and that it is to be found in every aspect of media production. When analysing the ideological dimensions of a news item such as this YT one you need to consider, therefore, the internal structure of ITN as a broadcasting institution, the codes of Construction that govern the production of the item and the *News at Ten's* team's view of its audience and of its own role. This is an important point, for all too often students simplify and distort these complex relations by seeing the owner's ideological position as the sole determinant, and this is clearly not the case.

If you wish to look at these issues of media bias in a more detailed way we suggest that you turn to the works of the Glasgow Media Group. These have provoked considerable controversy both within the media industry itself and also within the field of media studies. A large scale study of bias in TV news, begun at Glasgow University in the mid 1970s by the Group, aimed to show how the processes of selection, editing and presentation in TV news production tended to favour the establishment's view of events. In four subsequent books – *Bad News* (1976), *More Bad News* (1980), *Really Bad News* (1982) *War and Peace News* (1985) – the Glasgow Group claimed that British news programming did not live up to its own criteria of balance and impartiality.

Because many reporters and journalists operate from a pro-establishment position, the Glasgow group argued, so the programmes they produce reflect the politics of the *status quo*. For instance, in the reporting of industrial disputes any police violence will normally go unreported, whereas picket line 'violence' will be given maximum coverage. The media are also more likely to access the views of key establishment figures and experts than they are the opinions of, say, union activists. The Group also found that industrial coverage frequently presented the poor economic performance of an industry as being the fault of the workforce; management faults were rarely highlighted and other relevant issues, such as poor investment or the international economy, were rarely considered. As a result inflation was nearly always directly linked in news coverage to wage rises. Broadcasters, they concluded, were professionally biased towards consensual, middle-class values and that the given framework of reference in broadcast news is the norm and values of this class, with the result that the dominant ideology is constantly being reinforced through the news.

Having looked at the sort of factors that are likely to play a part in industrial coverage and at the rival arguments that exist concerning these areas of news output, now is the time to return to our news item in order to underline, in conclusion, the importance of such debates. We have seen that by including only comments from the relevant elected parliamentary representatives the coverage of the item is already subtly determined in a number of ways. Even if oppositional views were to have been included in the item, these would have been presented within a framework established by those opposing such views (the Conservative government Minister, Gillian Shephard, outlining the proposals of a 'loony left' political grouping, for example). So, although we would not argue that this item on the shortfall in training places tells us what to think about the issue, it does influence how we think about the issue in ways of which we may not be aware. Because information which contradicts the established consensus on youth training is not explored as a rational alternative to the dominant views the 'agenda' for subsequent debate is established in advance.

For example, the item assumes that 'we' all want the best for the British economy and for the young unemployed; and, of course, both the politicians accessed in this item claim that they want these things also, despite the differences between their political approaches. It is important that you remember, as you write about television news, that the Glasgow Group were not claiming that there is an establishment conspiracy in which broadcasters and powerful élites collude to brainwash the general public. Certainly it would be ridiculous to imply that the *News at Ten* production team meetings had the sole aim of deciding on how best to frame this item in line with the *status quo* and dominant ideology. If there is some bias in the reporting of items such as this one on the plight of this teenager who is now too old for youth training, and we think that there is, then this bias is a result of a whole host of 'unconscious' factors such as the class background of news producers, their professional training and so on. This notion of a bias that is 'nobody's fault' might seem a difficult and contradictory idea if you are new to this area. The attractiveness of the conspiracy thesis is that it paints a very clear black-and-white picture of the operations of the media industries as being in the service of the establishment/dominant élites. As we will see in the remainder of this chapter, such a view is far too simplistic for our purposes: there is no 'grand plot'. Nevertheless, the structuring of television news is such that it still reflects *status quo* values.

Step 6

Have I achieved a sufficiently complex sense of the media text?

In our fourth section we looked at the news values that played an important part in the selection and construction of the item on the fishermen's protest against government legislation. One of the things that strikes us is that we did not say very much about how the ideological themes at work within the news item are actually developed by the item's narrative. Myths and ideological themes are, as we have pointed out in a previous chapter, ideas and concepts – such as 'work' or 'the family ' – that enable people to make sense of society and of their place within it. Insofar as television news has to explain the broader significance of events by using these very same concepts it, too, is a manufacturer of myths.

Because the makers of *News at Ten* have a definite view of who their audience is, they fashion news stories accordingly. The fishermen's protest item is given a specific ideological inflection by introducing key mythic concepts and themes into the way in which the story is told. Obviously, you will want to identify these ideological myths in

the particular news item that you wish to analyse, but in the context
of the fishermen's protest story, we have identified the following:

1. 'Britishness'
This is evoked by the setting (the Thames, Tower Bridge and the
Houses of Parliament) but, more importantly, is developed through
the way the fishermen themselves are presented. The following stock
myths about the national British character are in play:

(a) '*The resolve of the Briton when his back is against the wall.*' Our
heroic fishermen are making a noble stand against faceless bureaucrats and the joint might of Government and Brussels, reminiscent of
the British stand against Hitler and Napoleon (the fishermen
themselves refer to their protest as their Trafalgar!).

(b) '*The innate reasonableness of the Briton.*' The fishermen are
presented as calm and responsible men, different in kind from their
more mercurial French counterparts in the lorry dispute.

(c) '*The Briton as seafarer.*' Britain has for centuries both fed itself
and defended itself from the seas that surround it. Any threat to its
fishermen is, therefore, also portrayed as a threat to this very British
heritage.

2. 'Work'
Because fishing pre-dates nearly all other forms of livelihood, so any
threat to it will touch upon such core ideological themes as a man's
inalienable right to provide for himself, his family and his
community. You may notice in passing how firmly entrenched
cultural sexist stereotypes are in the ideology underpinning the news
story. These are readily identified in the way in which the family is
presented in the news item.

3. 'The family'
To give the item a human angle the report focuses on the effect that
the restrictions on fishing days would have on a single Brixham
fishing family. This family, the Passmores, are no longer able to
continue in 'the livelihood of their forefathers', and Russell Passmore
has been forced to sell the family fishing boat. Again, issues to do with
(2), 'Work' are closely related here.

4. 'Community'

The overall treatment of the item gives the impression that Britain is itself a nation made up of thriving communities held together by shared goals and community values. These values are now being threatened by legislation which originally hails from Brussels, Europe and 'the foreigner'. It is interesting to note that the mining communities devastated by the pit closures of the mid-1980s were rarely given the positive treatment that this Brixham community receives in this item, presumably because the decision to close the pits came from a Government which was then at the height of its popularity. The closures brought about by Michael Heseltine in 1992, however, when the Government was less popular, were treated quite differently.

5. 'Tradition'

The general effect given is that the natural order of things, in which British fishermen set sail as they have done since time immemorial, has been interrupted by foreign meddling.

6. 'Individualism'

In this item the stress is not on fishing as a large-scale industry – which it is, of course – but on fishing as a form of individual enterprise. The small trawlers themselves connote 'family business' rather than corporate activity; had the item contained only pictures of large ocean-going factory ships then the ideological theme of individualism could not have been developed.

In our society these mythic concepts of nation, work and tradition are not isolated from one another; they join together to make a coherent picture of 'our' social reality which is termed the **dominant ideology**. This in turn provides an organising frame that influences the construction of the fishing item and 'naturalises' a number of concepts which are socially, politically and historically specific. This would seem to reinforce the notion that bias and mythologising in the media is indeed 'nobody's fault'. For example, the family is seen as the 'natural' form of human unit; the community is the 'natural' social grouping; 'man' has the 'natural' right to pursue his livelihood free of interference; the British parliamentary system is the 'natural' democratic one, and so on.

It is important that you are aware how such ideological messages are produced. Here, the news item operates in a subtle way by introducing a number of myths into what would seem to be a straightforward record of events. Thus, although a persuasive rhetoric is in operation throughout the item, the overall impression is one of ideological neutrality. This is because the techniques of news production encourage us to believe that the image of trawlers passing under Tower bridge is, quite simply, the unmediated truth captured by the ideologically neutral camera, a picture of a boat passing under a bridge and nothing more.

It is, however, precisely this ideological dimension of news production which many broadcasters most fervently deny when media analysts comment upon it. Broadcasters will usually claim that such actuality footage fundamentally guarantees the objectivity of the item, just because it is actuality. Such notions of neutrality and objectivity are the central sustaining myths in broadcast news, which generally claims to present us with a view of the world that is free of any bias. This 'ideology of objectivity' is a central sustaining myth within liberal humanist society, for it rests upon the distinction between real facts and personal interpretations, implicitly claiming for itself the status of a commonsensical view of the world, apparently free of any theoretical basis or bias. However, it is important to remember that all views of the world are constructed from just the kinds of myths we have considered above; what a commonsensical view of the world does is to hide its own processes of structuration so carefully that the Audience becomes unaware of their operation.

And this is really the central point of this chapter, and of our analysis of news. If this chapter achieves nothing else, we hope that it enables you to understand that facts just are not simply out there to be gathered. **The news is instead ordered, edited, organised and constructed by news producers, and this production is in turn influenced by the wider social, cultural, historical and ideological context in which it takes place. The way to see this for yourself, as ever, is to take a small extract of text and to analyse it in detail. Begin by looking for some sort of tension or conflict in the extract, seeing how it sets opposites against each other in the way we describe on pp. 133–4. Try to build your analysis from the extract itself, using the five key media concepts to help you explore how the news is constructed and what sorts of meanings it produces and how it affects its audience. All the time be conscious that you are seeking to produce an analysis rather than a general impression, an intelligent discussion rather than a series of generalisations.**

II ASPECTS OF THE MEDIA TEXT: AUDIENCE

IN the previous sections we have looked in some detail at the various factors that shape news items. What we want to do now is to pull some of these ideas together by taking a step back and considering the media aspect of Audience. A good way to do this is to look at the way in which the same news story was presented by two different news programmes: ITN's *News at Ten* broadcast and the BBC's *Nine O'Clock News*.

In this section, therefore, we will be comparing these two accounts of the same news story. To do this, we will be returning to the item on the French lorry drivers. The response that an audience will have to any item will be subtly influenced by both the images and the language that news producers have selected (the **paradigmatic dimension**) and by the way in which they have chosen to combine these together (the **syntagmatic dimension**). In media studies this practice of structuring material so that audiences are likely to interpret it in a particular way is called establishing a '**preferred reading**'. By using such weighted phrases as 'no sign to an end of the chaos' and 'militant drivers' to accompany pictures that themselves connote turmoil and chaos, the producers of the item are clearly 'preferring' that we interpret the issue in a certain way.

Now, if we accept the general assumptions that underlie the *News at Ten* team's presentation of the item then we are said to be making a 'preferred reading' of it. The *News at Ten* production team could have 'preferred' that we viewed the lorry drivers' action more positively by emphasising that the protest was against the introduction of legislation affecting the lorry drivers' livelihoods (which is exactly the treatment they give to the fishermen's protest), but they did not in fact choose to present it in this way. The news item can be said to have been 'encoded' in a certain way by the production team. This encoding is itself structured so as to guarantee that the audience will 'de-code' the item in line with the preferred reading.

In media studies the terms **encoding** and **decoding** are often used to describe the kinds of processes we are discussing here. The producers and editors of *News at Ten* are said to encode this preferred meaning when they assemble the item, and the audience to decode it as they watch – although, as we shall see, audiences do not always make such preferred readings.

The process of news production involves the selection and prioritisation of items, those which are considered to be of greater importance being featured first. In making decisions, for example, about running order, mode of presentation and emphasis, editors influence how audiences perceive events and also determine the nature of subsequent coverage. For example, in the changes that took place to the *News at Ten* format in April 1993 it is interesting to note how the new introductory sequence placed much more emphasis on the image of the Houses of Parliament and Big Ben, the latter providing the main motif for the new studio setting itself (see Figure 6.3). In the same way that a Levi sweatshirt has the authentic brand name emblazoned across it, so the new *News at Ten* format employs the Big Ben motif to establish a brand identity, with the clockface standing for both 'up-to-the-minute' and 'authoritative'. The introduction of a single, well-established newsreader, Trevor McDonald, further enhanced the identity and authority of the programme, thereby establishing the context in which the rest of the programme was to take place.

We will look now at the running order of the BBC's *Nine O'Clock News*. If you turn back to the opening section of this chapter, in which we outline the running order of the *News at Ten* broadcast, you will see that the *Nine O'Clock* format differs from that of the *News at Ten* broadcast in a number of ways. However, the first three items, all of which we have looked at in some depth, are shared between both programmes.

BBC 1: Nine O'Clock News

Item 1 : A report on the G7 summit and the response of G7 leaders to the continuing heavy fighting in Sarajevo

Item 2 : The French lorry drivers' dispute

Item 3 : The fishermen's demonstration on the Thames

Item 4 : A report on spending on the armed forces and the 'go-ahead' given for the Trident submarine

Item 5 : President Yeltsin's ban on the Communist Party

Item 6 : Controversy surrounding a Pakistan fast bowler's comments about a British umpire

Item 7 : Disturbances in Salford lead to shots being fired at a police vehicle

Item 8 : British Telecom's crackdown on obscene phone calls

Item 9 : Only one bid is received for the new Channel Five franchise

Item 10: A round-up of the main news

The most obvious difference between the two is that whereas *News at Ten* had a much lighter tone the BBC *Nine O'Clock News* sticks to 'heavier' items. For example, Item 7, which deals with the seemingly newsworthy disturbances in Salford, was not chosen for *News at Ten*, although the ratings battle for *Eldorado* was.

We will now look at some of the points that need to be taken into account when discussing any news item in relation to the topics of Audience and agenda-setting by focusing upon the main differences between ITN's and the BBC's coverage of the lorry drivers' dispute. The main similarities and differences between the two items are as follows:

1.   The *News at Ten* item concentrates solely on matters of violence and disruption. There is no attempt to put forward the drivers' views about the issues concerned. The BBC report, however, includes comments by French drivers and also a more detailed account of their view of the dispute:

> Working conditions are one thing, said this driver, but it's the points system we want scrapped. They say that the savage competition in the freight industry forces them to break the law, that it's unfair that they, who drive more miles in a month than some people do in a year, should only have the same six points to start with, that they work cruel hours for wretched pay. . . (BBC coverage).

2.   The commentaries in both items place more emphasis on the effect of the dispute on stranded British drivers than they do on its causes, so that the BBC report is, in some places, not unlike ITN's:

> That's bad news for those British still trapped in the nearby town of Cambray. Local people are feeding them, the conditions are grim. Last night there was a slim chance that the Paris talks could resolve this dispute; this evening though, that does not look likely. The confrontation appears capable of dragging on for many more days. . . (BBC coverage).

3.   In both items visuals are chosen which function rhetorically to influence the audience's interpretation. Pictures of motorways clogged with lorries and congested villages focus the audience's attention on the strike's effects on the 'general public'. The technical codes of Construction – camera angle, shot-size and editing style – play a significant part in the negative representation of the drivers' dispute. Many of the shots are purposefully visually chaotic, using dynamic compositions and low camera angles; the jumpy editing style adds to this effect.

4. The French government and the European Commission are presented as acting for the good of the general public. The ITN item also implies that most French lorry-drivers are opposed to extremism, that they value moderation and that they want the strike to come to an end. Such beliefs function to structure the framework of debate – the drivers are put in the position of having to justify their actions, whereas the Government is not:

> The Minister of Transport. . . said this agreement will provide better working conditions for drivers. It offered a shorter week, promises of alternative employment for drivers who lose their licenses, a review of the effects of the new points system on professional drivers, penalties for employers who encourage their drivers to break the speed limit. . . (BBC coverage).

5. The language used by the ITN presenters and reporters plays an important part in determining how we perceive the dispute. The following phrases play a decisive role in giving the story a particular slant; none of these occur in the BBC item:

(a) 'Sixty blockades set up by French lorry drivers. . .' ('blockades' suggests a military style action).

(b) 'there is no sign to an end of the chaos. . .' ('chaos' emphasises that the results were not wholly predicted by the drivers).

(c) 'an agreement worked out this morning was soon rejected by militant drivers. . .' ('militant' creates the impression that a hard core of politically motivated activists are in fact organising the protest).

(d) 'beseiged the city of Lyon for the best part of a week. . .' ('beseiged' is another military term, making Lyon seem the innocent victim of the drivers' selfish actions).

(e) 'There are still some signs of defiance. . .' ('defiance' suggests that the lorry-drivers are being single-minded, self-centred and unreasonable; for example, the same word is *not* used to describe the actions of the Government).

As we have seen already, the preferred encodings of news producers often successfully hide from the audience their own political slant. This is because the presentation of the news draws upon widely accepted ideological themes which we may easily see as being 'natural', 'the way things are' or 'just common sense'. There is, therefore, a very close connection between a preferred reading and the dominant value system within society; such readings also effectively close off the possibility of alternative or subversive readings.

However, not everyone in the audience will decode the preferred meaning; some, whilst accepting existing social values, will argue that particular groups within society are unfairly treated. A member of the British lorry-drivers' union, for instance, might accept that the French government have to ensure that the road network remains in operation but argue that the *gendarme's* treatment of the lorry-drivers was harsh and brutal. Because this person neither wholly accepts nor dismisses the dominant value system but instead 'negotiates' a particular stance in relation to it, his/her interpretation is referred to as a '**negotiated reading**'.

Finally, some members of the audience will reject both the 'preferred' version of events presented and the *status quo* values of the journalists and editors that determined the item's form, making what is termed an '**oppositional reading**'. Such a reading would see the lorry drivers' action as the justified expression of their political rights and take the police to be the violent repressive agents of the ruling class. A lorry-driver who was both a union activist and a member of a militant political group might well interpret the item in such a way.

Clearly, news items will always be different; it is to some extent this very difference that makes an event news. However, as we hope to have demonstrated in this Chapter, it is useful to have a few guiding ideas to help you whenever you start your own analysis of any particular news item. For convenience, we will reiterate these central issues here:

1. News producers make decisions about which items to include and which to reject (gatekeeping).
2. These decisions are made on a variety of grounds, amongst the most important of which are the views on 'newsworthiness' of journalists and editors (news values).
3. These values play an important part in determining how news items are covered (agenda-setting).
4. As a result of this certain key figures within society are interviewed and play an important role in defining the nature of the event (primary definers).

Finally, it must be remembered that the 'news industries' are themselves important social institutions within our society and that news coverage can set the agenda for political debate and policy-making. We cannot say, therefore, that the news simply passively reports important events; the structuring processes in operation within the news industries play a vital role in shaping all our perceptions of society.

In conclusion, we will return briefly to the changes to the *News at Ten* broadcast that we have already mentioned in passing. The format and scheduling of news programmes do tend to change fairly rapidly, and you may well be asked to examine these changes. Indeed, during the writing of this book both ITN and the BBC remodelled their broadcasts. When, over recent years the BBC invested heavily in paying for computer-generated logos and so on there was considerable criticism about the cost to the licence payer of such seemingly minor changes. It could be argued that such criticisms miss the point. First and foremost TV news is, like everything else that appears on television, a media product designed to attract and keep audiences. The small but significant changes in the format of *News at Ten* were made to these ends. By having a single anchor person and by using two images of the Big Ben clockface in 'windows' beneath the conventional news item window in the top right-hand corner of the screen, the visual identity of the programme was made much clearer. When two news readers were used, as in the broadcast analysed here, it was possible to mistake them for the presenters of another news programme such as *Newsnight*. In the revamped *News at Ten* we never see Trevor McDonald separated from the clock-face motif. And the studio setting itself is now the 'busy news building' that is used for ITN's early evening broadcast, a change which further helps programme, station and corporate identity.

We might conclude that the format changes carried out by both ITN and the BBC are a part of the quest to build audiences who are more likely to show loyalty to a particular station's news service. This reinforces a central point: in analysing any news item you will find yourself understanding more about the nature of the society which created that News item, and, implicitly, more about your own position within that society. Analysis of media representations of reality in the context of the news can therefore lead directly to questions about the structures of our social formation.

7

The TV soap: *Neighbours*

I CONSTRUCTING AN OVERALL ANALYSIS

SOAP operas had their origins in early American radio broadcasting, and the first daytime serial, *Painted Dreams*, was broadcast by WGN radio. In 1932 Proctor and Gamble, the detergent manufacturers, using a daytime serial domestic comedy for women, sponsored a programme involving *The Puddle Family* to advertise Oxydol, a washing powder. And so the term 'soap' was born. Over the next five years sponsored serial dramas dominated radio daytime programming: in 1935, on NBC radio alone, Proctor and Gamble sponsored 778 broadcast programme hours.

Given the immense popularity of the genre on radio it was quite natural that broadcasters should consider using it on television. The early television soaps were, like the daytime radio serials, transmitted five times per week and were aimed at female audiences. The success of the genre in the daytime schedule led executives to ask whether they might introduce prime-time soaps. Many thought that the slow moving plot-lines of soaps, together with their lower production values, would not hold a general audience. Thus, when prime-time soaps such as *Peyton Place* (NBC, 1964–9) were introduced, these had more action and higher production values.

Although the first British television soap, *The Grove Family* (BBC, 1954–7) attracted a loyal audience it was not until the arrival of commercial television in 1955 that the full potentiality of the genre was exploited. The medical soap *Emergency Ward Ten* (ATV, 1957–67) was Britain's first twice weekly serial, but it was *Coronation Street* (Granada, 1960–present), the longest-running British TV soap, that really proved the popularity of the genre. The BBC tried to respond to the successes that its commercial rival was having in this area of programming but its own productions failed to achieve long-term success. It was not until the introduction of *EastEnders* (BBC, 1985–present), with its controversial plot-lines relating to key contemporary social issues, that the BBC succeeded with the genre.

The success of the soap format was further confirmed by the success of two American prime-time serials, *Dynasty* and *Dallas*, which became known as 'super-soaps' because of their lavish production values. These were transmitted as season 'blocks', composed of a number of weekly episodes and were far more star-oriented than other soaps: J. R. Ewing (Larry Hagman) and Alexis (Joan Collins) are central to *Dallas* and *Dynasty* in a way that no character within, say, *Neighbours* is. When J. R. was mysteriously shot, the tabloid press was filled with speculation about his unknown would-be assassin. The resulting media hype was enormous – much to the delight of the programme-makers – and soon the issue was even being discussed in the serious press and on television news programmes. As a result, after the 'who shot J. R.?' hype, Hagman was able to argue for both a salary increase and a share in the profits of the show. It is interesting to note that, by contrast, when Ian Smith (alias Harold Bishop of *Neighbours*) decided that the fee he was receiving was insufficient he was simply written out of the script. He died 'lost at sea', leaving behind him the grieving Madge.

The popularity of Australian soap operas since the mid 1970s can be seen by looking at the range of titles below, all of which have been broadcast in Britain:

1975 *The Young Doctors*
1976 *The Sullivans*
1979 *Prisoner Cell Block H*
1981 *Sons and Daughters*
1981 *A Country Practice*
1985 *Neighbours*
1986 *The Flying Doctors*
1988 *Home and Away*
(All dates indicate the first Australian broadcast)

It is partly this popularity which makes the study of soaps so worthwhile. Certainly, you can expect that the study of a soap will form a part of most media or communications studies courses. Begin, as ever, by deciding on an episode to analyse, and approach it with a view to establishing some broad issues. We are going to look at an episode of the Australian soap, *Neighbours*.[1] *Neighbours* tells of the trials and tribulations of a group of families living in and around Ramsay Street in Erinsborough. The programme originally centred on the Robinsons, the Clarkes and the Ramsays and their various relatives and lodgers.

Step 1

After watching the programme, see if you can identify any kind of pattern or structure at work.

It is, as usual, a good idea to start by making a brief outline of the episode you are studying, noting its main events and themes. You will not, of course, include this in your final essay, but it will provide you with a good starting-point as it will focus your attention on the central issues and actions that you will need to discuss.

Our episode starts with Madge reprimanding Brenda for keeping Joe's children up late. We then cut to the Robinson household, where Helen and her new husband Michael are telling Jim about their honeymoon. Meanwhile Melanie and Joe, who are on holiday together as a result of winning a '*Blind Date*'-type competition, are having breakfast in bed. Back at the Robinson's, Jim tells Michael that he has discovered that he does not have a sister (Michael had been claiming that his wife, Louise, was his sister), and later we find out that Madge and Harold are also aware of his bigamy. A pop-video-style sequence of Joe and Melanie having fun at the holiday complex follows and we then return to the Bishop household, where Madge tells Harold that she feels that Brenda will not be able to run the coffee shop; however, when she discovers that Brenda kept Joe's children up late to show them why rules are necessary, she is won over by her astuteness. As the episode closes Jim gives Michael an ultimatum: either Michael tells Helen about the bigamy or he will. In the closing cliffhanger sequence Michael confesses his bigamy.

As you can see from this outline, the episode seems to have a very fragmented story-line. In order to prevent your essay becoming equally fragmented it is important that you identify, at the outset, the main plot-lines in the episode you want to study. Our episode is in fact composed of only three main plot-lines (a typical number for *Neighbours*). These are:

1. *Harold and Madge Bishop's preparations for their holiday*   Madge has begun to doubt whether Brenda will be able to run the coffee shop satisfactorily in their absence. Harold is eagerly anticipating their holiday, apparently oblivious of Madge's reservations. Fussy by nature, Harold is relishing the planning and organisation of the trip, to the amusement of Madge.

2. *Helen's marriage to the bigamist Michael*   Helen is rapturous about her honeymoon in Greece and Italy with Michael. In their absence Jim has been looking into Michael's background and has discovered that he is a bigamist. Madge and Harold know this and push Jim to force Michael to reveal the fact to Helen. In the final closing cliffhanger sequence Michael confesses to Helen.

3. *Joe and Melanie's holiday romance*   As a result of appearing together on a television '*Blind Date*'-type programme Melanie and Joe are on holiday together. Joe confesses his love to Melanie and, to his surprise, she admits that she loves him too. Joe reassures Melanie that his children like her and, when she expresses concern about hurting her fiancé, Simon, Joe comforts her by saying that it is not in her nature to hurt anyone.

These plot-lines are developed in some sequences but not in others. It is important, therefore, to break the episode down into a list of sequences, so that you can be quite sure about which plot-lines are developed by which sequences, and how. We have included the sequences at the end of this chapter, in order to avoid cluttering our analysis with a long string of sequence descriptions. Once you have broken the episode down into a list of sequences, you can then go on to identify which of the main plot-lines is developed in each sequence. So, before you go any further, turn to the end of this chapter (pp. 188–90) to see how we have done this.[2]

Now note which characters are involved in which sequence and plot-line and to what degree. One way of summarising this information is to write it out in continuous prose; however, you will find it more useful if you get into the habit of putting this information into chart form, indicating which characters appear in which sequence. A chart of this type is known as a **cross-plot**, and is a commonly used device in the pre-production and planning stages of video and film production. A cross-plot of the episode we want to analyse is shown in Table 7.1.

There are some important stylistic differences between these plot-lines. The first (the holiday preparations of Madge and Harold) has

Table 7.1 Cross-plot of sequences in episode examined

Story-line	Sequences														
	1	2	3	4	5	6	7	8	9	10	11	12	13	14	15
Plot-line 1															
Madge	X			X		X		*		X	X			X	
Harold				X		X		*	X	X					
Brenda	X		*		*									X	
Plot-line 2															
Michael		X		X	*		X					X			X
Helen		X		X	*		X					*			X
Jim		*		X			X					X			*
Plot-line 3															
Joe			X				X						X		
Melanie			X				X						X		

Key: X = Major role * = Minor role.

some of the characteristics of sitcom. The second (the holiday of Melanie and Joe), resembles a pop video and the third (Michael's bigamy) is highly melodramatic. This diversity is one of the main factors contributing to the success of *Neighbours* since it ensures that the programme has 'something for everyone'.

In order to help you to discuss the different types of soap that you might come across it makes sense to look first at some of their common features and at the ways in which our episode of *Neighbours* exhibits these:

1. *Soaps have no 'ending'* There will be no concluding episode of *Neighbours* in which all events are drawn together to produce a happy or meaningful ending. In consequence:

2. *Soap plot-lines are 'open-ended'* Because they are open-ended narratives soaps keep us guessing. We tune in to the next episode of *Neighbours* to find out what, for example, Helen's response to Michael's confession will be, and to see if our thoughts about the outcome were correct.

3. *Soaps have a number of independent plot-lines* Each episode of *Neighbours* will have a number of different plots, three being a typical number (*EastEnders*, on the other hand, may have as many as seven in any given episode). Some of these will be mundane and everyday, others melodramatic or comic.

4. *Soap plot-lines continue over a number of episodes* Whereas in a television series each plot-line finishes with the episode, soap plot-lines

may last for many months (as is the case with the romance of Joe and Melanie).

5. *Soaps employ cliffhangers*   The cliffhanger device is closely related to the open-endedness of soap plots. These cliffhangers can be major events – as when Michael tells Helen of his bigamy at the end of our episode – or more minor matters such as an emotionally charged moment.

6. *Soaps have temporary narrative resolutions*   Although soaps reach no final conclusion this does not mean that all narrative strands are left unresolved – marriages take place, business deals are successfully completed and so on.

7. *Soaps contain many references to past events*   Soap characters often refer to past events which regular viewers will remember. Such references to an accumulated past are another feature distinguishing serial TV soaps from other television series. In most TV series, characters seem somehow to forget, at least by the start of the next episode, what happened in previous weeks.

8. *Different soap plot-lines may have common themes*   Although there may be no direct relation between the different plots in our episode there are thematic links: the Joe/Melanie story and the Helen/Michael story both deal with the issue of relationships.

9. *Soap plot-lines involve events of differing magnitude*   We can identify three scales of events in soaps:

(a) Plot-lines dealing with the *big events*: births, marriages, deaths, tragedies, etc. The eventual marriage of Joe and Melanie, a hyped media event reported in newspapers and magazines, is an example.

(b) General plot-lines that deal with the *basic issues* on which soaps are commonly based: difficulties between the generations, problems between men and women, etc. The Madge/Harold plot-line is an example of such a plot-line.

(c) Specific plot-lines which *depend upon some external agency* for their resolution. These plot-lines can involve, for example, bigamy, seige, protest, demonstration, terrorism, etc. For such plots new 'short-stay' characters are usually introduced (e.g. Michael the bigamist). These quite often turn up again in later episodes.

10. *Use of gossip*   Gossip plays an important part in developing our episode, both revealing things to us and also making us think about what might happen in the future.

These basic structuring patterns develop the conflict or tension at the centre of the soap as drama. As soaps are essentially about communities and the individuals within them, the conflicts and oppositions that structure their narratives will reflect this. In the episode of *Neighbours* that we want to analyse in this chapter, for example, we feel that the basic conflicts and tensions at its centre are concerned with:

1. *Tradition and change* In plot-line 1 Madge initially objects to Brenda's new and different ways of doing things.
2. *Insider versus outsider* In plot-line 2 Michael as a bigamist, is clearly an outsider, somebody who must be rejected from the Ramsay street community.
3. *Head versus heart* In plot-line 3 we have the question of whether Melanie should listen to her heart and marry Joe or to her head and stay with Simon, to whom she is engaged.

However, you may not always find it so easy to identify the conflict or tension at the centre of a particular episode. If you are stuck, try considering one of the pairs of opposites shown in Table 7.2, since these are the types of conflicts or tensions you are most likely to come across when analysing a soap.

Table 7.2 Types of conflict and potential plot-lines

Opposition	*Potential Plot-line*
Order and Disorder	People may wish to live in an ordered society, but the reality is often untidy and fraught with problems
Community and the Individual	The individual must recognise that s/he is bound by the same rules as other members of the community
Maturity and Youth	Young people, in general, and headstrong adolescents in particular, have to learn to accept the values and wisdom of the adult community
Cooperation and Competition	Ruthless individualism and selfishness cannot lead to happiness

In *Neighbours* the majority of younger characters are not a part of a traditional nuclear family at all. They often live with relatives, friends of relatives or even relatives of their own friends – usually because their parents are either divorced or living far away. As a result, there is an emphasis on young people learning about things for themselves as opposed to being told about the world and their place within it by their parents. Because the problems they face are not seen from the perspective of an adult, younger viewers can relate more easily to the programme, for it is far less patronising than the traditional soaps. Typical adolescent-centred plot-lines we might find in *Neighbours* are:

1. How to relate to your parents.
2. The pros and cons of premarital sex.
3. How to form a relationship.
4. How to express your love for someone.
5. The responsibilities which are a part of adulthood.

Both 3 and 4, above, appear in our episode. This ties in precisely with the type of general tension or conflict we have identified in the programme as a whole: the tension between head and heart, between following your feelings and doing what you think best. Having focused in on this conflict, it is now possible to move on to a more detailed analysis of the episode.

Step 2

Analyse the opening sequence, or, if this proves unilluminating, a sequence from fairly near the beginning, featuring one or two of the major characters.

The sequence we want to analyse here is from the very beginning of the episode. It involves Madge and Brenda, the latter having been involved in looking after Joe's children while he was away on holiday with Melanie. Having watched this sequence several times, the area we want to concentrate on is Construction, simply because the sequence has been constructed in a way typical of this soap.

In this section we are going to introduce a way of talking quite precisely about the Construction of a particular sequence by considering it in relation to three areas: **performer space**, **camera space** and **lighting**. These terms are often used in the media industries but they are not very different, as you will see, from the technical codes and codes of *mise-en-scène* that we have already introduced. The reason we introduce them here is because it is quite likely that you will find them used in more technical analyses of media production. To make this clearer, we will be referring to line drawings of the sequence (see Figures 7.1 to 7.6).

1   Performer space
Performer space relates to the positioning of the characters, Madge and Brenda in relation to the camera. This can be done along two axes:

(i)   The **horizontal axis** (the **X axis**) which extends to the left and right of the camera (Figure 7.1).
(ii)   The **depth axis** (the **Z axis**) which extends toward and away from the camera (Figure 7.2).

What we immediately notice is that Madge and Brenda are 'blocked' along the X-axis, moving from one side of the scene to the other, rather than toward or away from us (see Figures 7.1 and 7.2). As a result we do not feel particularly involved in the unfolding action. As you analyse the programme more widely, you will find that this type of X-axis blocking predominates in *Neighbours*. The effect of X-axis blocking is to make us feel like members of a theatre audience; indeed, the changes from one Ramsay Street interior to the next are quite like scene changes at the theatre (the sequence will have been shot in a studio using a number of cameras, each with its own X- and Z-axis). Our drawings of the key shots in the sequence give you an indication of the typical structure of a studio based sequence using X-blocking.
    The way in which this axis blocking is used is important to the overall effect of a soap. In *EastEnders*, for example, performers tend to be blocked on the Z-axis, with action taking place on several 'planes of action' – foreground, middle ground and background. This Z-Axis blocking is particularly noticeable in the street scenes and along the long bar of the Queen Vic pub: people will move in and out of shot, walk between the camera and the subjects of the action, thereby creating the impression that a 'slice of life' is unfolding before our eyes. The effect of this is to enhance the day-to-day 'business' of the scene, and is a technique commonly used in fast-action soaps, such as police series. *The Bill* and *Hill St Blues*, as well as hospital series such as *St Elsewhere* and *Casualty* use Z-axis blocking extensively to create a 'busy' feel. The X-axis blocking we find in *Neighbours*, however, tends to create an impression of humdrum domestic life, and this fits in

Figure 7.1   *Neighbours* X axis

Figure 7.2   *Neighbours* shot 1 Z axis

Figure 7.3   *Neighbours* shot 2

Figure 7.4   *Neighbours* shot 3

Figure 7.5   *Neighbours* shot 4

Figure 7.6   *Neighbours* shot 5

precisely with the overall pattern or shape of the episode, in which we drop in on the everyday lives of the Ramsay Street regulars.

2 Camera space

The 'room' in which the action takes place is, as in most other soaps, a studio set in which the cameras are relatively free to move around, changing shot size and proximity as the sequence demands. There are two aspects of camera space that need to be taken into account:

(i) Shot size: LS, MS, CU, BCU   Our sequence contains more close ups (CUs) than normal. This intimate camera style is characteristic of TV soaps, being used to reveal the subtle plays of emotion on a character's face.

(ii) Camera proximity   the positioning of the camera in relation to the performer (in front, to the side, behind). Visual variety is achieved in our opening sequence by continually changing the camera angles and viewpoints (see Figures 7.1–7.6). This makes us feel that we are seeing something new even though a familiar location, the Bishop household, is being used.

3 Lighting

There are two different lighting styles that you will need to comment upon when discussing soaps:

(i) Chiaroscuro   When a single light source is used to create small pools of illumination surrounded by dark shadows the lighting is termed **chiaroscuro**. This is an artistic term used to refer to the distribution of light and dark masses in a picture. In our opening sequence the Bishop household is lit in this way by side-lamps creating a rather sombre mood, appropriate for the conflict between Madge and Brenda. This style of lighting is used extensively in *EastEnders*, where a single weak light bulb may seem to be the only light source, thereby creating an impression of gloom and pessimism which attempts to capture the despondency of inner-city life. In general the chiaroscuro style helps to increase the emotional and psychological depth of a sequence.

(ii) Notan   The sets in most soaps are brightly and evenly lit by studio lights, giving a flat, shadowless illumination known as **Notan lighting**. The resulting picture is bright (high-key) creating an

optimistic mood. Such lighting is often used in *Neighbours* and is one of the elements contributing to its up-beat feel.

You can now see just how important the codes of Construction are in establishing the everyday naturalism characteristic of *Neighbours*. The tensions and conflicts that arise in our episode cannot be satisfactorily described simply by attending to what the characters themselves say and do; camera angle, shot size, lighting, etc., all play an important part in the overall effect. For instance, in discussing this sequence, we might point out how the low-key lighting in the Bishop household creates a slightly sombre mood or how the protracted close-ups of Brenda's expressions as she reacts to Madge's criticisms enable us to gauge her thoughts and feelings without her having to say anything.

Step 3

Select a second sequence for discussion.

In this section we are concerned with sequence 7 in which we see Joe and Melanie at the holiday complex enjoying a number of activities – crazy golf, swimming, volleyball. It is not a typical soap sequence for it uses a montage style, is in condensed time (a number of hours being compressed into minutes), has no dialogue and uses non-diegetic music. These techniques seem more appropriate to a pop video than to a typical piece of soap programming, and this makes it an interesting piece to analyse in terms of the media aspect of Narrative.

Although a considerable number of episodes led up to this plot-line (plot-line 3), viewers did not need to see each one in order to follow it. This is because *Neighbours*, like other soaps, 'updates' its viewers by having characters gossip about relevant past events. This is not to say, however, that all soaps are obsessively concerned with the past; characters quite soon cease to mention events that are irrelevant to the present. Instead, *Neighbours* plots, like those of other soaps, invite us to recollect the past and to guess what will happen in the future. Two terms are used to describe these activities: protension and retention.

(i) Protension (predicting future events) Because soaps exhibit what is termed '**protensive indeterminacy**' (a rather grand term which simply means that we cannot predict the outcome of events) almost anything can happen – a promising relationship such as this between

Mel and Joe can founder. The syntagmatic structure of soaps is thus more 'open' than other genres such as police series, in which the outcome is always far more predictable.

Again, it is useful to use a chart to outline the likely future events, given the nature of the characters involved, as we do in Table 7.3.

Table 7.3 Likely future events given nature of characters involved

Character	Character	Narrative Potential
Joe	Melanie	
Has a young family	No family in the programme	How will Joe's children react if they marry? Will Melanie live up to Joe's former wife in their eyes?
Widower	Single	
Conventional	Extrovert	
Marriagable	Marriageable	

(ii)   *Retention (remembering past events)*   Our sequence encourages us both to recall past events (e.g. Joe's previous marriages and Melanie's broken romances) and also to relate these to earlier romances such as that of Charlene and Scott. It is at this level of association and connection (the paradigmatic axis) that soaps become particularly interesting, simply because we are encouraged, for example, to compare Melanie with Joe's previous wives, to consider whether she would make a good mother and to evaluate her as a potential partner for Joe.

These issues of Narrative can be usefully developed. For example, much that we learn about our plot-line comes through the agencies of the camerawork and editing, which have 'decided' *what* we should be shown, *when*, and *for how long*. As a result, any character's account of events is inevitably embedded within the larger framing story, presented through the codes of camerawork and editing. We might argue, therefore, that the camerawork and editing, which do so muchto hide their own important operations, are in fact the primary narrators, both in this sequence and in soaps generally. This would not, however, be totally accurate. All the codes of Construction might be said to narrate the soap because without them the events that we see simply could not be organised and presented. Nevertheless, some codes do play a more important part in such narration than others.

Editing, for example, which involves, along with other things, the organisation of time, is naturally of greater importance than, say, lighting.

The absence of dialogue and the pop music montage style is a characteristic of *Neighbours* and other television programmes aimed, partly, at younger audiences (*Baywatch* is another example). However, the introduction of such sequences is not merely a gimmick to attract younger audiences; considerable thought is given to the way in which they fit in to the episode as a whole and enable audiences to relate to unfolding events in different ways. Certainly, the soap still deals with the central tensions, conflicts and oppositions characteristic of the genre as a whole, but the innovative use of sequences such as this tap into the ability of younger members of the audience to make sense of media texts in new ways. Pop videos are extremely popular with young audiences, who respond to their fast cutting and unusual camera angles. These also have their own narrative organisation and this sequence, in which Melanie and Joe have fun together at the holiday complex, is a typical mini-narrative of this type.

Step 4

Select a third sequence for discussion.

The sequence we want to look at now is one which raises a number of important issues concerning the way in which soaps deal with moral issues. In this sequence (sequence 8), Madge, Harold and Jim are discussing Michael's bigamy and what should be done about this situation. Such scenes in which characters give their opinions about the behaviour of other characters occur regularly in soaps. In order to direct your thinking in a purposeful way when discussing scenes of this type it is a good idea to ask the following questions at the outset:

1. *Where is the sequence set and what sorts of things happen here?*
   The action takes place in the coffee shop run by Harold and Madge Bishop, which, along with the Watering Hole, is the main meeting place for characters.
2. *What do we know about the principal characters in the plot-line?*
   (i) Helen Daniels: Helen has been previously 'unlucky in love' and the seasoned viewer might have expected that all would not go well in her marriage.

(ii)   Michael Daniels: Michael is a distant relative of Helen's
first husband and he has been something of a dark horse.

3.   *Which other characters are involved, and what do we know about them?*
We know that Brenda, a fairly recently arrived character, is
working class, happy-go-lucky and down-to-earth. Madge is
always quick to speak her mind but beneath the forthright
appearance she is a caring and concerned person. Harold Bishop,
Madge's husband, is correct, proper and a little over fussy. He is
also a humorous character and would not seem out of place in a
sitcom.

It is important to note that the information that we glean from this
sequence – Michael's bigamy – has already been relayed to us on a
number of occasions as different characters discussed it. Such
exchanges are termed '**syntagmatically redundant**' because they
tell us what we already know; nevertheless, they also tell us in whom
characters choose to confide and this, in turn, tells us quite a lot about
them. Again, we can see that in the soap, gossip is not redundant, but
is instead central to the Narrative process.

Some writers have argued that the moral universe of the soap is an
intrinsically female one and, further, that women have a different
sense of morality than men. For men, individual rights and social
rules are, it is argued, the key dimension of the moral order, whereas,
for women, moral issues are tied to relationships and responsibilities.
Thus, in terms of our plot-line, we would expect Jim and Harold
simply to adopt a moral position over Michael's bigamy whereas
Madge may seek to probe such issues more deeply, considering them
mainly from the perspective of interpersonal relationships.

As soaps often deal with the kinds of moral issues that are found in
this plot-line it is important to understand the way in which these
issues are presented to us. It is interesting to note that there are no
point-of-view (POV) shots (sometimes referred to as **subjective
shots**) in this sequence. Such shots are often used in fictional genres
to draw viewers into the action but they are rarely used in soaps, and
there are none here. Instead, **objective shots** are used throughout
the sequence – the camera does not view things from the perspective
of any one character. As a result, we are prevented from identifying
with either Madge, Harold or Jim. It is important that such
identification does not take place because this would shift our
attention away from the areas of relationships and the community
that are the central concern of the soap genre, forcing us to

concentrate on the thoughts, feelings and moral sense of a single individual.

Although Madge, Harold and Jim unanimously condemn Michael's behaviour they are not, as yet, agreed on the best course of action and the main function of this sequence is to show how this is achieved. If any one of these characters was made central to the story-line (making them first-person narrators), the complexity of such interpersonal negotiations would be more difficult to foreground. A different form of narration was used in the early radio soaps which employed voice-over narration to explain events (mainly because of the difficulties audiences experienced in understanding multiple-character soaps broadcast in the medium of sound). Such narration is termed **extra-diegetic** because the person relating events to us is, quite literally, outside the unfolding story or diegesis. Because of the power of this person to impart information that we take to be the truth such narration is often termed omniscient, being 'voice of God' in style. Such a narrative style is out of keeping with the general tenor of the soap genre, however, and as a result it was kept to a minimum in radio soaps. If it were used, in our sequence, to comment on the characters themselves, it would be much harder to become involved in their various views and thoughts.

Any analysis of a sequence such as this one must take into account all the broader factors discussed above. Clearly it is not enough to say that Madge, Harold and Jim are worried about what to do about Michael and Helen. For example, we are also finding out:

(i) The moral hierarchy within the soap   Madge, Harold and Jim are deemed appropriate characters for discussing such weighty ethical matters whereas Brenda is not (she remains in the background in this sequence);

(ii) The relationship between characters   Each of the three characters involved in our sequence thinks that the opinions of the others is worth taking into account;

(iii) Relationships between present and past events   Both Madge and Jim have had marital problems in the past and, if we know of these, we will relate Helen's present difficulties with their previous experiences.

It is clear, then, that the story provides us with information in a fairly complex way; had first person or omniscient narration been employed, for instance, then our feelings about events would be subtly changed. You need to be aware, therefore, as you begin to write about soaps that the impression that they make on you depends upon many factors which you may not notice on a first viewing, simply because soaps are structured in such a way that you become involved in their unfolding and fascinating story-lines.

Step 5

Select a fourth sequence for discussion.

So far we have seen how the media aspects of Construction and Narrative can be used to analyse our episode. What we now need to do is to spend some time considering how these two aspects can themselves be brought into even sharper focus by looking at the aspect of Categorisation. It is very important to consider just how we might begin to classify and to categorise TV soaps. Yet as soon as we think about this in any detail we realise how difficult it is; a gritty, down-to-earth soap such as *EastEnders* seems quite different from a glitzy, sophisticated soap such as *Dallas* (with *Neighbours* itself resembling neither). Given these difficulties, we suggest that you use the framework we introduce in this section to help you to clarify your thinking about soaps as a genre.

We will look first at the wider cultural knowledge and the specific knowledge of the genre that any member of the audience must possess in order to make sense of the final sequence (sequence 15), in which Michael finally admits that he is still married. The points that we make are certainly not exhaustive, but they do have the advantage of being sufficiently flexible to allow you to talk about nearly all forms of soap.

1   Genre conventions and cultural knowledge

Clearly any viewer must be able to:

(i)   Understand the conventions of the soap genre   This sequence is a 'cliffhanger' and a viewer would need to know what the implications of using this convention are. Quite simply, we would expect the following episode to explore the outcomes of this sudden revelation for Helen. If this matter was dealt with only cursorily, or even not dealt with at all, the regular viewer would feel cheated.

(ii)   Understand the social rules and codes of behaviour operating in the soap   Michael has deceived Helen by bigamously marrying her. Therefore a viewer must be able to comprehend the nature and consequences of such actions. An obsession with social norms and codes of conduct is characteristic of the genre and when Michael breaks these, by bigamously marrying Helen, he meets with universal disapproval. Nevertheless, not all soap plot-lines are built around such simple stark moral oppositions. More often, as we listen to the differing views of the characters, we realise that there is more than one side to a story. It might be argued, therefore, that soaps are, on the whole, broadmindedly liberal, for they tend to acknowledge the complexity of human affairs.

(iii)   Understand the motivations and personal qualities of the main characters in the soap   To understand the full implications of this sequence a viewer would need to know certain things about Helen's character and background. For example, we know that Helen is a mature and stable person who is also thoughtful and sensitive and this leads us to predict certain outcomes to the plot-line that are in keeping with her character. Viewers are thus continually involved in guessing and developing possible scenarios for the subsequent episode(s).

2   Genre and character types

As we pointed out above, a knowledge and understanding of what each character is like, how s/he is likely to behave in a particular situation, and what we know of the character's past and hopes for the future are all important in soaps. Helen is at the centre of the plot-line of which our sequence is a part, so we are now going to look at the ways in which you can analyse her character and her role in the episode and the programme as a whole.

(i)   Character biography   As you will often need to write in detail about a soap character it is a good idea, at the outset, to construct a character biography like that in Table 7.4 overleaf when preparing an essay.

Helen's previous social standing was 'single person', which meant that she could be involved in stories relating to romance and marriage. We will now look a little closer at her personality.

(ii)   Character traits   A character trait is a facet of an individual character's personality that belongs uniquely to them. Helen is

artistic, and *Neighbours* scriptwriters have often built plot-lines around this trait. She has had a failed relationship with a crooked art dealer, a romantic entanglement with an 'outback' artist, and she fell in love
with a terminally ill, rich art-lover who bequeathed her the money to set up an art scholarship. In this episode Helen and Michael have just returned from a honeymoon that consisted of tours of the major art galleries and museums in Italy and Greece.

It is often useful, when studying a character, to construct a character trait chart like Table 7.5, in which the positioning of the cross indicates the degree to which a trait is exhibited.

3   Soaps and melodrama

We will conclude this analysis of sequence 15 by considering the relation between soaps and melodramas, the genre to which they relate.

The sequence involving Michael's confession contains the following features characteristic of melodrama:

(i)   The polarisation of good and evil   Melodramas frequently offer a picture of a Manichean world, showing how the forces of good and evil operate in our daily lives. In Neighbours, Helen's goodness is frequently emphasised by involving her in story-lines in which she becomes caught up with a cunning self-serving character.

(ii)   The emphasis on personal life and relationships   Melodramas and soaps chart the evolution of characters through familiar social rituals.

Table 7.4   Constructing a character biography

Character	Helen
Age	Sixties
Ethnic group	White
Class	Middle
Marital status	Single (bigamously married to Michael)
Parental status	Had two daughters. One was married to Jim Robinson but died, the other is a successful business woman in the USA
Domestic situation	Until marrying Michael Helen kept house for Jim and looked after his children (her grandchildren)
Work	Runs chauffeur business and oversees an Arts scholarship fund

Table 7.5 Constructing a character trait chart

Intelligent	X			Slow witted
Sociable	X			Unsociable
Warm	X			Cold
Active	X			Passive
Excitable			X	Calm
Hard			X	Soft
Dominant		X		Submissive
Pleasure orientated		X		Business orientated
Modern		X		Old fashioned
Mature	X			Immature
Moral	X			Immoral

   In this sequence we see Helen, who has moved through the stages of romance, engagement and, as she believed, marriage, facing single life again as a result of Michael's bigamy. This story-line is contrasted, in this episode, with that of Joe, who has suffered the loss of two previous partners and whose burgeoning romance with Melanie seems sure to end in marriage (which in fact it does). Even when *Neighbours* deals with wider social and political affairs such as the threatened closure of a local school – a story-line which was running at the same time as our episode and which is briefly mentioned in it – it will always concentrate on the effect such affairs have on the people involved. We would never expect to see, for instance, an analysis of broader events within the Australian educational system.

(iii)   Music   'Mood music', a basic feature of the melodrama, is used in our sequence to underline the emotional moment of Michael's confession of bigamy.

(iv)   Dramatic intensity   Family life in Ramsay street is never stable for long and the conflicts and heightened emotions found in our episode are typical of its melodramatic excess. Television critics often deride performances such as Helen's in this sequence, with its long stares of disbelief and harrowed expressions (all emphasised by the use of close-up shots), as 'ham acting'. Such criticism fails to accept the nature of the soap as a genre, and is really like criticising characters in a musical when they break into song. Melodramas and soaps seek to deal with the 'reality' of inner emotional life, as opposed to the realities of everyday existence. Certainly it is true that Helen, in this

sequence, gives a rather melodramatic performance; nevertheless it is the 'truth' of her emotional response that is uppermost, and it is here that melodramas and soaps find purchase upon our imagination.

Television soaps present everyday life in such a way that its moral dimensions and emotional aspects are emphasised, the main aim being that we recognise the authenticity of the feelings and experiences they present. They are not, therefore, simply an escape from the realities of daily life, but are, on the contrary, an amplification of the emotional dimension of everyday existence.

(v)   The domestic basis   Nearly all the crises that we find in soaps and melodramas have a family or domestic basis. This is why the action largely takes place either in the home (as in this sequence) or in public spaces in which the 'extended family' of the soap community can meet (Lassiters, the Waterhole or the Coffee Shop).

4   Genre and intertextuality

All genres exhibit what is known as intertextuality. This complicated sounding term refers simply to the fact that any media text (such as our episode of *Neighbours*) is 'read' in relationship to other texts. *Neighbours* has the main characteristics of a TV soap but it also has some of the qualities of a sitcom; in categorising it as a soap we are simply deciding which of its characteristics are the most significant. Increasingly, other television genres have adopted some of the aspects of the soap/melodrama form. As a police series, *The Bill* focuses on crime detection; however, it also deals with the relationship between characters in the confined world of the Sunhill police station, with its heightened emotional atmosphere. Furthermore, the extended family of the soap is mirrored by the 'Sunhill family' of police officers, with the station itself functioning as a family 'home'. There have also been a number of interesting soap hybrids over recent years. *Casualty* is a hospital-series-soap, while *Jimmy's* could probably be described as a documentary-hospital-series-soap! It is highly likely that this trend will continue, for it has proved an extremely successful way of winning large audiences at key points in the weekly schedule. The popularity in the early 1990s of the youth pop-soap, *Baywatch*, confirmed this.

There are a number of important conclusions that we must draw from our consideration of genre and classification. First, in terms of Narrative we have seen how the media industries organise their output into recognizable television genres – the soap, the sitcom and the police series – whose very generic status functions to contain and to regulate stories. What we mean by this is that although innumerable *Neighbours* plot-lines are possible – spy plots, underworld plots, etc. – only those which conform or relate to the 'typical' soap narrative will be employed. The reason for this, of course, is that an audience will only be drawn to this soap if the stories that it has to tell work within familiar codes and conventions. Although there is, as we pointed out above, an increasing trend towards hybridisation, it is important to emphasise that these new combinations, in order to succeed, must very carefully intertwine the conventions of each. If an audience is merely presented with an *ad hoc* combination of stylistic and generic forms the media text will hold no interest.

In part II of this chapter we will return to the media aspect of Audience in order to develop some of these points. Before this, however, we will look now at the aspect of Agency, for some of the facts relating to the genesis and scheduling of *Neighbours* will inform our discussion of Audience.

Step 6

Have I achieved a sufficiently complex sense of the media text?

Having examined soaps in relation to the important issues of Narrative and Audience we will now move on to the aspect of Agency. This area is often neglected by students when they write about soap operas, principally because the stories themselves can be so fascinating to discuss. However, it is always important to think about the various organisational factors involved in the making and transmission of any programme, and in order to do this successfully we suggest that you adopt the procedure of breaking down this aspect into the two areas, creative activity, and production and organisation as outlined in Chapter 2.

1   Creative activity

We will look first at the work of those responsible for developing the original programme. Ian Holmes, President and managing director of the Grundy organisation, and Reg Watson, head of TV drama at Grundy, decided to introduce a new soap during the 1984 season. Watson, the creative force behind *Neighbours*, thought that they should focus on everyday problems rather than heavy social issues:

I wanted to show three families living in a small street in a Melbourne suburb, who are friends. Humour was to play a big part in it and the important thing was to show young people communicating with older people. The characters will make mistakes. Quite often people do silly things and make stupid mistakes in their lives.

Watson had previously worked in the UK, where in 1964 he created the classic soap *Crossroads*, which ran for 24 years. In 1973 he returned to Australia to work for Reg Grundy, who was expanding his media portfolio from quizzes and gameshows to drama. At Grundy Productions Watson was the creative ideas man responsible for such serials as *Sons and Daughters*, *The Young Doctors*, *Neighbours*, and *Prisoner: Cell Block H*.

What we can see from this is that a single individual often plays a key role in the birth of a soap; Tony Warren, Phil Redmond and Julia Smith/Tony Holland were equally important in bringing, respectively, *Coronation Street*, *Brookside* and *EastEnders* to the screen. Their creative role and vision of the programme should not be neglected when discussing the issue of Agency.

2   Production and organisation

The Grundy Organisation, the Australian television company responsible for *Neighbours*, has produced, over a thirty-year period, more than eighty quiz/game shows and twenty-two drama series – more hours of TV than any other independent television company in the world. By 1990 an average of seventeen hours per week of British TV air time was given over to Grundy programmes, the majority of which were soaps.

Soaps are one of the most popular television genres; in the UK alone about 80 million viewer-hours are spent each week watching them. They are also popular with production companies and broadcasters for a number of reasons. First, they are comparatively cheap to produce as the same sets can be re-used many times; second, they are less of a financial risk because the size and demographics of their audience is known in advance; third, soap actors have contracts and fixed salaries (the short length of *Neighbours* contracts and its modest salaries have resulted in some stars leaving to pursue a stage career); and finally, the soap audience is a loyal one – even though viewers may miss episodes they still watch the programme on a fairly regular basis.

A number of factors of this kind lay behind the decision to introduce *Neighbours* to the British audience. In the first place the programme was thought to be suited to the tastes of the 1980s British audience. Barry Brown of the BBC's Purchased Programme department, who brought the soap to the UK stated:

> I thought it would appeal to women because it is a classless society. Living standards in Australia are high, and it's good to see ordinary people like Max the plumber or Des Clarke the young banker, living well without money problems.

Furthermore, financial considerations obviously played a significant part in the decision to introduce the soap. In 1988 five twenty-three-minute episodes of *Neighbours* cost the BBC a mere £27 000, whereas its own *EastEnders* was costing £40 000 an episode to produce. *Neighbours* proved to be a sound investment: in the first three weeks of 1988 its daily viewing figures were around 14 million and it occupied five of the ten places in the British top TV programmes.

3   Scheduling

When *Neighbours* went on air in Australia on 18 March 1985 it was aimed at the early evening audience who, up to that point, had only game shows and cartoons to choose between. Unfortunately, because of its scheduling and format, the soap had problems with its viewing figures almost from the start. Ian Holmes responded to these difficulties by convincing the executives of Australia's national Channel 10 Network that they could make the soap work better than Channel 7 (the network who were about to axe *Neighbours*) by making changes to its format, its characters and, most importantly, to its slot in the schedule.

Neighbours moved to the Channel 10 Network where the executives decided to screen it at 7p.m. and introduce more humour into the story-lines; according to a Grundy executive, '40 percent of the content was to be sitcom based.' However, the ratings were still low and the station's promotion chief had to be brought in. An intense publicity campaign followed that involved *Neighbours* personalities making regular appearances in Sydney shopping centres. This marketing strategy succeeded and soon millions of Australians were following it each weekday evening.

When *Neighbours* was first broadcast in Britain in October 1986, BBC executives were surprised by the fact that it quickly acquired an audience of approximately 6 million for its afternoon screening at 1.30p.m. The executives soon started to think about how *Neighbours* could be used in a prime-time slot to gain larger audiences, and, having decided to keep the lunchtime slot, they introduced in January 1988, a repeat showing at 5.35p.m. This attracted school-children who were by this time, back home. *Neighbours* doubled its viewing figures almost immediately, and by February 1988 was attracting 16.25 million viewers; only *EastEnders* was more popular, with an audience of 24 million (although by October 1992 this figure had dropped to 17 million).

It is easy to be blind to the way in which each of the above forces shaped the final form of *Neighbours*. These factors are, however, real and important ones, for they take us from the area of textual analysis to contextual analysis. The above factors relating to Agency may seem to you, at the outset, rather remote and abstract. Nevertheless, as we have seen, it is possible to analyse just how these organisational, institutional and financial factors play a central role in determining the final form of the programme. For example, using the above information alone, it is clear that television schedulers have to build the audience for the programme, and to do this they need to take many social, cultural and domestic factors into account. The success or failure of any media product is not determined solely by its own intrinsic qualities, but relies also, as we have seen, on careful media planning.

Students who are new to media studies often assume that the episode of a soap that they see on the screen is the realisation of the scriptwriter's ideas. This is, of course, true in one sense, simply because everything must start with a script of some kind; on the other hand, however, the writers of the script have to be very clear about the constraints within which they are working, all of which relate to the media aspect of Agency. Once you have begun to appreciate the close relationship between Agency as creative activity and Agency as organisation and institution you will be able to write about this area of media analysis as we have here. And this will allow you build a structured response to any text, using all the information you have gathered to feed in to your understanding and analysis of the text before you.

The danger in writing about soaps, of course, is that you will pay too much attention to the characters and stories, and too little attention to the way that the programmes achieve their effects and what makes them such successful products. The way to avoid drifting into character or story summaries

is to remind yourself of the sort of tensions soaps deal with (see Table 7.2) and how they are constructed. Work on a series of extracts that allow you to analyse not only their use of audience expectations of the soap genre, but also how soaps fit into the larger cultural framework of society.

II ASPECTS OF THE MEDIA TEXT: AUDIENCE

LOOKING back over our analysis so far, we are struck by the fact that although we have noted the spectacular success of *Neighbours*, particularly with younger viewers, we have not really accounted for why this should be so. We will concentrate in this section, therefore, on the media aspect of Audience.

Within weeks of *Neighbours* being shown on British TV pupils began to arrive late at school, having stayed home to catch the early morning or lunch-time instalment of their favourite soap. This caused something of a '*Neighbours* scare' in the press, with some articles portraying young people as hooked on a soap which was the TV equivalent of junk food. We need to put such worries in context. Almost since television began critics have voiced similar concerns. We will look now at the four most-commonly voiced concerns about the effects of TV, for they are views which you will often come across in communications and media studies.

1 'Television requires little sustained mental activity'

Some critics claim that because most TV programmes do not demand the same level of concentration as, say, a novel or a symphony, they are little more than 'chewing gum for the eyes' or 'flickering wallpaper', and that their audiences are little more than couch potatoes, uncritically consuming throw-away narratives.

2 'Television is addictive and can become a "plug-in-drug"'

The almost obsessive interest that some younger *Neighbours* fans have shown in their favourite soap stars (particularly during the heyday of Kylie Minogue and Jason Donovan), together with their craving for *Neighbours* memorabilia, fuelled fears that they were hooked on the programme.

3 'Television influences behaviour'

The fact that the 'Jason-look' and the 'Kylie-look' could be found in places as far apart as Brisbane and Barnsley and that Australian slang such as 'this arvo', 'tinnies', 'barbie' could be heard on British streets would seem to confirm this view. Indeed, if this view were incorrect, it would be questionable whether television companies would be able to attract such huge revenue from advertising.

4 'Television is a threat to family life'

It is often said that TV destroys family conversation and some have gone so far as to claim that the television set itself has itself become a child-minder, enabling parents to leave their children with the Ramsay Street regulars as they get on with something else.

These, as we said above, are common views you will encounter. As such, they are just the kind of views you may well be asked to discuss in an exam, or in an essay or project. To do this, you will need to consider the information about *Neighbours* and its audience, given in Table 7.6. This chart confirms the appeal that the programme has for the younger audience: over one-third of its total UK afternoon audience (17.35 million) are in the under-15 group.

Table 7.6   The percentage of under-15s watching the lunch-time and tea-time broadcasts of *Neighbours*

| | *13.30–13.50 (Wk 3–4)* | | | | | *17.35–18.00 (Wk 3–4)* | | | | |
	Mon	*Tue*	*Wed*	*Thu*	*Fri*	*Mon*	*Tue*	*Wed*	*Thu*	*Fri*
Age 4–7	1	2	2	2	3	10	9	9	10	9
8–11	1	1	1	1	2	11	12	11	12	13
12–15	3	2	3	3	3	14	14	12	13	13
All Children	5	5	6	6	8	35	35	32	35	35

Source: BARB/AGB (Wk 3–4) 1988.

This chart confirms the appeal that the programme has for the younger audience: over one-third of its total afternoon audience (17.35 million) are in the under-15 group.

The television industry must be familiar with the characteristics of its potential audience and be able to find out how much they enjoy and appreciate their product. A regular questionnaire asking viewers for their feelings about programmes is sent out by BARB, which broadcasters use for scheduling and general programming purposes. The BARB Reaction Service uses these responses to produce an Appreciation Index (or AI) which measures the audience satisfaction in percentage terms.

EastEnders is a good example of a soap whose improved AI performance was responsible for the rapid increase in its viewing figures. In its first month its AI was 58 (February 1985), after 3 months 70, and after 6 months 80. Its viewing figures soared, as a result, to 23 million. By 1989, however, it had been beaten in the AI index by *Neighbours*. Table 7.7 shows the Appreciation Index for the five main British soaps broken down into demographic groups:

Table 7.7   Appreciation Index for five main British soaps

	Overall AI	Male	Female	Age			Social Grade		
				12–34	35–54	55+	ABC1	C2	DE
Neighbours	78	74	80	80	75	77	76	79	79
Brookside	76	73	79	78	72	76	76	75	78
Emmerdale Farm	76	75	78	73	76	79	74	75	78
Coronation Street	76	71	78	74	74	77	73	75	77
EastEnders	71	67	74	71	70	73	68	71	74

Source: BBC 1989: no 34 (BBC (1989) *Annual Review of Broadcasting Research*, no. 15 (London: John Libbey, 1989).

[We outlined the way in which BARB breaks audience down into social Grades in Chapter 2, so look back to pp. 23 if you can't remember what each Social Grade in the above chart represents.]

Although the AI rating gives us an idea of audience preferences it does have some limitations. Because the results are based on responses to programmes that the AI panel have themselves chosen to watch (which means, of course, that it is highly likely that they like them!) the AI is always likely to be high, usually coming somewhere between 60 and 80. Furthermore, the calculations are based on limited coverage, with only about one-third of the programmes currently broadcast being used for AI surveys. Consequently, any conclusion that we may draw from such data needs to be tempered by a recognition of its imperfections. AI ratings give a good general indication of popularity but they are certainly not accurate enough to enable us to make irrefutable claims about the quality of programmes.

Having looked in a general way at the issue of audience appreciation as measured by the AI index, we will now look in a more focused way at the nature of the pleasures that soaps offer their audiences. In the 1940s a number of mass media researchers in America tried to identify the kinds of pleasure that radio soap operas offered their large audiences. Whereas earlier researchers had been mainly concerned with the harmful effects that the mass media may have on their audiences this new approach looked more closely at how people used the media and at the pleasures they derived from such use. This approach became known, as a result of this emphasis, as the '**Uses and Gratifications Theory**'. Four basic categories of need and gratification are most often identified:

(i)   The need to be diverted and entertained   We all 'use' TV as a form of enjoyable distraction. As we watch this episode of *Neighbours* we can escape from our daily routines and problems and become absorbed in the problems that Michael has caused Helen, in the burgeoning romance of Melanie and Joe and laugh at Madge and Harold's holiday preparations.

(ii)   The need for social interaction and personal relationship   Many people often switch on the television when they are in the house alone simply for company. Furthermore, we may come to look upon the regular cast of *Neighbours* as almost personal friends. Finally, insofar as we talk to other regular *Neighbours* viewers about the programme, it serves in some ways to cement personal relationships.

(iii)   The need to establish, maintain and assess one's sense of personal identity   Comparing the actions and beliefs of TV characters with our own is a natural process. By asking themselves 'What would I do in Joe's/Melanie's/Helen's/Jim's situation?' viewers are exploring and developing their own sense of personal identity.

(iv)   The need for information   We all use television to find out what is going on in the world. Whilst this category of 'need' is of less direct relevance to understanding *Neighbours*, soaps such as *EastEnders* and *Brookside* – which deal with contemporary issues such as unemployment and homelessness – can provide their audience with important information concerning these matters.

The emphasis that the 'uses and gratifications' approach placed on the active involvement of audiences with media texts was perhaps its most significant contribution; there are, however, a number of problems with it as a method of analysis. Because it concentrates on the gratifications that *Neighbours* might offer a viewer, wider social and ideological factors are ignored: clearly it is important to ask where these 'needs' come from and how and why they are sustained. Such questions go beyond the sphere of the individual's social and psychological needs. Furthermore, the approach ignores the fact that soaps, as media texts with their own structure, cannot be 'used' in any way that one pleases: media texts have structures of their own with which their audiences negotiate.

Soaps are conventionally associated with female audiences because of the domestic nature of their plot-lines. Daytime soaps are also scripted in such a way that they fit in with their female audience's daily domestic routine. Because women may be looking after a young child one moment and cleaning the next, soaps are structured in such a way that they do not require continuous attention (hence the importance of gossip as an 'updating' device). A number of stimulating and intriguing debates surround the issue of the relation between soaps and the female audience. However, given the constraints on space, all we can do here is to outline the main arguments. Some writers have claimed that because women are socialised in a particular way – being more likely to have a better understanding of family life, relationships and so on – so they are more able to appreciate these areas in soaps. Others have pointed out that gender differences also play a significant part in determining how we relate to TV characters: because women tend to have a wider number of roles – wife, mother, full/part-time employee, cook, cleaner and bottle washer, etc. – their own sense of personal identity is likely to be less rigidly defined than that of men. As a result, so it is often claimed, soap characters become, for their female fans, something of an on-screen 'family', people they may care about but do not identify with in any strong way.

In this final section we have given you a lot of information relating to the media aspect of Audience. But it is important that you remember that such details are only useful if you do build them into your developing argument. A simple listing of viewing figures or scheduling details is clearly not sufficient. As a media studies student you are expected to show how the audience is 'constructed' and positioned by market researchers and broadcasting organisations in the way that we have here. You will also need to account for the important role played by television in the creation of popular culture within our society, which is why we have focused particularly on the younger and female audiences of *Neighbours* in this section. Rather than present a simplistic view of the media as manipulators of the minds of their audience we have sought to show how different people negotiate their own meanings from TV soaps.

Notes

1. Details of the programme discussed in this chapter are as follows: Neighbours, Grundy Television; TX: Australia 1991, UK, 1992 (BBC1); Executive in Charge of Production: Peter Pinne; Executive Producer: Don Battye; Script Supervisor: Kay Kolle; Script Editors: Barbar Angell, Jason Daniel; Assistant Producer: Jan Russ; Production Manager: Reita Wilson; Television Presentation: Mike Frost, Tony Blake; Created by: Reg Grundy.

2. Sequence synopsis:
   Opening Sequence (repeated cliffhanger) The holiday complex (Plot-line 3).
   Title Sequence This consists of a simple street map of Erinsborough with the title *Neighbours* superimposed over it.
   Sequence 1 The Bishops' house at night (Plot-line 1). Madge reprimands Brenda for keeping Toby and Sky (Joe's children) up late. Brenda is due to take over the running of the Coffee Shop and her behaviour leads Madge to question whether she will be able to manage this.
   Sequence 2 The Robinson house (Plot-line 2). Helen and her new husband Michael have returned from their honeymoon in Greece and Italy. For some reason Jim looks slightly awkward.
   Sequence 3 Joe's hotel bedroom (Plot-line 3). Melanie and Joe are having breakfast in bed together. Romantic orchestral music accompanies their conversation.
   Sequence 4 The Bishop household (Plot-line 1). Harold and Madge make arrangements for the day as Brenda listens.
   Sequence 5 The Robinson household (Plot-line 2). Helen, her new husband Michael, and Jim discuss the tragedy of Josh's loss of eyesight in a recent accident. Jim then mentions that he has written to Michael's cousin, Alf, who had told him that Michael did not have a sister (Michael had been claiming that his wife was his sister).

Sequence 6   The Coffee Shop (Plot-line 2). Harold suggests that Brenda gets help in their absence. Madge and Harold talk to Helen and Michael and the awkwardness of their conversation indicates that they know that Michael is a bigamist.

Sequence 7   The holiday complex (Plot-line 3). In this pop-video-style montage sequence we first see Joe and Melanie pull up in a golf buggy, jump out and start a round of crazy golf. A highly romantic song dominates the soundtrack. After a few seconds on the golf course the shot dissolves to the swimming pool where Melanie emerges from the water to kiss the sleeping Joe. The sequence continues with them playing volleyball, and tennis, kissing on a pedalo and feeding ducks.

Sequence 8   The Coffee Shop (Plot-line 2). Gossip on Michael's bigamy.

Sequence 9   The Robinson household (Plot-line 2). Harold points out to Jim that Helen must be told about Michael's bigamy. Jim agrees to tell her.

Sequence 10   The Bishop household (Plot-line 1). More arrangements for the Bishops' planned holiday. Madge's expressions again show that she is not convinced about Brenda's ability to cope in their absence.

Sequence 11   The Bishop household (Plot-line 1). Toby says he will go to bed. Madge points out that it is not yet his bedtime. Toby admits that staying up late and doing what you wish is 'not all it's cracked up to be'.

Sequence 12   The Robinson house (Plot-line 2). Jim tells Michael that he knows about his bigamy and offers an ultimatum: either Michael tells Helen or he will.

Sequence 13   The holiday resort (Plot-line 3). Melanie and Joe discuss their future together.

Sequence 14   The Bishop household (Plot-line 1). Madge realises that Brenda had kept the children up late the previous night to show them why rules are necessary. Madge admires her astuteness and it is clear that the relation between them is much improved.

Sequence 15   The Robinson household (Plot-line 2). Michael tells Helen of his bigamy. A plaintive woodwind accompanies his confession. This sequence is the closing cliffhanger and will be repeated at the start of the next episode.

Credits   The credits roll over an exterior shot of Ramsay Street. Signature tune. This jaunty, sing-a-long *Neighbours* tune played no small part in establishing the programme's popularity in the early days. Very few British soaps then being broadcast actually had words accompanying the title music, unlike the *Neighbours* signature tune. The simplicity of the song made it memorable, and being repeated five times a week probably helped, too!

8

Writing an essay: the game show

I PREPARING AND WRITING A PROJECT FOR MEDIA OR COMMUNICATION STUDIES

WHEN you begin to put together an essay or project for media or communication studies, it is important that you appreciate, at the outset, what you are trying to achieve. This can be summed up in a single formula: **in any essay or project you are trying to build a clear argument either from the evidence of a media text itself or from your analysis of an important media issue.** If you follow the advice in this chapter, you will be able to research, prepare and write fluent, coherently-argued essays which will be analytical and personal responses to the topic you have to address.

However, we are also aware of the practical problems faced by students when preparing the hard data upon which their essays or projects will be based. Because of this, we have chosen to give you detailed practical advice here, rather than merely offering some stylistic tips. Also, in order to give our comments greater focus, we will be analysing television game shows and quizzes in this chapter to demonstrate how you can organise a response to this form of media output.

As we saw in Chapter 2, Construction is always a good place to start, because it can help us to identify some fairly straightforward points. The simplicity of the points themselves can provide a ground for more detailed analysis. Usually, you will need either to produce a clear, detailed synopsis of the sequence you wish to analyse, or to produce a storyboard of the opening sequence, or to take photographic stills from the television to accompany your project.

Although taking photographic stills from a television is quite a straightforward process, students often make simple mistakes which lead to very unsatisfactory results. Most commonly, a photographic image taken from a television screen will be virtually indecipherable, because of a series of bars across the screen. These bars cannot be seen on the television when you take the photograph, but they are certainly there when you process your film! The reason for the appearance of the bars is the speed at which the television tube, or screen, is scanned by an electronic beam twenty five times per second. There is an easy way around the problem, however. All you have to do is this:

1. Use a 35mm camera with a 50mm lens and a 100 ISO colour film or 125 ISO black-and-white film. Do not use a fully automatic camera. You will need to use a camera which allows you to set the shutter speed and lens aperture. Mount the camera on a tripod or on a solid support.
2. Position the camera at a distance that will make the TV screen fill the viewfinder (ensuring that the camera is square on to the screen) and focus the image.
3. Make sure that no lights are being reflected on the screen (close the curtains and turn off the room lights if necessary).
4. Set the camera to 1/15 second and f5.6 (ask your teacher or a technician if you are unsure about this). The 1/15 second setting is slower than the time taken for the beam to scan the tube, and this means that you will miss the bars scanning down the screen. We have found that 1/15 second is the slowest practical speed to use. If you use a shutter speed slower than this, then the resulting image is likely to be blurred because of movement on the screen.
5. Using the pause button on your VCR pause the tape at about twenty seconds before the image you wish to photograph.
6. Set the tape into play mode and return to your camera and wait for the correct frame to arrive and carefully press the shutter (use a cable release for this to avoid camera wobble).

You can then use your stills to analyse the opening sequence of a programme, just as we have been recommending all along. A good way to begin on this analysis is, as ever, to note the kinds of information connoted alongside each image.

Blockbusters: opening sequence

Image 1   The World
Connotations   World events, knowledge, facts, truth.

Image 2 A hexagon motif (the *Blockbusters* scoreboard grid)
Connotations Science and mathematics. These hexagons are produced using computer graphics and fly through three dimensional space. This suggests Star Wars type sci-fi movies
Image 3 The flying hexagons move through a futuristic cityscape in which the buildings are hexagonal
Connotations Advanced civilisation, progress
Image 4 The flying hexagons move down a corridor which we take to be located in the studio and return to the *Blockbusters* scoreboard
Connotations It is as if the hexagons have returned to the 'mothership' of the studio (in the game itself each hexagon represents an item of knowledge)
Image 5 Swirling sculpted reliefs of Isambard Kingdom Brunel (the great Victorian engineer), Albert Einstein (the physicist who developed the theory of relativity), God the Father (copied from Michaelangelo's Sistine Chapel figures)
Connotations 'Our' great Western tradition with its engineering prowess (Brunel), science (Einstein), art (Michaelangelo), and religion (God the Father)

Another way to take a visual image from a television screen involves the use of a computer running suitable software. The precise details of how a televisual image is taken from the screen will depend upon the software you are running, but, simply stated, what happens is that the video input is converted by the computer to digitised information, capable of being displayed on a computer screen. This can then be either stored on disk or downloaded via a suitable printer to provide a print-out of the visual image. You will have to check with your teachers and technicians whether you have access to a computer and the software necessary to extract an image in this way, although it is clear that the use of personal computers in media and communications studies will become increasingly important in the future as a means of storing and retrieving graphic images. Whichever method you use to extract hard data in the form of visual stills, however, you must always return to the job in hand: the analysis of the media text. It is the way that you analyse the television output that will really impress the examiner, not just the quality of your stills or computer-generated images.

II   BLOCKBUSTERS

IN an analysis, for example, the main points that we would bring out in an essay on the opening to this programme are:

1. Its attempt to fuse the worlds of knowledge and culture with the world of youth culture;
2. Its ethnocentricity – 'our' culture, history, traditions and religion are brought to the fore.

These simple insights can then be developed in many different ways. If we wished to explore the programme's appeal to a youth audience we could point to the way in which the opening sequence imitates both the graphics of an arcade video game and the imagery of a sci-fi movie. On the other hand, if we wanted to discuss the opening sequence in a broader way that would allow us to connect this media text to its wider cultural context, we could point out that the use of such established icons of western civilisation and culture as Michelangelo and Einstein function to define art and knowledge – core concerns of the quiz show – in terms of Western culture. Having identified these central issues, you are now in a position to develop your analysis further.

Most of the writing with which you will be involved in media and communications studies will ask you to develop an argument. Many students find this type of essay intimidating because it asks them to do more than either impart information or to give a subjective response to a media text. Information and personal interpretation do play a part in writing such an essay, but their role is, mainly, a supporting one. Your main objective in writing an essay is to develop a thesis or argument in order to explain your interpretation of a certain programme or media issue, based upon your own close analysis.

In order to find a thesis or argument relating to a television game show we need to ask some general questions that relate to our five media aspects. For example, if we now turn to another type of quiz show, *Mastermind*, we can see, just by looking at the opening sequence, that we can consider the programme in terms of its setting, the NVC of the game show host or the type of camera work, all of which relate to our media aspect of **Construction**. If we decided to look at *Mastermind* in terms of this media aspect we would note the following issues:

1. the use of a university or historic setting for each episode;
2. the isolated spotlit *Mastermind* chair in which each contestant will be put to the test;
3. the slow zoom in on the contestant's face as s/he answers the questions;
4. the darkness of the auditorium (once the question sessions begin);
5. the positioning of the question-master, Magnus Magnusson, to the front and side of the contestant.

Alternatively, we may ask, focusing on the aspect of **Audience**, what it is about the game show that holds our attention. Here we would note the following points:

1. *Mastermind* invites its audience to participate. The viewer also can 'win' or 'lose' as s/he answers questions with the contestants.
2. *Mastermind* invites its audience to judge the performance of others. As the camera slowly zooms in on the contestant we can assess their ability to stand up to the strain of the inquisition.
3. The studio audience remain silent witnesses to the performances of others. This ties in precisely with Construction (setting, props, etc. – polite applause is all that can be allowed in the hallowed University setting) – but implies other things about, for example, the nature of the audience for the programme, who, it is assumed, will appreciate the air of solemnity and gravity that surrounds the proceedings.

Our five controlling concepts enable us to say a number of things about *Mastermind*. First, in terms of Construction, its fixed format – hardly anything has changed since it was first broadcast in the 1970s – make it relatively easy to discuss in terms of the technical codes of camera work, lighting, etc. Second, it successfully involves its Audience by emphasising the formal, almost ceremonial, testing that the candidates endure. Third, its simple Narrative structure can be understood almost immediately – four contestants, time limits, specialist topic followed by general knowledge and so on. Fourth, it can be Categorised as a particular form of television output and compared with other quiz shows. And finally, in terms of Agency, the programme can be discussed in terms of its position within the BBC schedule.

III   TYPES OF TASK IN AN ESSAY

OF course, deciding which aspect of the game show it is that you want to consider will influence the way in which you approach the topic: an essay on *mise-en-scène* in quiz shows will be organised differently from an essay in which you want to compare the way in which different game shows relate to the issue of Audience. The main point to remember is that you must find the organisational structure that is most appropriate for the topic that you want to analyse. This is because the various media studies essays that you will tackle as part of your course will all involve different kinds of intellectual tasks. The following are the ones that you are most likely to encounter:

1. *Interpretation*   This is one of the main activities with which Media Studies students are engaged, which is why we have chosen to concentrate on it throughout this book. By examining the signs, codes and narrative organisation of media texts we are able to comment on their 'meanings'. Remember that such meanings are always plural: no media text, as we have pointed out many times, has a single meaning.
2. *Clarification*   Some essay titles in media and communications studies will require you to clarify what is meant by a particular concept contained in the title itself. If, for instance, you were asked to comment upon the claim that television game shows were a threat to 'quality' programmes, you would have to outline the nature of the 'quality' debate by making reference, where appropriate, to such notions as high and low culture and to the various theoretical approaches taken to the issue.
3. *Evaluation*   This is the type of essay which asks you to look at some controversy in media studies. You may have been set the following essay topic: '*Game shows are banal, trivial and an insult to their audience. Discuss.*'

There are many ways in which you might approach this question. You may, at the outset, point out what can be said in support of such a view: game shows are indeed simple and formulaic. If you start by noting what can be said in support of such a view you are indicating that you understand why someone might hold such an opinion. This is often better than merely attacking their position as wrongheaded.

Similarly, let us suppose that your teacher or lecturer gave you the following essay topic: '*Game shows, Soaps and repeats are likely to pose a significant threat to quality television over the course of the next decade. Comment.*' This is a common type of question, and one which is commonly poorly done by students. The best place to start is by looking closely at the title and asking yourself a number of questions relating to it.

1.   What exactly is a game show?

It is important, at the outset, to identify the main characteristics of this form of television output. Competition, fun and prizes are always involved, and the proceedings are supervised by a game-show host. Traditionally, British game shows have tended to be fairly light-hearted affairs, in which taking part rather than winning is the main objective. American game shows, on the other hand, tend to be fiercely competitive, winning being the sole aim. In the 1980s a number of ITV game shows followed the raucous style of the American programmes on which they were based. Although these have waned in the 1990s, BBC game shows have, in the main, remained focused on the camaraderie brought about by the occasion.

2.   Why might game shows be taken to constitute a threat, and to what?

Game shows attract large audiences and, therefore, substantial advertising revenue. This, combined with the fact that they are relatively cheap to produce, using a standard format and setting, makes them more economically viable than other forms of programme. They thus pose a threat to more expressive 'quality' output which may generate less advertising revenue. Like any other industry within capitalist society, the television industry involves (a) substantial capital investment; (b) high technology; (c) job specialisation and (d) production and distribution. Each of these factors, all relating to the media aspect of Agency, are important determinants of the final form of any game show.

In order to understand more fully the nature of this apparent threat we could therefore go on to consider the important differences that exist between the USA and the UK in the organisation of television scheduling. In the USA the larger viewing channels tend to schedule the same genres in the same time-slots; a game show in the USA would be up against a rival game show and a police series against a rival police series. This is done because each of the channels is in direct competition for the same demographic audience group. As a result, the viewer is left with a narrower choice of programmes than the ones available in the UK. However, it could be argued that the competition resulting from having programmes of the same genre scheduled against each other has led to a general improvement in their quality. At the time of writing, British television has far fewer channels than are available in America. Also, the public-service ethos of the BBC is still a significant force in broadcasting in this country, although the changes brought about by the Government and by John Birt since his appointment as Director-General of the BBC in 1992 look set to change this ethos significantly.

3. What is 'quality' television?

Most people take 'quality' to mean documentaries and serious drama. Many column inches will be devoted in the media press to such output and it will be accorded the same status as any other significant artistic or cultural form. Defenders of quality television see game shows as mindless nonsense, a view which others condemn as highbrow and elitist. It is certainly true that we all judge, evaluate and criticise media texts; indeed, one of the main pleasures that television offers us is that it enables us all to become critics, expounding our views and judging the outpourings of the media industries in just the same way that, say, Clive James does. It is therefore quite ironic that most media studies textbooks fail even to raise the issue of quality when dealing with television. It is often argued that we cannot discuss the issue of quality because of the very personal nature of evaluative criteria – who is to say what is good TV? It is understandable, therefore, that many writers within the field of media studies avoid these issues altogether. This can represent a real problem to a student, simply because the student is quite likely to be asked to discuss the very issue which most media theorists themselves carefully and neatly side-step.

All too often, students 'solve' the problems caused by this thorny issue of quality by asserting that a game show, say, is 'just as good as' a television adaptation of *King Lear*, which, if you think about it, means very little. The phrase 'as good as' is, in fact, being used here in such a way as to imply an élitist view in asking the question at all. While we would be the first to criticise the snobbery shown by those who claim that television programmes are intrinsically inferior to other works of art, we do not feel that it is sensible to redress the balance by giving everything an equal status. As a media studies student you need to recognise at the outset both the complexity of this issue of quality and also that there is no one measure by which we may compare and judge cultural forms as different as Elizabethan

tragedies and game shows. Media texts are produced in circumstances that are very different from those that characterise the
production of novels, plays, poems and paintings; they are also
funded in different sorts of ways and seen by a different kind of
audience. Therefore, when attempting to discuss a game show in
terms of issues of quality, we need to bear in mind a number of factors
that relate to the media aspect of Agency. It is, in consequence, very
important that you examine the precise wording of any question or
topic that makes some reference to the issue of quality in order to be
sure about precisely what you are being asked to do.

4. Why is the next decade of particular significance?
Clearly reference is being made here to the numerous changes that
are taking place in both the media industries themselves and also in
broader Government legislation. On the one hand, it might be
argued that satellite and cable television, together with increasing
deregulation, will lead to greater choice and an increase in minority
programming. On the other hand, there are clear indications that
financial forces within the media industries themselves will ensure
that repeats and cheap programmes such as game shows will fill the
schedule.

There is something to be said for both sides here and it would be
rash to think that we can, at this moment in time, predict the outcome.
For this reason it can sometimes be better, in an essay, to weigh up the
pros and cons and to leave the reader to decide. More often, though,
you will need to decide whether the evidence supports one side of the
argument more than the other, and you will, as a result, have to come
out on that particular side when you conclude your essay.

Another thing to remember is that there is not such a thing as an
easy question or a difficult question. The above question on game
shows seems a fairly straightforward one, and this can deceive
students into thinking that their answer can be loose and chatty. The
point to realise about questions, however, is that they are always
asking you to consider one or more of the key media aspects –
Construction, Audience, Narrative, Categorisation, Agency – that we
have dealt with in this book. In order to help you to organise your
answer, lecturers and examiners select a particular aspect or aspects –
in this instance those of Agency and Audience – and you must take
care to concentrate on those aspects in your essay. But your answer
must, where appropriate, be informed by a larger sense of the topic
that the other five media concepts will allow you to consider.

PLANNING YOUR ESSAY

WE will now look more closely at how to analyse a game show, moving from your first tentative notes to an essay draft. Start by analysing a short sequence from near the beginning of the programme, then select a second, a third, a fourth sequence, just as we have done in each of our chapters. This will help you to clarify your thinking about the programme by seeing a larger pattern at work. Suppose, for example, you have been set the following topic:

'Comment on the main differences between a specialist high-brow television quiz programme (such as Mastermind*) and a popular game show (such as* The Generation Game*). In your answer you should focus on any broader cultural issues (such as gender or class) that you consider to be relevant.'*

What you are being asked to do here is to contrast two related forms of media output, an activity that clearly involves you in tackling issues related to the media aspect of Categorisation. This aspect often presents students with particular difficulties because it demands a good working understanding of the other media aspects of Audience, Narrative and Agency. It is important that you remember that the Categorisation of media texts should not be a pigeon-holing exercise, and in fact no hard-and-fast line can be drawn between the quiz and game show forms. Nevertheless, there are considerable differences between the two forms you have been asked to look at. Your first task, therefore, is to identify these differences (bearing in mind that you are also required to discuss these programmes from a broader cultural perspective). This is how you can go about writing an essay on this topic:

1. *Watch and rewatch the quiz programme and game show you have selected*
   This first step is an extremely important one. Having recorded the programmes on video you will need to watch them through a number of times, even if they are programmes you have seen many times before.
2. *Identify the topic* To do well in media or communication studies you need to acquire the ability to recognise the central topic in questions such as this. It is clearly not enough to put down everything that you know about quiz programmes and game shows. You have been asked to comment upon the differences between two related forms of media output, and to write about

these in relation to the issue of class, gender, etc. The question set points toward this specific topic, and, however well you write, you will gain no credit unless you actually discuss this. The question we have given here might seem relatively easy. The point to realise about such questions, however, is that they are always asking you about central issues relating to one or other of the key media aspects. As we have already pointed out, in order to help you to organise your answer, lecturers, teachers and examiners often indicate a particular aspect or issue – in this instance Categorisation – and you must concentrate on this aspect. **Nevertheless, your answer must also be informed by a larger sense of the topic that the other key media aspects allow you to consider. This might seem difficult, but it is not: all the earlier chapters of this book have stressed the importance of understanding the broader structure of a media text, how it deals with wider ideas or issues that are central in our culture, such as class, gender, and the family.**

3. *View the programmes again*   You now need to start looking for the main elements that enable you to categorise these media texts, as this is what the question is asking you to do. As programmes produced for television they will share the codes and conventions that typify this medium. A preliminary consideration of any differences between them at the level of Construction will therefore be a good place to start. Next you might turn your attention to the programmes as entertainment media forms (as opposed to dramas or documentaries). Certainly they are both entertaining in their own ways but there are significant differences in the kinds of pleasure that they offer their audiences. By noting just what you think these differences are, you will be able to refine your analysis of their Categorisation. Clear notes are all you need to write at this stage. Here are the sorts of things we would note about different quiz and game shows:

(a) Looking first at the area of *mise-en-scène* analysis (a dimension of the aspect of Construction), we notice a number of differences between the visual appearance of popular game shows and 'highbrow' quizzes. Popular game shows tend to have brightly lit, elaborate, colourful settings, whereas subdued colours and lighting and relatively simple sets are the norm for quizzes of the 'highbrow' type.

(b) Moving on to technical codes (another dimension of Construction) we note that both quizzes and game shows make frequent use of close-up shots of the contestants. However, such shots play a slightly different role in each. Close-ups are used in quizzes to reveal whether contestants can survive the ordeal of quick-fire questioning without showing emotion; in game shows, on the other hand, they are employed to emphasise the emotional responses of contestants.

You have now watched a game show and a quiz show, and noted some basic differences at the level of Construction in order to prepare your answer to this 'compare and contrast' style essay. In comparing the two shows, it is interesting to note that they both depend upon questioning some aspect of the contestant's knowledge. But how, precisely, is knowledge defined by each show? In quizzes such as *University Challenge*, *Mastermind* and *The Krypton Factor*, based on general and specialist knowledge, the honour of winning is more important than any prize that may be attached to this. Knowledge and skill are thus deemed valuable in their own right and you might wish to connect this to issues of Audience by pointing to the slightly more middle-class nature of such programmes. This is quite easy to do. Clearly, *University Challenge* offered its audience the opportunity of seeing the country's 'brightest and best' – future leaders of industry, politicians, and so on – compete against each other; in *Mastermind* the erudite display their abilities while, in *The Krypton Factor*, yuppie-type-strivers utilise the array of conceptual and physical skills that have secured their success within their respective professions.

Having identified this aspect you may then go forward and link it to the definition of success as being the result of 'individual effort' (which is itself an interestingly middle-class attitude). To back up this point you can point to the fact that these quizzes test the contestants' ability to recall facts quickly and accurately and under pressure. You can then enlarge on this theme by pointing out that knowledge is defined in such programmes in a way that links it with traditional ideologies of education: answers are either right or wrong, and, as a result, no questions can be set which suggest that there may be more than one interpretation of events. You might then go on to point out that alongside this broadly middle-class framework such programmes also exhibit a meritocratic aspect. Everyone, it seems, has an equal opportunity to win if they have the talent and ability. This is why much was made of the success of Fred Housego the London taxi driver who won *Mastermind*, and who went on to become, for a while, something of a media celebrity. Any differences that might exist between contestants in terms of their class, educational or cultural background do not, it is made to seem, determine their performance on the show.

Having looked through the current television schedule you note that there are a number of quizzes based not on the specialist knowledge that we have just considered but upon 'common knowledge' and popular opinion. Examples of these are: *Play Your Cards Right, Family Fortunes, Blankety Blank*. Okay, you might be saying, these seem to be more light-hearted but what exactly should I say about them? A good way to deal with this issue is by considering just how knowledge is defined within these programmes. Frequently, public opinion replaces factual knowledge, the 'correct answer' being one which an opinion poll of a particular group ('we asked one hundred bus drivers', or 'we asked the studio audience') revealed. Since popular common sense – what we all know – replaces specialist knowledge, everyone has an equal chance of winning. And this, of course, will enable you to return to the areas of class and ideology at which you looked in the more formal quiz programmes.

In media studies the concept of hegemony is often used to discuss this whole issue of common sense, of everything that we take to be unarguable, natural and true. It is, therefore, a concept you are likely to employ when analysing quizzes of this type. The first point that you might make here is that 'public opinion' quizzes of this kind came to the fore in Britain in the 1980s, a period when the politics of Thatcherism was dominant or 'hegemonic'. Many writers are agreed that one of the key reasons for the success of this particular hegemony lay in its support for the beliefs, values and innate good sense of the 'man in the street', as opposed to the opinions of 'boffins', 'bureaucrats' and other 'so-called' experts. It may be appropriate for you to claim, therefore, that some of the quizzes of the period reflect this hegemonic move in their focus on popular, rather than specialist, knowledge.

After you have thought about the nature of television quiz programmes and the issues of class and hegemony, you can clarify your ideas still further by contrasting TV quizzes with game shows such as *The Generation Game, Blankety Blank, The Price is Right, Bob's Full House* and *Celebrity Squares*. One of the first things you might notice is that these feature ordinary members of the public competing for big prizes. In others, single contestants battle it out. The next thing that may strike you is that the game show is more light-hearted, often using the games and contests as a pretext for comic banter between host and contestants. Having noticed this, it is now quite straightforward to return to the broader theme of working-class culture and to make some point about this issue.

For example, British game shows such as *The Generation Game*, a 1970s hit that was resurrected in the 1990s, tend to celebrate values that are central to traditional working-class experience. They are not far removed from such traditional forms of working-class entertainment as the music hall, bingo, variety theatre and seaside end-of-the-pier shows. In order to show that this is the case all you have to do is to point out that such game shows show considerable concern for the loser: taking part, being willing to be made to look a fool but accepting this like a 'good sport' is generally more important than winning. Placing *The Generation Game* in relation to earlier forms of entertainment in this way will enable you to write about this game show in a much more perceptive light, allowing you to discuss a variety of cultural, social and historical factors. American game shows, in contrast, tend to be more harshly competitive (the American game show *Family Feuds* was re-christened *Family Fortunes* in order to make it fit for the British market), and winning is everything.

Clearly, such differences are determined in important ways by the differences between the political and ideological frameworks of the two countries (the 'dog-eat-dog' ethos of some Japanese game shows takes this primitive raw competition even further). The ability to relate a quiz or game show to prevailing political and ideological trends in this way, is one that students often find difficult to achieve; it seems hard enough to write about a quiz or game show in terms of Construction or Categorisation without also having to relate these media aspects to wider cultural trends. Nevertheless, if you wish to proceed to more advanced responses to essay assignments you will have to gain confidence in this. To begin with you might point out that because most contemporary capitalist societies 'naturalise' both democratic ideologies (which assert that we all have an equal chance to reach the top) and meritocratic ideologies (that insist that only those with talent and ability will 'make it'), so viewers tend to assume that quiz-show winners succeed as a result of their own merits. In consequence, they tend to forget about the social and cultural inequalities that exist between, say, the working class and the middle class.

The concept of hegemony is also likely to be useful to you here, for it enables you to emphasise the fact that ideology is an active process: although game shows strive to position certain groups of viewers – housewives, for instance – as powerless consumers, it has to be recognised that their consent to their own subordination can never be fully secured. This, you may then go on to point out, is because a complex process of negotiation between the game show and its audience is always in operation: the viewer is actively involved in making meanings, s/he does not passively receive a fixed message. Thus, although a game show may, in itself, be the bearer of a materialist ideology, making it seem that all that matters is wealth and possessions, its viewers may be at odds with and may challenge this outlook. In conclusion, you can emphasise the fact that although the dominant class may always have the upper hand, its influence can be resisted by some sectors of society.

After thinking about the ways in which game shows and quizzes differ in terms of their definition of knowledge, you might then want to look at the way that the treatment of contestants differs in these two forms. You will almost certainly notice that quiz-masters such as Magnus Magnusson and Bamber Gasgoigne are much more restrained than game-show hosts such as Bob Monkhouse, Terry Wogan, Michael Barrymore and Bruce Forsyth. Although the latter may seem to dominate the proceedings more, it is noticeable that any power relations between host and contestant are played out in a 'fun' way. For instance, Bruce Forsyth's catchphrase, in the early stages of his career, was 'I'm in charge', a send-up of the posturing, dominant, self-important boss that working-class audiences would appreciate.

When the game-show host walks onto the set he is greeted by applause and it is his task to see that things run smoothly; the hard work that went into preparing the show must not be noticeable, an air of easy exuberance must pervade the show. The host explains the proceedings and introduces the contestants and is the only one who can talk directly to the camera. This gives him the opportunity to establish a rapport with the viewing audience. If contestants were to do this the special 'I–You' relationship established between viewer and host would be lost.

The next thing you are likely to notice is that there are very few female presenters on quiz or game shows (Angela Rippon in *Masterteam* and Sarah Kennedy in *Busman's Holiday* are the exceptions). Generally the hosts are male, white and middle-aged, their personality being central to the creation of the show's atmosphere. This is an important moment, for you have now arrived at an important stage and can start to put together your earlier comments on class, which emphasised that television defines what appears to us to be normal, natural and simply 'common sense' with an analysis of issues of gender by pointing out that game shows usually only have women as assistants (*The Generation Game* being a good example of this). This is not to say that the media are simply the mouthpiece for the ruling class or the patriarchy; nevertheless it is clear that such views and values are quite likely to be unconsciously encoded by the white male, middle-aged, heterosexual, middle-class professionals who occupy many of the positions of power within the media industries

Having looked in detail at the style of the game-show host and at the broader issues of class and hegemony we will look finally at the differences between the treatment of quiz-show contestants and game-show participants. First, we notice that the latter are much more at the mercy of the show's host who may, if s/he so chooses, embarrass him/her. Second, we perceive that at one moment the host acts as the boss of the show, putting contestants in their place, whilst at others he acts as a jolly uncle (a dual role that has its origins in the end-of-the-pier-show). The contestants, in turn, are encouraged to show off their personalities and to act in a showbiz way; they are usually given time by the host to say something about themselves, and this is just what happens in traditional variety shows. We find out that they are just like us, and, as a result, we can identify with them and wonder what we would do in their position.

What you will have begun to see by now is the way in which you can make some quite broad social and cultural comments on a game show based on the evidence of fairly specific aspects of a programme such as the style of the introductory sequence, the mode of address of the game-show host, and the role of the contestants. The whole point of this chapter is to suggest that this same method will help you to answer any question, and answer it really well. This is what is so good about this kind of systematic approach: it allows you the freedom to develop your own ideas; having a clear essay method allows you to be inventive because you know that you are building a sensible argument from the evidence of the game show itself. As ever, the five key aspects of media studies – Construction, Audience, Categorisation, Narrative, Agency – provide you with a basic framework on which to build your analysis.

Now you have etablished the main areas you wish to cover and decided on their ordering, your task is half done. You have arrived at a thesis, mustered relevant evidence, and begun to organise your final essay. You will, of course, revise your thoughts as you re-read your own notes or first draft of your essay. Do not think of these initial efforts as a waste of time; it is only by re-thinking and modifying your material as you proceed that you will arrive at a more coherent presentation of your ideas about a media text. Having completed the research and produced the outline of your essay you can begin a final draft.

V   WRITING YOUR ESSAY

BEFORE moving on we will remind you once again of the essay topic. This was 'Comment on the main differences between a specialist highbrow television quiz programme (such as *Mastermind*) and a popular game-show (such as *The Generation Game*). In your answer you should focus on any broader cultural issues (such as gender or class) that you consider to be relevant.'

Now that you have decided on the general outline of your answer, you now need a clear argument, which will serve as the basis for this essay asking you to compare quiz and game shows, focusing on broader cultural issues. Your thesis will be a claim relating to the programme's meanings and effects in relation to the media aspect of Categorisation. Do not make the mistake of thinking that this argument (or thesis) has to be the last word on the essay topic you are tackling. In your first paragraph, then, you can outline the basic argument you are going to put forward. Your thesis might be that, in their different ways, quiz programmes and game shows celebrate *status quo* values: quizzes because they celebrate a very traditional view of knowledge, and game shows because they exalt the consumerism of capitalist society. Clearly, such a thesis is a very general claim about the programmes you are discussing, and your analysis will need to develop and refine this argument. So we have on the one hand a clear statement about the nature of such programmes, but on the other some areas to develop in the rest of the essay.

The second paragraph can then be devoted to comparing the formality and restraint of the 'serious' quiz programme with the light-hearted informality of the game show. First, you will need to say something about the media texts you have chosen to study. Your opening paragraph will have identified the issue for discussion, now is the time to refer specifically to concrete details to back up this argument. After that, start to discuss what strikes you as particularly important in the extract, given your thesis. You are looking for points relevant to the question. Having described and analysed the extract in this way, you then need to tie the paragraph together with a sentence or two of conclusion. These will need to confirm the validity of your impressions and analysis so far, but will also need to lead on to other aspects that you think are important to the question.

So, in this second paragraph, you might, for instance, consider the different ways in which knowledge and skills are defined and celebrated in the programmes you have chosen to look at. The winner of a *Mastermind* heat receives the polite applause of the audience and the warm but restrained congratulation of Magnus Magnusson. The winners of *The Generation Game* on the other hand are likely to get a hug from Bruce Forsyth and rapturous applause from the audience. Always make sure that you stand back and sum up what you have established so far at the end of a paragraph by forcing yourself to write two or three sentences of conclusion. This will ensure that you are answering the question that has been set, and will help to push along an argument in your essay.

These concluding sentences will trigger off your next paragraph. For example, the logical starting-place for your next paragraph on this essay topic in which you are comparing game shows with quizzes might be a contrast between the celebration of taking part, being a 'good sport' and family or communal values in a game show such as *The Generation Game* with the emphasis on individual success found in quiz programmes such as *Mastermind* or *The Krypton Factor*.

In the next three or four paragraphs you can work your way through the various aspects of the quiz programme and game show which you identified earlier, such as the way in which the contestants are treated or the difference between game-show hosts and quiz-programme question-masters. Again, describe the extract, then comment on its significance in relation to the question. As your answer progresses, providing you take care to sum up at the end of each paragraph, you should discover that you are getting to grips with the larger issues of class and culture in relation to the programmes you are studying.

The questions to ask yourself at the start of each paragraph are, 'is there another aspect to this question that I have not considered yet ?', and 'is there something that contradicts what I have said so far?'. This will help you to give your essay a real sense of analysis, as you weigh up the evidence and try to refine your opening paragraphs into a more subtle discussion of the question. By the time you reach your concluding paragraph there should be very little left to say, as the thoroughness of your analysis along the way will have covered all the worthwhile points.

You might, however, feel a little hesitant about writing your concluding paragraph, as, having worked through a number of extracts, you will have developed a substantial and detailed argument and may not know what to put to round it off. All you have to do is to sum up the answer to the question set, the answer you have finally reached. It is important to remember that your lecturer or examiner will want to see you finish your essay in a tight and controlled way. This clear statement of your central argument is, therefore, very important; consequently, you should avoid spending your last paragraph describing a relatively minor aspect such as lighting or editing style.

VI TACKLING DIFFICULT AREAS

THE time will come when you want to make your essays more sophisticated than the relatively straightforward one that we have just described. Although the aims of such an essay are fairly obvious, you will need a considerable amount of practice to see clearly what you are aiming for in an essay of this nature, and to arrive at the point where you can easily demonstrate the argument you want to make. Your progression to more in-depth answers can only be a natural development over a considerable period of time, as you become more assured in your understanding and application of the five media aspects we have considered in this book.

The objective of a more complicated essay on quiz programmes and game shows should be to show the complexity of these media texts. This is not to say that they are in themselves making a profound statement: it is as well to keep in mind that you are dealing with a highly formulaic entertainment genre here. Nevertheless, like all other media texts, they can give rise to almost endless new analyses and interpretations.

The first point that we wish to make is that you cannot accomplish this task of writing a more complicated essay overnight. Confidence must clearly precede sophistication. As you analyse more media texts, the likelihood is that you will find that you begin to say more complex things in your essays. In this section, we will look briefly at how you can develop some ideas by discussing quiz programmes and game shows in terms of the media aspect Audience, extending and integrating these two areas of concern by relating them to a fairly complex media concept that we have not introduced as yet: **discourse**.

A discourse is, quite simply, a socially constructed way of considering a particular topic. The term is used in media studies when discussing the way in which established 'common-sense' ideas about gender, race, class, age and the family are dealt with by the media. Thus we might say that an episode of a quiz show articulates dominant (i.e. middle-class) discourses concerning class, while game shows articulate dominant discourses relating to the family. A discourse thus involves a number of shared assumptions which appear in its formulations (i.e. in a quiz or game show), assumptions of which those who articulate this discourse (an individual or a broadcaster) will be largely unaware.

Discourses can be thought of as signifying systems (see our comments in Chapter 3 on semiotics) responsible for the production of meaning in society in general and the media in particular. As a game show is likely to be made up of a number of discourses – relating to class, gender, pleasure, consumerism, etc. – your first task is to identify those in the particular programme you may have chosen to study. Next you need to consider just how viewers make sense of or 'read' such a text. In terms of our key media aspect of Audience it is clear that each viewer's consciousness will also be composed of a number of discourses enabling that viewer to make sense of both the media text and also her/his wider experience. The activity of 'reading' the game show is, therefore, a complex negotiation between the discourses articulated by the media text and the discourses of the reader (which relate, of course, to their own social experience).

Answering any media studies question that requires you to take into account discourse theory can be quite challenging because you are not only being asked to establish how a media text articulates certain views on class or gender but also to reflect on your own values and beliefs as being elements of other, wider, social discourses. This is a difficult task and some students never come to terms with the problems associated with it. They may well be able to see that something can be said about the game show in terms of gender, but they often find it harder to introduce the range of subtle insights into the construction of meaning that discourse theory suggests. To help with this, it can be a good idea to try to state in broad terms what sort of view of the world the particular programme is supporting or encouraging; it might be argued that a game show such as *The Price is Right* articulates capitalist discourse insofar as it celebrates wealth and consumerism and that quiz programmes circulate discourses relating to middle-class culture insofar as they limit knowledge to topics such as literature, history and the lives of great men (as opposed to darts, football and punk rock). Further, it is possible to claim that both these programmes circulate patriarchal discourses: *Mastermind*, by making Magnus Magnusson appear the personification of the truth and knowledge that he assesses and *The Generation Game* because of the way in which females are always placed in the role of assistants to the male quiz-master. Even if you are able to identify complexities of this order, it can prove hard to describe these cogently in an essay. Reconciling the need for clarity with an understanding of the discursive density of a game show can prove extremely testing. But this is where it helps to keep to the sort of simple format outlined in this chapter, building up your argument in a structured and systematic way.

It will, of course, take some time for this sort of analytic expertise to develop, and you can only adopt the approach outlined here if you are very confident about what you are doing. Your main aim in media studies is to provide a solid analysis of a media text, not to indulge in terminological pyrotechnics. You should remember, therefore, that the sole purpose of using more advanced concepts is to clarify more complex issues relating to a media text. Never fall into the trap of thinking that you can just learn a list of some rather fancy terminology with which to baffle the examiner; knowing your subject does not equal merely knowing the technical names of a few concepts.

VII DEVISING YOUR OWN ESSAY TITLE

YOU may, at some point in your studies, be given the opportunity of devising your own essay topic. This is most likely to happen at a later stage in your course when you may well be asked to prepare a research essay. Unfortunately, the initial enthusiasm that students commonly have for their topic can quickly turn to despondency when they confront the problem of structuring their thoughts in a coherent way. The overall method we have been recommending in this book will help you to achieve a sense of direction and structure, but there are other things you should consider when you begin to put together your own essay topic.

In the early stages of tackling a self-devised topic you will almost certainly need to talk to your lecturer or supervisor if you are to come up with an essay title that is both well-defined and also realistic in terms of its scope. If you are dealing with a subject in which you are very interested you will, quite understandably, want to put down all your thoughts. However, if you do this it is almost certain that a formless essay will be the result. You may certainly discuss many topics but your essay will lack focus and direction.

In order to prevent this we would advise you to tackle a self-devised essay as follows:

1. *Define your initial area of interest*   At this early stage your topic can be a very general outline; you may wish, for instance, to try to account for the considerable popularity of television game shows. Do not worry too much if this initial idea sounds rather vague. Defining your topic is a process and it may be some time before you decide what your final direction is to be.

2. *Specify your topic*   A media research essay is an in-depth analysis of a particular issue or media text. So the point here is: do not try to cover too many topics. Instead, restrict yourself to a detailed consideration of just a few major issues.

   In this second stage of specifying your topic you need to outline carefully exactly what you will be considering. If your initial area of interest is game shows and the aspect of Audience, you will need to decide just what you will say about this topic. You will certainly need to consider the following areas:

   (i)   The nature of the pleasures that game shows offer their audience.
   (ii) The effects of game shows on their audience. (It might be argued, for instance, that shows such as *The Price is Right* encourage consumer culture.)
   (iii) Mode of address. Here we might consider how game-show hosts on different shows talk to the viewing audience.

(iv) A consideration of the demographics of the game-show audience.

(v)   How viewers from different groups – gender, race, class, educational background and so on – make sense of programmes.

Any one of the above would be an appropriate avenue for research. But if you pick more than one of these for consideration you are likely to have problems with the organisation of your essay – unless the topics are closely related.

Having reached a conclusion about which angle you are going to pursue you next need to decide which game show/s to target. Topics such as (iii) (above) would require you to look at a number of game shows in order to comment adequately on mode of address. Others, such as (v), would demand a more detailed account of a single programme.

One way you can make your argument more persuasive in a self-devised research essay is by comparing one game show with another – *Blockbusters* with *Mastermind*, say. You should always remember that the essential subject of such an essay is the shows themselves, the act of comparision being an analytical tool enabling you to discuss their respective qualities. For example, if we were planning to compare *Blockbusters*, a game show aimed at a younger audience, with the adult show, *Mastermind*, we could begin by listing the similarities and differences that strike us. First, both have middle-aged male question-masters (Bob Holness and Magnus Magnusson). Second, both are competitive: *Mastermind* with its specialist topics and interrogative style; *Blockbusters* with its quick-on-the-buzzer pressure. However, there are some important differences. The winners of *Blockbusters* are sent on fabulous holidays, whereas the prize awarded to the final victor at the end of the *Mastermind* series is simply an engraved glass bowl. Clearly the reason for this is that in *Mastermind* it is the status and respect gained through standing up to arduous questioning over a number of episodes and emerging the victor that is of central importance. If a fabulous prize such as a round-the-world tour or a Mercedes car were awarded this would suggest that the pursuit of material goods was more important than the pursuit of knowledge as an end in itself.

When writing such comparative essays you should always make a note of what is happening at the level of Construction (*mise-en-scène* and technical codes) in both programmes. Keep turning back to

Chapter 2, where we discuss these issues in depth, until you are thoroughly conversant with these codes. To begin with you are bound to wonder which technical codes are the most relevant and you will be tempted to describe every zoom or cut that occurs. You need, therefore, to think carefully about which codes play an important role visually and are, therefore, pertinent to the argument that you are making. You may choose, for example, to concentrate on the technical code of lighting. The use of high-key lighting in game shows is important because it helps to produce the happy and optimistic atmosphere essential for such shows, while high-contrast lighting will produce a quite different effect (see Table 8.1).

Table 8.1 Lighting codes for quiz and game shows

	Mastermind	*Blockbusters*
Lighting style	Chiaroscuro	Notan
Visual effect	High Contrast	High key (bright)
Connotation	Drama	Light-hearted fun

But whichever aspects of the two programmes you choose to develop you need to remember that brilliant ideas do not in themselves make brilliant essays. A brilliant idea must be thoroughly substantiated from the evidence of your analysis.

And that really takes this book back to the point at which it began. You may be totally baffled by a TV programme, or you may be bursting with original, provocative and challenging ideas, but your case about the programme as you work it out in an essay will only really stand up if you prove everything from the evidence of your analysis of the programme itself.

Further reading

ONE of the biggest problems that students new to the area of Media and Communication Studies face is not so much how to find books on the subject, but rather, to know which books they may safely leave to one side: some may be too specialised, some simply may not be very good. All media studies students have experienced the frustration of tackling a complex analysis that moves quickly between difficult arguments, employing all the while, a dense and apparently arcane vocabulary. This can be a particularly discouraging experience, and you should remember that there really is no reason to struggle on with a singularly inaccessible text when there are others to which you can turn. It is a good idea to try to organise your study in such a way that you are tackling the more accesible works first, only moving on to deeper and more complex forms of analysis when you feel confident to do so.

Media studies textbooks are useful, but only if you use them in the right way; they should complement your own thinking about a media text rather than serve as a substitute for individual thought. You need, therefore, to go further than summarising standard positions. The most important thing to remember is that your arguments will only stand up if they are based on your own thoughts, impressions, insights and analysis.

Generally speaking, there are two times when you are most likely to need to turn to media and communications studies textbooks. First, after just viewing the programme, when you might need some help both in sorting out your general ideas and in identifying the central themes and concerns of the genre; second, after you have done a lot of your own work on the programme and feel that your own thinking might benefit from some additional stimulus. But which books do you choose? There are several things worth considering, before you commit your time and energy to reading one of the many books you can find on television. Here are a few hints:

(i) **Date of publication**

Approaches to television studies have changed considerably over the past thirty years. Although it would be extremely presumptuous to call books and articles written in the 1950s or 1960s 'out of date', it is unlikely that either the attitudes expressed in them, or the theoretical models they employ, will be representative of current debates in the field. They may, however, have historical relevance or certain important ideas that were developed and refined at a later date. If this is the case, you will probably find that their theoretical stance is summarised by more modern texts.

(ii) **The author**

Most books contain some information about their author. This can be quite useful in helping you to decide if it is the sort of book you are looking for. Books on television are written by journalists or television critics as well as by academics, and journalists and TV critics are much more likely to provide a personal, impressionistic, or even anecdotal view, than they are to provide a detailed, analytical response. Do not write these books off, however. Such works often contain many useful facts and interesting insights, which may be of use. Even so, they will be unlikely to contain any detailed analysis that relates to the five key media aspects with which we have been concerned in this book. Most of the texts you will need to consult will, therefore, be written by academics within the field of television studies.

(iii) **The publisher**

Some publishers produce large, glossy, behind the scenes, coffee-table accounts of television programmes aimed at regular viewers of these shows. Such books can be quite useful, because they may contain detailed information about the programme which is not easily obtainable elsewhere. These naturally differ from academic works produced by a publisher for a particular specialist field. In the main it is the latter that you will most often use.

If this is the first book on television that you have read or if you are fairly new to the subject, you will probably want to start with some general introductory texts. *More than Meets the eye* by Graeme Burton (Edward Arnold, 1990) deals with the key media aspects in an accessible way and provides useful summaries of some of the main debates. If you are finding it difficult to grasp the principles of visual analysis, then *See What I Mean: An Introduction to Visual Communication* by J. Morgan and P. Welton (Edward Arnold, 1986) can help you with this (but read our Chapter 2 again first). A more advanced work that provides an overview of contemporary television theory is John Fiske's *Television Culture* (Routledge, 1987) which locates TV within the wider domain of popular culture. Since Fiske adopts what is essentially a viewer-centred approach (stressing the way in which audiences construct meanings), this book can provide a useful springboard into an analysis of the active involvement of the audience in making meaning from media texts. Once you have got hold of these broad overviews of the current debates in media studies and the position of TV in contemporary culture, you will want to look in more detail at the five key media concepts which we have been using in this book.

John Izod's *Reading the Screen* (Longman, 1984) is a good place to start on construction/media languages. This book not only contains some very useful technical information, but is also written in an extremely accessible style.

On audience, probably the best introduction is *Television, Audiences and Cultural Studies* by David Morley (Routledge, 1992) which is not only an excellent survey of the developments and current state of audience studies, but also includes some original, thought-provoking and detailed analysis of this field.

An extremely useful discussion of television narrative is *Visible Fictions* by John Ellis (Routledge, 1984). This book deals with both film and television, and is very good on the differences between the classic narrative structure of the feature film and classic TV narrative patterns.

Categorisation/genre can present students new to the area of media and communications studies with problems, and this because – as we have tried to make clear in this book – each genre tends to partake of characteristics of other genre. Perhaps the best book to turn to on this is *Channels of Discourse Reassembled: Television and Contemporary Criticism* by R.C. Allen (ed.) (Routledge, 1992). This book is particularly useful on genre because it contains a collection of essays which give a representative overview of the various approaches to the subject, and can help to clarify your own thinking on the topic.

Our final media aspect, Agency, involves – again, as we have pointed out in this book – many quite different factors: institutional, organisational, technological, artistic, legal and economic. A good place to start is with a book which has by now become almost a classic exposition of the topic: *Hazell: The Making of a TV Series* by Manuel Alvarado and Ed Buscombe (BFI/Latimer, 1978). Although it is some years since the programme on which the book is based was broadcast the work still stands as an excellent model for anyone wishing to tie together the areas of creative production with those of economics and organisation. For a more general discussion of the different stages in the production process, *The Making of a Television Series* by Philip Elliott (Constable, 1974) is an excellent introduction. A more recent book which addresses the complex relationships within Agency is *Screening the Novel: The Theory and Practice of Literary Dramatization*, by Robert Giddings, Keith Selby and Chris Wensley (Macmillan New Insights, 1990), which focuses on the various processes of negotiation involved in the re-creation of a media product. The interviews with members of the production team give a unique insight into the various tensions present within any media realisation – but again, re-read our Chapter 4 on *The Bill*, before you tackle any of these books on Agency.

Related to this issue of Agency are two other areas, which you may be asked to consider: the future of the medium, and the connections between media, power and control. On the first of these issues, try Chris Dunkley's *Television Today and Tomorrow: Wall to Wall Dallas?* (Penguin, 1985) which is a very readable and persuasive account of the direction in which he sees TV moving. On the question of media, power and control, you should look at *Questioning the Media: A Critical Introduction*, a series of essays edited by John Downing, Ali Mohammadi and Annabelle Sreberny-Mohammadi (Sage, 1990), which is good at presenting various, conflicting approaches to the issue.

Of course, as you will soon find out when you start looking along the shelves of your library, television has attracted a huge amount of academic analysis. The first thing to remember is that you cannot read all of it. Instead, it is much more important that you read selectively, and in a directed way. The books which we have recommended here should help you to get to grips with television and its various aspects by sending you back to your own analysis to try out some new ideas. And that really is as good a way as any of judging the quality of any book you read on the subject: see if it sends you back to the text to explore it further for yourself.

Glossary

THE first thing you will probably notice about this Glossary is that it is fairly long. The second thing we hope you will notice is how useful it is, containing not only a brief explanation of technical terms used in the course of this book, but also a brief explanation of terms you will probably encounter in other books on media and communications studies.

Aberrant decoding: A term used to describe what happens when the message received by a member of an audience differs from the meaning intended by the broadcaster (or any other encoder). This usually happens when the encoder and decoder do not share the same beliefs and values.

Accessing: The inclusion, in news and current affairs, of statements or interviews given by individuals who are not employed by the broadcasting organisation.

Action: Any movement in front of the camera.

Actuality: Footage that records real events as they happen.

Adaptation: A screenplay based upon a stage play. See **Dramatisation.**

Agenda-setting: In making decisions about the running order, mode of presentation and emphasis of news items news producers not only influence how audiences perceive events but also, more importantly, determine the nature of subsequent coverage. This process is known as Agenda-setting because the editor's view of what is important and worthy of comment and analysis becomes our view of what is significant in the day's events; a programme editor could therefore be said to set the agenda for subsequent coverage.

Ambient sound: The sounds that are normally found in a particular place (e.g. traffic noise in the street, birdsong in the countryside and so on). Notice, too, that the ambient sound characteristic of a church will differ considerably from the ambient sound characteristic of a bedroom. In such cases, the ambient 'sound' will not in fact be heard, while the difference between sounds heard within their respective ambient settings will be considerable.

Anchorage: A term which refers to the way that words fix the meaning of visual images. Captions, titles and voice-overs make us 'read' in a particular way images that may otherwise be open to a number of different interpretations.

Angle: The direction and height of the camera from the subject.

Arbitrary signs: Where the relationship between the signifier and the signified is established purely by convention, the sign is termed unmotivated or arbitrary. The written or verbal sign 'dog', for instance, bears no necessary relation to that animal, which is why it can be replaced by '*Hund*' in German and '*chien*' in French.

ASA: Advertising Standards Authority.

Audio track: The sound portion of a video tape.

Backlight: A light source that is positioned behind the subject in order to separate the subject from the background.

BARB: Broadcasters' Audience Research Board: A company jointly owned by the BBC and ITCA that collates viewing figures for programmes and monitors audience response to programmes.

Beat: A moment shorter than a pause but longer than a cut in a script or televisual.

Bias: Distortion of an issue resulting either from individuals being unaware of all of the relevant information or from them deliberately presenting a partial or prejudicial account.

'Bible': A series format, including details on characters, past events and stories, possible future developments, script requirements, production facilities and structure.

Big close-up (BCU):   This is obtained when only a part of the full face is shown, such as tear-filled eyes or a smiling mouth. Such shots are usually reserved for dramatic moments because they can reveal to us the inner emotions of a character.

Binary opposition: These are basic oppositions – masculinity:femininity, logic:emotion – that are fundamental within a culture and which form the structuring oppositions of the narratives of many television genres. In the news, for instance, the binary 'us:them' is used to structure stories (e.g. striking railway workers (them):stranded commuters (us).

Business: This refers to the activity a particular character is given in a script or televisual, e.g. sawing wood, pouring a pint of beer, etc.

Cable TV: The transmission of television signals via a cable as opposed to broadcast waves.

Camera script: The version of the script given to camera operators and other technicians on which the director has blocked out his or her camera shots and movements. See **Rehearsal script**.

Cardinal functions: These are narrative functions that have to do with the posing of enigmas, the introduction of disruption and the setting of riddles. Such functions serve to maintain the viewer's attention and are central to the narrative.

Catalytic functions: These are narrative functions which are responsible for prolonging the pleasures of suspense by introducing 'breathing spaces' into the narrative.

Cathode ray tube: The picture tube in a television.

Chiaroscuro: A lighting technique in which a single light source is used to create small pools of illumination surrounded by dark shadows. The chiaroscuro style helps to increase the emotional and psychological depth of a sequence.

Chroma key: Sometimes known as **Paintbox**, this is an electronic technique that uses a blue screen background to unite separate pictures. Often used for special effects and in news broadcasts to block out one part of the screen so that another image can be imposed upon it.

Cliffhanger: An exciting scene ending designed to ensure that the audience watches the next episode or stays tuned in after the commercial break.

Close-up: Usually a head-and-shoulders shot.

Codes: A system into which signs are organised in such a way as to convey meanings.

Combination: See **Syntagmatic axis**.

Common junction point: Many programmes on the two commercial TV channels (ITV and Channel 4) or on the two BBC channels (BBC1 and BBC2) start at the same time. Such 'common junction points' are often used to inform the audience of what is about to be shown on another channel, 'And now a choice of viewing on BBC. . .' and 'Over on BBC2 in 5 minutes is. . . meanwhile here on BBC1. . .' are familiar phrases. 8.00p.m. and 9.00p.m. are the most frequent common junction points in the evening schedule across all channels and these are the times when the programmers are trying their hardest to attract the peak-period audience.

Common sense: A term used to describe any knowledge whose 'truth' is taken as being self-evident. It is important to notice that in communications and media studies it is suggested that such knowledge, rather than being natural and unarguable, is deeply ideological. It then follows that because the mass media in general operate with common-sense views of reality they perform a hegemonic function. See **Hegemony**, below.

Commutation test: This test is carried out when analysing any media text in order to ascertain whether a particular element in a syntagm carries a meaning. To carry out the test one simply has to exchange one element for another in the same paradigm.

Conspiracy theory: An approach to the mass media that argues that the media are owned and controlled by a dominant élite who use the media to maintain the *status quo* by presenting only their views of issues and events.

Construction: (technical codes) these include: shot size; camera angle; lens type; composition; focus; lighting codes; editing codes; colour and film stock codes.

Continuity: The creation of the illusion of coherent time and space from shot to shot in a sequence. Continuity editing is a style in which the editing process itself becomes largely invisible.

Content analysis: A statistical method that identifies and quantifies the content of mass media messages. Typically such research seeks to describe general trends relating to the representation of particular groups; a study might focus on, say, the number of businesswomen shown in advertisements over a particular period or the number of black characters in British TV soaps.

Contrast: see **Lighting**.

Cultural effects theory: A communications model which suggests that the influence of any media message will depend upon the social and cultural situation and background of the audience.

Cultural imperialism: A term used to describe the process whereby economically powerful countries (such as the USA) develop a cultural and political control over less-powerful countries.

Cut: The simplest form of edit: one shot finishes and the next begins. Film is physically cut (hence the term) and pasted together. In video this operation is achieved by switching (cutting), either live or at the editing stage, from one camera to a second camera which is recording a different scene or a different angle of the same scene.

Cutaway: Any shot within a sequence that is not itself central to the action but which can be included without upsetting the audience's understanding of the space and time of the sequence. For example, in a sequence showing a circus high-wire act the inclusion of shots of the audience would be cutaways.

Decoding: the process of interpreting a message. Usually satisfactory decoding depends not only on an understanding of the words or images employed but also a sharing of the beliefs and values of the encoder (see **Encoding**).

Deep focus: A technique in which both objects near to the camera and those far away are equally in focus.

Depth of field: The nearest and furthest distances from the camera at which objects are acceptably sharp.

Denotation: The straightforward relationship that a sign has to its referent. The word 'dog' and a photograph of a dog both denote a particular type of animal.

Deregulation: The reduction of controls over broadcasting by governments. This can involve splitting a monopoly communications institution into separate firms, relaxing the legislation relating to the ownership of broadcast stations, or other measures.

Deviance: A term used to describe social behaviour which is considered unacceptable. Any actions that have been labelled as deviant tend to become the focus of media coverage (see **Labelling theory**).

Diegesis: A term used in narrative analysis to refer to the simple telling of events as narrative.

Diegetic sound effects: 'Inclusive' sound. That is, any sound that originates from the story space itself and is not artificially added to it.

Director: The person who has the final responsibility for the creative realisation of a television programme.

Direct broadcast satellite (DBS): Any satellite with a signal strong enough to be received by a domestic receiver.

Dissolve: In this, one picture is faded out while another is faded in on the screen. For a moment, both pictures are mixed on the screen. The dissolve is sometimes used instead of the fade (which it resembles stylistically) to indicate the passage of time between one shot and the next or some relationship between the two images.

Diversification: Most large media institutions have sought to stave off the financial risks associated with the media business by diversifying into other forms of business.

Dramatisation: The fictional reconstruction of a real event. Also used to describe the process of transferring a story from a novel to television.

Dub: The adding of sound (such as music or a commentary) to the final cut.

Effects theory: A general term used to refer to mass media research that focuses on the effects of the mass media on their audiences.

Sometimes known also as the **Hypodermic needle model**.

Elite: Used in media studies to refer to a small group of people in control either of society or of a particular part of it.

Encoding: The process of communicating a message by means of written, spoken or visual signals which are combined according to particular codes.

ENG (Electronic news gathering): A technique for gathering news using lightweight video cameras. The technique gives an impression of immediacy and has been imported into many drama productions, such as *The Bill*, which is shot almost entirely in ENG mode.

Establishing shot. The opening shot/sequence, generally showing the location (and therefore usually a long shot).

ETV: educational television.

Executive producer: The person responsible for securing the finance for a programme or series of programmes.

Exnomination: This literally means 'un-named'. The term was introduced by Roland Barthes to describe the process whereby certain core values within a society are deemed to be so widely held that they do not need to be named. For example, while there are often art exhibitions devoted to Contemporary Women's Art or Contemporary Black Art, there are few exhibitions with titles such as Recent Men's Art or Recent White Art. The masculine gender and white 'race' are un-named/exnominated because these are taken to be the dominant powerful groupings within society. This is a useful concept in media studies because it helps us to understand how agency functions: in a news broadcast a management or government position is frequently exnominated (their view being put by the news reader), whilst a union view of an issue is nominated (using an interview with a named union official).

EXT: Exterior.

Extreme long shot (ELS): A shot in which the subject takes up only a small part of the frame; the setting itself is the main thing that we see. Because of this such a shot is often known as an establishing shot because it establishes what scene or location we are looking at.

Eye-level shot: A shot taken from the same level as the subject.

Faction: Dramatised documentaries in which fiction and fact are mixed.

Fade: This may be either to fade in, allowing a blank screen gradually to be filled by the picture, or to fade out, in which the picture grows dimmer until the screen is left blank. The fade is usually employed either at the end of one scene and the beginning of the next or to indicate that what is being seen is only a part of what actually happened.

Flashback: A change in the story order to show events that have taken place earlier.

Folk devils: Social groups who are thought to be a threat to the core values of society (e.g. Skinheads, Mods and Rockers, Punks, etc.).

Fourth wall: The absent fourth wall of a television set.

FX: Effects

Gatekeeping: Within media and communication studies news editors are known as 'gatekeepers' because they 'open the gate' to certain stories while 'closing the gate' on other information. The concept of gatekeeping is a useful one because it highlights the important processes of selection and rejection. However, as a general model for explaining the news process, it tends to minimise the complexities involved. The term 'gatekeeper' suggests that the final form of a TV news item is determined solely by the news producer and duty editor, whereas in reality a number of practical constraints (the availability of equipment or a key interviewee) and day-to-day operational routines will have influenced the kinds of decisions taken about what news can be covered.

Genre: Recognised groups into which media output can be classified and categorised.

Glasgow Media Group: A group of academics based at Glasgow University whose studies on bias in TV news since the mid-1970s have provoked considerable controversy both within the media industry itself and also within the field of media studies. 'The Group', as they have become known, aimed to show how the processes of selection, editing and presentation in TV news production tended to favour the establishment's view of events. In four books – *Bad News* (Routledge, 1976), *More Bad News* (Routledge, 1980), *Really Bad News* (Writers and Readers' Publishing Cooperative, 1982), *War and Peace News* (Open University Press, 1985) – the Glasgow Group claimed that British news programming did not live up to its own criteria of balance and impartiality. Because many broadcasters operate from a pro-establishment, consensual middle-class position, so the Group argued, the programmes they produce reflect the politics of the *status quo*. As a result the media are more likely to access the views of key establishment figures and experts than they are the opinions of, say union activists.

Hammocking: This involves placing a programme (such as a documentary) which will appeal to a 'minority' audience between two more popular ones so that it can benefit from both the inheritance factor and the pre-echo.

Head-and-shoulders (HS): see **Close-up**.

Hegemony: This term, as developed by the Italian Marxist Gramsci, refers to the ability of dominant classes and élites to exercise cultural leadership in such a way that they can maintain power by consensus rather than constraint. By portraying the views of the ruling class as simply being common sense the media help to win the consent of subordinate classes to inequalities in class relations. Hegemony thus functions to naturalise ideology.

High angle shot: The camera looks down at the subject.

Horizontal integration: The acquisition, usually by takeover or merger, of one media organisation by another media organisation of the same type. For example, when a number of small television production companies are taken over by a powerful rival company. See also **Vertical integration**.

Hypodermic needle model: See **Effects theory**.

IBA: Independent Broadcasting Authority. Previously the regulator for UK commercial TV and radio. Replaced, by the ITC (Independent Television Commission).

Iconic signs: Signs which resemble the things that they represent.

Ideology: An ideology is a set of beliefs and ideas that provide individuals and groups with a framework for thinking about key social issues and making sense of the world around them. Ideological beliefs are different from purely personal thoughts and preferences for they are, in essence, shared with others. Because people are generally unaware that they hold such beliefs – seeing them as just 'common sense' – so their ideological positions are more a set of unconscious assumptions about 'the way things are' than a set of explicit conscious beliefs. Ideology is a concept which has developed from Marxist Theory, where it is used to consider the way in which any set of ideas upholds the class structure of a society. Thus within a bourgeois capitalist society, according to the Marxist, the media uphold the ideologies of the dominant or ruling class. The concept of ideology is, therefore, central within the areas of media and communication studies for it introduces the key idea that the media do not simply provide us with a window onto the world but rather interpret events in an ideological way.

Indexical sign: A sign which is connected with the thing it signifies but which does not represent or picture this in the straightforward and direct way that iconic signs do. For example, because we associate Churchill with his cigar and Napoleon with his hat each of these historical individuals can be evoked by these objects, which function as indexical signs.

Inheritance factor: Any television programme can expect to 'inherit' a reasonable proportion of the audience already watching a particular channel.

Institutional voice: Any voice which speaks on behalf of the broadcasting organisation (a news reader for instance). This is thus the opposite of an accessed voice.

INT: Interior.

Intelsat (International Telecommunications Satellite Organisation): This agency, based in Washington, regulates the world's main satellite networks.

Intertextuality: A term used loosely to describe the interplay between one media text and another.

Impartiality: Broadcasters are required, by Parliament, not to be seen to be taking sides in the reporting of public affairs. Usually this is achieved by attempting to include a range of viewpoints, and to take into account the relative weight of particular positions. The notion of impartiality is tied to the concept of objectivity and to the view that a balanced, neutral, value-free representation of events is possible. Within media studies there has been much questioning of these basic assumptions, with some writers claiming that the very notion of impartiality is an important prop for the *status quo* insofar as it rules out the inclusion of radical viewpoints that may question the very nature of the current political consensus.

Iris out: This was very common in early silent movies. The frame gradually reduces to a small circle and then disappears, the whole screen being then left black.

ITC: Independent Television Commission.

ITN: Independent Television News.

ITV (Independent Television): This term is usually used to cover all the commercial television organisations.

JICTAR: Joint Industry Committee for Television Advertising Research. A body measuring the audience ratings for ITV.

Key: see **Lighting**.

Labelling theory: A theory that argues that a deviant act is any behaviour that people 'label' as deviant. Deviance, therefore, is not a quality that is intrinsic to particular social acts (such as those of , football hooligans) but is the result of a process of social labelling; something which is deviant when committed by one group may not be when committed by another. The mass media play an important part in transmitting such labels. 'Hooligans', 'militants', 'rioters' 'terrorists' are frequently the main characters in news items in the media, where they acquire the status of folk devils. See **Folk devils.**

Laugh track: Also known as 'canned' laughter, this is a pre-recorded tape of laughter that can be used on TV programmes where no live audience is present (or when more laughter is required). This is used much more on some programmes than on others.

Library: see Stock footage.

Lighting: (i)   Lighting key refers to the brilliance of the picture as a whole. A picture which is fairly bright is described as high key, one which is dark is said to be low key. (ii) Lighting contrast refers to the tonal range of a picture. A low-contrast picture is one which has a much narrower range of tones, with many greys but no areas of deep black or bright white; a high-contrast picture will have a dramatic appearance, with strong shadows and bright highlights.

Lip sync: When the movement of a character's lips and the words on the soundtrack are synchronised.

Live: Broadcast 'as it happens'.

Long shot (LS):   A shot which contains the whole human figure.

Low angle shot: a shot in which the subject is above the viewer.

Media imperialism: A term describing the domination of developing countries by the media and communication systems of Western capitalist societies.

Mediation: In contemporary society much of the information that people receive is mediated through various institutional and economic forces; the mass media act as intermediaries between different social groups and classes and also between events in the world and audiences. Because all reporting involves selection/ rejection, editing, and so on, news items cannot be said simply to reflect events in the world on a particular day. As a result, an individual's views are inevitably influenced by the values and ideologies of the media as mediators.

Medium long shot (MLS):   A shot which is half way between MS and LS.

Medium shot (MS):   This is obtained when the subject is cut off just below the waist by the bottom of the frame. In such shots the subject and the setting normally occupy approximately the same area of the frame. This shot is frequently used in TV work as a transition shot between long shots and close ups, because to jump suddenly from one to the other would be abrupt and disorientating to the viewer.

Metaphor: Used in media studies to describe a 'visual' figure of speech in which the unknown is described by relating it to the known. For example, in advertising, metaphoric images are frequently used to give the viewer an idea of the qualities of the product: an anti-perspirant advertised in a setting of mountain streams would assert qualities of coolness, even though the anti-perspirant may not be cooling in itself.

Metonymy: A figure of speech in which an attribute or aspect of a thing is substituted for the thing itself. Television news can be said to function metonymically insofar as the images that it includes in an item – a protesting striker say – will be taken as representative of the whole strike.

Mid close up (MCU):   A shot which is half way between CU and MS.

Mise-en-scène: This French term has been assimilated into English and means 'the fact of putting into the scene' and has its origins in the theatre, where it applied to stage direction. It later came to be applied to the cinema and it is for this reason that *mise-en-scène* analysis looks at only those aspects which overlap with the theatre: setting and props, the behaviour of the figures or actors, costumes and make-up.

Mix: see **Dissolve**.

Moral panic: A term which describes the way in which the media respond to particular forms of deviant activity. See **Deviance**, above.

Myth: In today's society the mass media are amongst the most significant carriers of contemporary myths – ideas about glamour, romance, success, sophistication, and so on. Communication can only take place because encoders (producers of media texts) and decoders (audiences) both draw upon certain key social myths: myths about work and leisure, men and women, about the young and old and so on. Myths, therefore, only come alive when we appropriate them, when they resonate with our own values and beliefs. Such values should more properly be considered as intersubjective rather than as personal for we share them with others and use them to make sense of our lives and of the world around us.

News gatherers: Journalists and correspondents are often referred to as the 'news gatherers' because they collect the information that 'news processors' (i.e. editors) process.

News values: The professional values that influence the selection and presentation of news items.

Noddies: Often used in interviews, in which the interviewer is shown nodding in agreement with what the interviewee is saying, so that the person speaking is seen from the viewpoint of a third person standing a little behind and to one side of the listener. As a result the back of the head and shoulder of the listener can be seen.

Non-diegetic sound: Any sound from a source outside the story space.

Non-verbal communication (NVC):   A general term used to describe communication by means of posture, dress, gesture or facial expression.

Notan: A style of lighting in which a set is brightly and evenly lit by studio lights giving flat, shadowless illumination. The resulting picture is quite bright (high-key), and therefore creates an optimistic mood.

OB: Outside Broadcast.

Organic plot: A plot which is structured in such a way that it attempts to hide its own processes of structuration. In such plots there does not seem to be any strict logic to the ordering of the sequences, and, because of this such plots have something of a 'slice of life' quality; events seem to grow and develop in a natural ('organic') way around the characters.

PA: Production Assistant.

Paintbox: See **Chroma key**, above.

Pan: From 'Panoramic', and meaning to swivel the camera without changing its angle or base height.

Paradigmatic analysis: An analysis of a media text (or, indeed, any other type of text) which looks at how the component elements of the text relate to elements that were not chosen. If low camera angle, chiaroscuro lighting and deep focus were used in a particular shot one could talk about each of these in terms of other choices that might have been made from the codes of camera angle, lighting and focus respectively. The paradigmatic dimension is, for this reason, sometimes referred to as the axis of selection.

Performer space: The positioning of the characters in relation to the camera. This is achieved along two axes: (i) The horizontal axis (the X axis) which extends to the left and right of the camera; and (ii) The depth axis (the Z axis) which extends toward and away from the camera.

Point-of-view shot (POV):   A shot showing the scene from the perspective of a character.

Political economy analysis: An approach to media analysis which emphasises the way in which economic institutions and political factors interact to determine communication processes.

Polysemic: Capable of multiple meanings (visual texts are often described as polysemic because they can be 'read' in different ways).

Post production: Usually regarded as synonomous with editing, this is the time after production during which everything is done that is needed to finish the televisual realisation.

Post synchronisation (post-sync):   The practice of adding dialogue, SFX or music to mute tape that has already been shot.

Pre-echo: A term used by TV schedulers to describe the fact that a percentage of the audience of a programme will tune in early. It is then quite likely, if they enjoy what they see, that they watch all of this programme on the following week.

Pre-production: Everything that needs to be done before something is shot – script preparation, budgeting, set construction, etc.

Primary definers: Socially accredited commentators such as the police, professional bodies and official union spokespersons regularly appear in news broadcasts, providing 'authoritative' comment on issues with which they are directly concerned. Such 'official' figures, who help to provide an atmosphere of authority, are termed primary definers because the agenda for subsequent debate is often established by them. Because primary definers promote and defend the values and beliefs of the organisations they represent their influence on news coverage is such that this stays within the confines of the *status quo*.

Prime time: The period during which most TV sets are in use.

Producer: The person who oversees the production of a programme, hires the writer/s, director and actors and organises the finances.

Propaganda: The deliberate manipulation of information in order to achieve particular political objectives.

Public service broadcasting: The organisation of broadcasting through a Government corporation (as with the British BBC) which is itself relatively independent of the Government. Such broadcasting is termed 'public service' because it aims to provide the general public with a broad service that is entertaining, educative and informative. Its ethos differs, therefore, from that of the commercial television companies whose primary consideration is to capture large audiences that can then be 'sold' to advertisers.

***Reductio ad absurdum* plot (reduction to the absurd)**:   Plots in which a simple human error or character fault is magnified so that problems multiply and everything ends in chaos. Usually we are made aware of this error or mistake in the opening minutes; the *reductio* is often built up around a simple human mistake such as picking up the wrong parcel.

Rehearsal script: The writer's imaginings. The script as it comes from the writer and before production details (such as camera angles, etc.) have been added by the director.

Reithian: A term used to describe a range of attitudes to the nature and purposes of broadcasting that were established within the BBC under the leadership of the first Director-General, Lord Reith. For Reith the broadcast media were, first and foremost, tools for the education and enlightenment of the population. This concept underpins the notion of **Public service broadcasting** (q.v.).

Reverse shot: A shot taken from an angle of approximately 180 degrees opposite from the one which preceded it. Such a shot is frequently used when two characters facing each other are in conversation.

Scene: One or more shots that take place in a single location, and deal with the same action.

Scheduling: A term used to describe the practice of ordering programmes in such a way that the maximum audience is attracted. Schedulers use **Hammocking** and **Tent-poling** techniques to achieve this. See under those headings.

Selection: See **Paradigmatic analysis.**

Semiotics/semiology: The study of the ways in which signs communicate meaning and of the various rules that govern their use. Its specialised vocabulary aims to describe just how the various signs and codes that are to be found in all media texts work to produce meaning.

Sequence: A group of linked shots or scenes that together comprise a major statement that develops the story. This term is normally used to describe a reasonably large segment of a television programme.

Serial: A continuing story told over a number of episodes. Most serials have a definite beginning and end. Soaps, however, might be described as 'unending' serials because they always begin in a state in which events are already underway and end without a straightforward resolution.

Series: A set of television programmes in which episodes share the same situations and characters but are separate from the others in the series in terms of their plotlines.

Set: Any interior or exterior location where a television programme is shot.

SFX: Sound effects.

Shooting script: A list of scenes in the order in which they are to be shot. This is unlikely to be the sequence in which they are finally assembled.

Sign: This is a composite entity made up of (i) the physical or material thing that is perceived through the senses, and (ii) the meaning that this thing has for us. In semiotics the former physical entity is referred to as the **Signifier** and the latter concept or meaning as the **Signified**.

Signified: see **Sign**.

Signifier: see **Sign**.

Slot: The amount of time allocated for a programme e.g. thirty minutes, forty minutes, etc. The actual running time will be shorter than this to allow for commercial breaks.

Soft focus: An image which is not sharply focused. This effect is usually achieved through the use of a particular lens or filter.

Solo performance sitcom: A phrase used to describe sitcoms in which a single character's performance takes centre stage.

Special effects (SP–FX):   Any unusual or extraordinary effect that must be specially created.

Standard lens: A lens that gives the various objects and people in a shot approximately the same proportions in relation to their distance from us as we would expect in real life.

Stereotyping: The act of classifying particular individuals and groups in a simplistic and judgemental way (the 'dumb' blonde, the 'crazed' drug addict, etc.).

Stock footage: Canned or existing film or video material that can be used in a new production. Also known as **Library**.

Storyboard: A pictorial sketch of how each shot should look and how it links with the next one. A blank Storyboard page is reproduced on p. 72.

Structured plot: Plots which depend, for example, on characters making sudden discoveries, or stories being resolved by what might otherwise appear to be somewhat unlikely coincidences.

Subcultures: Groups within a main culture holding their own values and beliefs, and which oppose those of the main culture (e.g. Punks, Rastafarians, etc.).

Subjective camera: See **Point-of-view (POV)**.

Symbol: Any sign that stands for an object or event as a result of members of a community agreeing over its use, rather than by any representational relation to what it denotes.

Synchronic and diachronic: These terms relate to the dimension of time – an extremely important issue in the study of television, for obvious reasons. Synchronic analysis proceeds by isolating a set of signs within a media text at a particular moment and discussing these independently of the part that they will play in the unfolding story. If we turn from this to discuss how they function across time then we are considering it from a diachronic perspective. This should alert us to the fact that there are some useful connections between these two pairs of terms, paradigmatic and synchronic; syntagmatic and diachronic. The paradigmatic axis of selection, for example, is a synchronic one: it is simply the set of signs from which the Sign has been chosen, since there are no temporal relations between them. The syntagmatic axis of combination is a diachronic one and therefore involves time – whether the thirty seconds of a TV advertisement or the two hours of a feature film.

Synechdoche: A figure of speech in which a part is substituted for the whole (as in 'wheels' or 'motor' for a car) or, more infrequently, the whole for a part (as in 'the police have arrived' instead of a policeman or policewoman has arrived).

Synopsis: A summary of the plot outlining the main content.

Syntagmatic analysis: An analysis of a media text (or, indeed, any other type of text) that looks at the relationship of component parts of the text to each other and to the whole. A syntagmatic analysis of a narrative looks at the way its sequences relate to each other and how these relations generate meaning. Such an analysis is concerned with surface as opposed to hidden meanings: *what* happens, *where*, *when* and *how* are the main issues. A syntagmatic analysis of a single image looks at the way in which the elements within it are combined to produce a message. The syntagmatic dimension is, for this reason, sometimes referred to as the 'axis of combination'.

Target audience: Very important for advertisers and schedulers. The Broadcaster's Audience Research Bureau (BARB) carries out audience research, classifying the population in terms of regions (because of the regional nature of ITV) in the following categories: Males and Females by age (0–15, 16–24, 25–34, 45–54, 55–64, and 65 +) and by class (A, B, C1, C2, D, and E). Men are classified as working/not working, and women/housewives (not always synonymous categories) as 'working' or 'not working'. This breakdown allows both advertisers and schedulers to target particular audiences for specific programmes or products; indeed, programmes are often commissioned specifically to fill a particular slot.

T/C: Telecine. Taped or filmed scenes that have been shot prior to the studio production.

Tent-poling: A scheduling strategy whereby a very popular programme, such as a crime series, will be placed at the peak of prime time while less-popular programmes, such as documentaries, will be 'hung' around it. This technique is used to capture viewers who tune in to their programme early or continue watching after it has finished. See **Hammocking**.

Three shot: A shot including three people.

Track: To move the camera forwards, backwards or sideways on wheels. These wheels are known as a dolly.

Treatment: A written outline of how the final programme will look and a description of how this is to be achieved.

Two shot: A shot including two people.

Two-way cable TV: A system which allows viewers to 'talk back' via a console.

TX: Transmission date.

Uses and gratifications theory: An approach to the study of the mass media, first developed in the 1940s which emphasised the fact that audiences actively make use of the media to 'gratify' particular 'needs' (hence the name). Because this theoretical approach took the audience to be composed of individuals using the media for their own ends it represented a break from earlier 'effects' theories (q.v.) which concentrated upon the influence of the mass media on an audience construed as intrinsically passive and malleable.

UTX: Recorded but untransmitted material or programme.

Verisimilitude: Appearing to be real.

Vertical integration: The concentration of raw materials, production, distribution and sales in the hands of a single organisation. A television company, for instance, will pay for the script, own the studios, pay for the programme to be made, and own the means of distribution (broadcasting systems).

VCR: Video cassette recorder.

Vision mixer: The person responsible for mixing or cutting between cameras.

Voice over (VO):   Any dialogue or narration in which the source of the voice is not seen.

VT: Video tape.

VTR: Video tape recording.

Zoom: This may be to zoom in or to zoom out from a subject. This is achieved by using a zoom lens, which is capable of being refocused while in use.

Index

237